Fulfilling America's Promise

FULFILLING AMERICA'S PROMISE:

Social Policies for the 1990s

Edited by

JOSEPH A. PECHMAN

with the assistance of

MICHAEL S. MCPHERSON

Contributors
HENRY J. AARON
MARY JO BANE
HENRY J. BRUTON
LARRY CUBAN
EDWARD M. GRAMLICH
JOHN F. KAIN
PAUL E. PETERSON
UWE E. REINHARDT

*A book from the
Williams College
Center for the Humanities
and Social Sciences*

CORNELL UNIVERSITY PRESS
Ithaca and London

Library of Congress Cataloging-in-Publication Data

Fulfilling America's promise: social policies for the 1990s/edited
   by Joseph A. Pechman, with the assistance of Michael S. McPherson
   contributors, Henry J. Aaron . . .[et al.].
      p. cm.
      "A book from the Williams College Center for the Humanities and
        Social Sciences."
   Includes bibliographical references and index.
   ISBN 0-8014-2631-6 (alk. paper: cloth)
   ISBN 0-8014-8059-0 (pbk.)
   1. United States—Social policy—1980– .   2. Human services—
United States. 3. Social change.   I. Pechman, Joseph A., 1918–1989.
II. McPherson, Michael S.   III. Williams College. Center for the
Humanities and Social Sciences.
HN65.F85   1992
361.6'1'0973—dc20   91-55562

To Sylvia Pechman

Contents

Preface   ix
    MICHAEL S. MCPHERSON

Introduction   1
    JOSEPH A. PECHMAN

1   Policies for Public Schooling in the 1990s   25
    LARRY CUBAN

2   American Health Care at the Crossroads   50
    UWE E. REINHARDT

3   Housing for Low-Income Households:
A Defense of Demand-Side Subsidies   85
    JOHN F. KAIN

4   Welfare Policy after Welfare Reform   109
    MARY JO BANE

5   Silver Threads: Pension and Health Policy
for an Aging Society   129
    HENRY J. AARON

6   Foreign Aid to the Less Developed Countries   158
    HENRY J. BRUTON

7   Social Needs and Tight Budgets:
Why Not Try Economic Efficiency?   198
    EDWARD M. GRAMLICH

8   The Politics of Social Policy in the 1990s   227
    PAUL E. PETERSON

Contributors   259

Preface

In this volume, eight social analysts assess recent trends in and future prospects for social policies in the United States. In subjects ranging from education to foreign aid, the authors examine the difficulties of reconciling social need with economic and political constraints. No one can predict with confidence the path that American public policy will take in the 1990s, but it is our hope that the essays presented here will contribute to educating the American people about the alternatives that lie before the nation in these critical areas.

This volume had its origins in a series of lectures arranged by Joseph A. Pechman when he was Bernhard Distinguished Professor in Economics at Williams College during 1988–89. Professor Pechman had assembled the essays and drafted an introduction before his untimely death in the summer of 1989. Since then, I have taken responsibility for overseeing revisions of the essays and seeing the volume through publication.

Financial support for the project was shared among several entities at Williams: the Bernhard Professorships, the Center for the Humanities and Social Sciences, the Lecture Committee, and the Department of Economics. Invaluable assistance in arranging the lectures and editing the volume was provided by Christine Naughton and Gwen Steege.

Joseph A. Pechman devoted his life to the improvement of American public policy. Joe brought enormous energy to his dual commitments to liberal social values and rigorous analysis of public policy that marked his long and exceptionally effective career. His clear thinking and his vigorous leadership will be sorely missed.

MICHAEL S. MCPHERSON

Williamstown, Massachusetts

Fulfilling America's Promise

Introduction
Joseph A. Pechman

The nation will soon be forced to address many social issues that have been neglected in the last decade or so. This neglect is in part the result of the heavy emphasis on increasing defense expenditures while cutting federal taxes by many billions of dollars. It is also a counterreaction to some of the attempts made during the 1960s to improve the welfare of the less fortunate in our society. Whatever the cause, the federal government is now spending less on social programs—other than social security—than it spent ten years ago as a share of the total budget and of gross national product (GNP). The American people are not now less compassionate than they were then, but the fiscal decisions that their political leaders are making in Washington suggest the leaders think so. The major purpose of this volume is to contribute to more enlightened and effective social policies in the last decade of the twentieth century.

The exact range of topics that fall under the umbrella of "social policy" is certainly debatable. The approach adopted here is to focus both on areas that involve investment in the future capacities of the nation as a whole—notably education and health care—and on areas concerned with the well-being of especially needy populations—welfare, housing for low-income households, and the aged. In addition, in a world of increasing interdependence, foreign aid, the United States's investment in the poor of other nations, represents a major contribution to resolving international social problems. The volume concludes with chapters on how to pay for the improved policies and on the political prospects for more effective social policy.

The discussion of these issues suggests that throwing money alone at the problems will not necessarily solve them. What is needed is an understanding of the structural problems that inhibit good policy in these areas and how to alleviate these problems. While the solutions advocated here by particular authors would surely not command universal assent (indeed, it is plain that the authors here would in at least a few areas disagree among themselves), each essay reflects a thoughtful and informed response to the issues and should be helpful in pushing the discussion forward.

PUBLIC SCHOOLING

Policymakers almost universally acknowledge that perhaps no area of social policy is more troubled than the nation's public education. Despite repeated efforts at reform, much remains to be done in our elementary and secondary schools to bring students up to the level of achievement and comprehension needed in a modern industrial economy. On standardized tests, American students do far worse than those in other advanced countries and little better than students in the Third World.

In the early 1980s, there was something of a consensus that mediocre student performance was caused by weak standards inherited from the turbulent 1960s and 1970s, inadequate instructional time in academic subjects, and poor instruction by teachers. The remedies were largely of an incremental nature: stricter graduation requirements, more homework, more testing, a longer school year, and crackdowns on absenteeism. These and other reforms were adopted in many states in the 1980s, but the results are discouraging. In Larry Cuban's assessment, the available evidence suggests that the reforms helped a minority of motivated students who were college bound but failed to work for the majority. Schooling of the poor worsened, and the gap between the haves and the have-nots widened. High dropout rates persist and functional illiteracy continues among high school graduates, particularly among minority groups.

Nor has the 1980s reform movement changed much in the classrooms, where teachers must implement the higher standards. There are examples of effective teaching and administration by dedicated educators who manage to create constructive and stimulating environments for their students. On the whole, however, according to

Cuban, little has changed in the classroom either for college-bound students or for those who enter the labor force on graduating from high school.

Cuban sees excessive emphasis on improving test scores rather than on learning as an equally disturbing development. Scores have improved as a result of better coaching and preparation of students for tests, but students have not been learning more. Too many high school graduates do not have the skills to solve problems and to participate responsibly and flexibly in a working environment.

The 1980s school reforms have not been successful, in Cuban's judgment, because they have been largely incremental in nature, rather than fundamental. Incremental changes try to improve the existing organization, rather than alter the ways in which teachers and students actually perform. Such changes include recruiting better teachers and administrators, raising salaries, improving textbooks, scheduling class work more efficiently, and using new methods of evaluation. In contrast, fundamental changes would alter the basic ways in which the schools operate. One of the most fundamental changes in American education occurred in the mid-nineteenth century, when the graded school replaced the one-room schoolhouse. The graded school revolutionized curriculum, instruction, organization, and governance of schools. The graded school was highly successful in promoting basic literacy among the nation's children. But the public, employers, and political leaders now demand more. There is a growing awareness that students should be better equipped to solve problems and exercise initiative when they go to work. Despite improved test scores, the incremental changes adopted in the 1980s have not achieved these objectives.

Cuban reviews three strategies, which have emerged in the last few years, for making fundamental changes in schooling. These strategies share a faith in the need to apply a business model to schools and are often blended together in proposals for changes. The first is to restructure the system so that principals and teachers in the schools, rather than state and district officials and school-board members, make key educational decisions. The second is to introduce market-type competition into the schools to break the monopoly now exercised by the school hierarchies. The third is to make the school a center of integrated social services, rather than exclusively a center of teaching. A good model for such integrated centers is the Head Start program, which was introduced in the mid-1960s for 4-

and 5-year-olds from poor families, to improve the ability of disadvantaged children to succeed in school and in the workplace.

These approaches are improvements over the failed policies of the 1980s and offer hope that fundamental school reform is on its way. But Cuban believes the success of the new programs, too, is at risk. Too often, proponents confine their attention to the strategy itself, rather than to what they hope to achieve. Many of those enthusiastic about these approaches risk converting a means to an end. They frequently do not understand the complexity of schooling and ignore the beliefs, norms, and relationships that combine to create effective schools. Nor do they have a clear vision of the kinds of places the new schools should be. Without such visions, reforms will be ineffective.

The objective of education policies for the 1990s should be, in Cuban's view, to bring about fundamental change in the practice of schooling. The reform strategies that have recently emerged are promising, but educators need to carefully examine and hone them to produce the desired results. An intractable deficit paralyzes the federal government, which encourages incremental, inexpensive solutions, rather than basic alterations in the structure of schooling. As a consequence, the responsibility for devising and implementing fundamental reforms and for mobilizing the resources necessary to implement them has come to rest on state and local officials. Cuban argues that the social stakes riding on better schools for children are crucial for our society and that the opportunities for genuine improvement are real.

HEALTH CARE

Uwe Reinhardt paints a disturbing picture of the present state of health care in the United States. This country possesses the greatest wealth, abundance, and technology of any industrialized country, yet its health-care system does not produce measurably better health than other industrial countries and fails to provide health-care coverage to a significant minority of its population. What brought about this uniquely U.S. paradox? The answers, claims Reinhardt, lie in the institutional structure of the U.S. health-care system, the ineffective methods of cost control, and the political difficulties of financing expansions in the system.

On the supply side, over ten million Americans are now directly or indirectly involved in the health-care business, although less than one million are physicians, dentists, and pharmacists. On the demand side, individuals, private insurance companies, businesses with health plans, and the government paid 99 percent of the health-care costs in 1987. The total health-care bill that year accounted for 11.3 percent of the GNP, the highest in the developed world.

Fully 15 percent of Americans do not have health-care insurance, and many plans leave significant gaps in coverage. One-third of the uninsured are children, and an equal share have income below the poverty line. These people cannot afford private insurance, and neither Medicare nor Medicaid, the two programs designed to finance health care for the aged and the welfare population respectively, cover most of them. While Medicaid has a wide range of benefits, its eligibility standards are strict and vary greatly among the states.

Over 70 percent of annual health-care costs are incurred on behalf of 10 percent of the population. These individuals are likely to be seriously ill at the time of treatment and do not seek out the most efficient combinations of price and quality. They also have neither the medical knowledge nor, if they are insured, much inclination to "shop around." This asymmetry of knowledge and motivation gives health-care providers a pricing advantage and generates considerable variability in local physician and hospital fees.

Through Medicare and Medicaid, the federal government accounts for 40 percent of health-care expenditure. Initially, Medicare retrospectively reimbursed hospitals for all costs incurred, giving no incentive to avoid waste. In 1983, the government switched to prescribed payments based on "diagnostically related" groupings. Medicare has always paid physicians on the basis of their own fees or the average fees in the market, a cumbersome, expensive, and capricious system.

In contrast, the states determine most Medicaid payments. Hospitals and nursing homes receive a specified rate per day, and physicians are paid an established fee. The physician payments are usually far below market rates or the rates set by Medicare and lead many physicians to avoid or limit the number of Medicaid patients.

Even though they serve a large market size, and so conceivably could have leverage in influencing health-care costs, Medicare and Medicaid have not slowed the growth of those costs. In Reinhardt's assessment, by unilaterally reducing or halting payment increases, the programs create a two-tier market that motivates health-care providers to avoid patients covered by government programs. Also, private employers suspect that lower government payments shift a disproportionate share of costs into the prices they are charged for employee health insurance. In contrast, Canada successfully controls prices through the universal, comprehensive health-insurance system administered by the provincial governments.

If health care is a private good, individuals should bear its costs; if, however, health care is a required social good that should be available equally to all citizens—as Reinhardt argues it should be—then the government should be responsible for the distribution of health care. The government can distribute health care, and limit costs at the same time, through regulation and price controls. Although Americans view health care as a social good, they have not supported government intervention to achieve an equitable distribution of health care. The result is a failed compromise between a free market and a regulated one.

Recently, a "pro-competitive" strategy gained prominence. It attempts to use free market forces to achieve efficiency in health-care pricing. Reinhardt identifies two problems with this approach: first, there are no reliable indexes of "quality" and "costliness" in health care; and, second, as with other market goods, free market health care will inevitably be distributed on the basis of ability to pay, a consequence Americans do not accept. Thus, the competitive strategy has not improved the efficiency of health-care delivery and has not slowed rising costs.

There appear to be two viable options for extending health care to cover those who are not now insured. The government could mandate business coverage of all employees and expand Medicaid to cover everyone else, or it could simply transform Medicaid into a fail-safe insurance system for all Americans not insured elsewhere.

Mandating employer benefits would cover three-fourths of the currently uninsured without any government spending, but it would add to business costs and might have serious effects on prices, output, and employment. Alternatively, a fail-safe net would eliminate the implicit cross-subsidies in the present system without coercing business to provide insurance. Reinhardt suggests that payments of such insurance should be based strictly on income and could be made progressive to discourage higher-income individuals from joining. Those not participating, however, would be required to share in the costs of insurance for low-income families and individuals through their payments to the general revenues. Such a system would increase health-care costs by about 2 to 3 percent, a price that the nation could easily afford.

In Reinhardt's view, the alternatives facing policymakers are simple: to muddle through with continued waste, overcapacity for some, and no care for others; to create a universal health-care system that controls costs and provides access to health care to all groups in the population; or to create a two-track system consisting of private insurance for the large majority of Americans and public financing for the poor. Unfortunately, the United States is now at a stalemate between the conflicting goals of health providers, insurance companies, business, politicians, and those who use health-care services. Resolving this stalemate is a vital issue for the nation in the decade ahead.

HOUSING FOR LOW-INCOME HOUSEHOLDS

The recent emergence of a highly visible homeless population, the explosive growth in housing prices in some metropolitan areas, and the savings-and-loan crisis have renewed interest in U.S. housing policy. John Kain identifies three basic questions for federal housing policy. How much subsidy should the government provide? What is the nature of the housing problem, and is it getting better or worse? And given the level of government spending, what is the most cost-effective method of allocating the funds?

The variety of federal, state, and local housing subsidies—mostly uncoordinated—makes the answer to the first question difficult. The federal Department of Housing and Urban Development spends approximately $10 billion a year, and the Tax Reform Act of 1986 for low-income housing provided another $2.7 billion over five years. Welfare programs combine to spend $10 billion a year on housing. All told, about 8 million people receive some of these benefits, through income maintenance, housing assistance, or a combination of the two. In addition, 5.3 million low-income renters and homeowners receive assistance amounting to $15 billion a year. Despite the recent emphasis on more cost-effective demand-side subsidies, which provide rental assistance to families eligible for appropriate programs, most of these individuals live in housing units produced under costly, ongoing supply-side production programs. During the Reagan years, there were substantial cutbacks in these programs, which were only partially offset by a shift to demand-side subsidies.

Recent studies suggest that the rental prices measured in the Consumer Price Index underestimate recent increases in rental costs and that the number of rental units under $300 a month shrank by one million between 1974 and 1983, even as poverty-level renter households rose by 300,000. The loss in units is due both to increases in rental costs and to the upgrading of units.

The percent of very low income households (those with income of less than $5,000 a year) and low-income households (those with $5,000–$10,000 a year) receiving housing assistance went up between 1974 and 1983, but, because subsidized units did not go up as rapidly, the number of eligible households not receiving housing assistance grew by 2.4 million. The growth of the gap accelerated in 1983 as supply-side programs, which were started before the Reagan cutbacks, were completed. The shares of very low income and low-income individuals receiving aid began decreasing in the mid-1980s and, unless a change in policy occurs, this trend will continue.

There is, in Kain's assessment, a simple answer to the question of how to allocate the funds efficiently: Almost all housing subsidies should be demand-side subsidies, not production or supply-side subsidies. Dysfunctional and other problem families and individuals are exceptions who may need the government to provide housing for them. Demand-side subsidies work better because they are less costly than supply-side subsidies and would encourage greater conservation of the existing housing stock, yet would not significantly affect the level of market rents.

The Congressional Budget Office, the Experimental Housing Allowance Program, and several private studies show that cash or voucher subsidies are half as costly as unit production or rehabilitation. This judgment is based on studies of the relative costs of the two types of programs in many parts of the country over the past fifteen years.

Demand subsidies are based on "fair market rents" (FMR), the cost of living in modest but decent housing in the local rental market area. In 1983 a new voucher program began, which, unlike previous programs, allowed tenants to live in housing costing more than the FMR, with the renter paying the difference; if they live in housing requiring less than the FMR, renters keep the difference. These modifications will make the program easier for households to find satisfactory housing, although the average ratio of rent to income may increase somewhat.

A common objection to demand-side subsidies is that they drive up market rates at the low end of the rent distribution. In fact, Kain reports, studies of the effects of full-scale, demand-side programs in two medium-size cities (Green Bay and South Bend) concluded that almost all rent increases were due to general inflation. Over time, rent increases for participants were only 4–5 percent higher than the expected market rents, and even these small differences reflected the elimination of discounts in units owned by relatives of the subsidized families.

In the two test cities, demand for housing units increased only 8 percent. Three facts can explain this modest increase: recipients of housing assistance occupied just one-fifth of eligible dwellings, 75 percent of families originally living in substandard housing chose to repair their units rather than move, and low-income renter households spent half their income on housing, as opposed to the nationwide average of one-quarter. Another study of twenty-one urban markets concluded that only in Miami, with its large refugee population, would rents react significantly differently from the two test markets.

About ninety percent of very low income and 94 percent of low-income renters already lived in "physically adequate" housing in 1985. If FMRs were increased by only 10 percent, the supply of housing units potentially eligible for subsidy would increase by about 2.7 million. These units would be produced under a larger demand-side program by preventing the deterioration of units currently renting at levels above the FMR or by upgrading currently substandard units.

Thus, the March 1988 call by the National Housing Task Force to expand federal production of housing is, in Kain's view, probably a mistake. He sees the principal housing problem not as inadequate housing, but rather as inadequate income. Fewer than 10 percent of very low income households lived in inadequate housing in 1985, but 23 percent of these households spent more than 30 percent of their income on housing. Use of the more cost-effective demand-side programs would permit the federal government to provide housing assistance to about twice as many deserving low-income households for any given level of spending. Whether the Bush administration, or its successor later in the decade, can be induced to move in this direction is not clear, but Kain presents powerful arguments that doing so would enhance both the efficiency and the equity of the nation's housing policy.

WELFARE POLICY

The passage of the Family Support Act in 1988 was heralded by many political observers as a major improvement in the welfare system of the United States. Its purpose is to encourage parents to obtain education, training, and employment to avoid long-term dependency on welfare. Nevertheless, Mary Jo Bane urges us to consider whether this reform of the welfare system will actually achieve its objectives.

The basic welfare program to assist needy families is Aid to Families with Dependent Children (AFDC), which provides cash assistance to about 3.7 million families, with children, who are under the poverty line. Approximately 90 percent of recipient families consist of children and their mother. No matter what their earnings or family size are, two-parent families are ineligible in all states if the parents are working, and in twenty-two states even if both parents are unemployed. While one-third of recipients leave the rolls after one or two years, 30 percent stay for at least eight years. Only about one-fifth of recipients who leave welfare work their way off; instead, most marry, reconcile, or otherwise join with a working adult.

The transition from welfare to work is difficult to make because the lost benefits and the costs of going to work often make a low-wage job financially impossible for the single mother. In many cases, the increases in income from employment are not enough to pay for the lost Medicaid and child care. Moreover, AFDC administration is oriented more toward verifying eligibility than toward helping individuals locate jobs and become self-supporting. The result is that only about 7 percent of recipients work, and hardly any are in training programs.

Until 1981, the AFDC disregarded a share of welfare recipients' earnings when calculating assistance, but since then work programs and requirements have replaced monetary incentives as work encouragement. In 1967 Congress created the Work Incentives program (WIN) to encourage work. Partly because WIN never provided much funding, states often complied with the minimal letter of the law by registering recipients for the program without actively helping them. Bane judges that WIN was, with a few exceptions, a failure.

During the 1980s some states began their own programs to help people achieve self-sufficiency. Massachusetts, for example, established a separate, voluntary program that encouraged clients to participate in education, training, and employment activities and provided services such as day care and transportation. This program succeeded in getting client participation and seems to have improved the lives of welfare clients. An evaluation of seven such work-welfare programs, not including that of Massachusetts, however, found that the earnings and employment of participants improved only moderately.

The main vehicle of reform in the Family Support Act is the Job Opportunities and Basic Skills (JOBS) program, which is similar in many respects to the programs originated by Massachusetts and other states. Unlike WIN, JOBS requires participation, not just registration, and covers more individuals than WIN did. The goal of JOBS is self-sufficiency, and states must develop plans to teach basic and jobs skills and provide support and child care.

However, Bane notes, the state programs were developed locally, and it is not clear that mandating development of programs from Washington will achieve the same success. Some successful state programs are voluntary, which means that both recipients and the state make a commitment to each other; mandatory participation under JOBS may not result in the same commitment from either party. Unlike some regions of the country, Massachusetts had the advantage of low unemployment and high starting wages when this program started, making success easier for those willing to invest in themselves. Finally, the federal government provides only modest funding for compliance with the Family Support Act. Thus, the success of the reform is far from guaranteed.

Even beyond these hurdles, the new system may in many cases simply transform the welfare poor into the working poor. While the Family Support Act provides extensions of Medicaid and child care after the person stops receiving active program assistance, recipients receive the benefits for only a limited period of time. The reform also fails to address the high effective taxation of recipient's wages by AFDC. In short, Bane concludes, it does not deal in a fundamental way with the work/welfare dilemma facing single mothers.

Despite its faults, Bane views passage of the Family Support Act as a political triumph for welfare reform. There is, however, more to be done. The next step is a policy that will permit individuals to support themselves above the poverty line without welfare. Changes such as health insurance for low-income mothers, an expanded earned income credit, and, especially, guaranteed child support will help to reduce reliance on welfare to the minimum possible. Such changes will require a larger commitment of funds by the federal government.

Retirement and Health Policy for the Aged

If the authors' assessments of current policy toward schooling, health care, and housing are fairly bleak and that toward welfare mixed, Henry Aaron's reading of the evidence on policies toward the aged is much more reassuring.

The demographic history of the United States has been turbulent for well over a century, and current projections indicate more of the same in the decades ahead. The proportion of the U.S. population below age nineteen has been falling since the 1880s, interrupted only by the baby boom between 1950 and 1970. Correspondingly, the proportion of those fifty-five or older has been growing for well over a century. And, in the next twenty years, there will be an explosion in the percentage of people over seventy-five.

The elderly are entitled to receive retirement and health-care benefits through social security. Many people worry that the burden imposed by the elderly on the working population will be very heavy, and some believe that it will be excessive. Can America afford to pay the benefits? How can the nation plan now to fulfill the promises to the aged embodied in current legislation and widely supported by the members of the working as well as the retired population?

Aaron argues that a population cohort can impose economic burdens on another only if its members consume more in their lifetimes than they earn. The ratio of workers to beneficiaries, which is the usual measure to dramatize the costs generated by the elderly, gives almost no information about the economic burdens they will impose on others. If, for example, every person relied exclusively on private pension plans, their pensions would come entirely from their own savings, and they would not be imposing any burden on the working population during their retirement.

It is true that current retirees are receiving a high rate of return—about 6 percent—on their contributions to the social security system, but, notes Aaron, this is only a transition feature as the system matures. When Congress enacted social security, the working population at the time was "blanketed in" to receive the full statutory benefits, even though they would make contributions to the system only through the part of their working lives remaining after the program began. As the population has aged, the number of retirees who received such "bargains" has declined; ultimately, this cohort will disappear. Since members of the baby-boom cohort will be making social security contributions throughout their working careers, they will receive a real rate of return of only about 2 percent, which is not exorbitant by the standards of private pension plans. In other words, the baby-boom generation will be paying fully for their social security benefits as well as for their private pensions and thus will not impose any burden on future workers for their retirement income. In fact, the taxes baby boomers will pay during their working lives will generate a large reserve fund that will not be exhausted until well beyond the mid-twenty-first century. This reserve will add to national saving, raise the capital stock, and increase the nation's productive capacity.

By contrast, Aaron argues, currently scheduled payroll taxes will be grossly insufficient to pay for promised Medicare benefits. Moreover, many private employers have not set aside adequate reserves to pay for the health benefits promised to their retirees. Thus, unlike the retirement programs, public and private health-care programs for the aged are being financed in ways that will not add to national saving. According to current projections, future generations of workers will be forced to reduce their consumption by at least 4 percent to finance the baby boomers' health benefits. This burden can be avoided only if taxes and premiums are raised to pay for the health benefits currently projected over the next several decades.

An even more serious burden that the baby boomers and others active today are imposing on future workers is the federal deficit on the government programs outside the social security and Medicare trust funds. This deficit, running at $190 billion in 1988, is projected to exceed $200 billion in the 1990s. By refusing to pay for current government services, this generation is using up the nation's saving to pay for current consumption rather than to finance a larger productive capacity. Aaron's preferred solution to this problem is to eliminate the non-social security and Medicare deficit by reducing government outlays, raising taxes, or by doing some of each.

A serious attack on the deficit, argues Aaron, should include two social security changes that will not fundamentally alter the present system. First, the government should tax social security retirement benefits like private pensions. This would mean raising the percentage of total benefits subject to the income tax from half to the percentage not contributed by the employee (85 percent for current retirees) and taxing the subsidy value of Medicare insurance coverage. Second, the government could increase the social security retirement age from 65 to 67, which could become effective in less than twenty-five years, and align the age for receiving Medicare entitlement with the higher retirement age when it becomes effective.

Aaron thus concludes that current public and private programs for the elderly are working well. There is no case for cuts in the retirement programs because they are too costly or too generous. While action will be needed soon to put the Medicare program on a firm financial basis, the most important way to reduce burdens current workers will place on future cohorts of workers is to eliminate the large non-social security deficit that is draining national saving and obstructing economic growth. This diagnosis of course raises the question of whether the deficit can be tackled without obstructing progress in those areas of social policy, such as schooling and health care for the poor, that badly need attention.

FOREIGN AID

What about social policy beyond the nation's borders? Plainly, a treatment of the social policies of other nations falls outside the scope of this volume. Yet, one important area of U.S. social spending is directed toward alleviating the social problems of other nations. This is the vexing topic of foreign aid. Henry Bruton argues in his paper that this area of federal policymaking requires fresh thinking and a renewed sense of purpose as much as or more than it needs additional funding.

Poor people, notes Bruton, exist all over the world, but there is a large group of countries in which most people are poor. These lesser developed countries (LDCs) are lagging far behind the industrialized countries in per-capita output and wealth, and the prospect is that they will continue to lag for many years, or even decades, to come. U.S. policies toward the LDCs must be part of the social agenda primarily for humanitarian reasons: It is simply immoral and unjust for many to enjoy a high standard of living while others live in abject poverty elsewhere. It is also important to help the poor nations because widespread poverty generates tension and unrest and undermines international security.

Recent economic history raises doubts about the growth prospects of the developing countries. From 1950 to 1980, the growth of output and foreign trade in both developed and developing countries was on the average higher than it was in the nineteenth and early twentieth centuries. Since 1980, however, growth everywhere has declined, particularly in the developing countries. With only a few exceptions (notably Japan, Korea, and Taiwan), the LDCs did not narrow the gap between them and the developed world even when they were growing rapidly, and there is little prospect that they will do better now that growth rates have declined. Thus, the notion of "catching up" to the West in the foreseeable future is impractical and even misguided. Under the circumstances, argues Bruton, the objective of the developed countries should be to help the LDCs achieve a level of economic development that is compatible with their own capabilities, institutions, and traditions, rather than to catch up to the West. Reducing poverty and establishing more flexible and responsive economies are much more immediately achievable objectives.

The formula for economic development that was influential in the late 1940s and the 1950s emphasized capital formation as the key to economic growth. Countries with high per-capita income and wealth provided more capital per worker than those with low per-capita income and wealth. Hence, all that seemed necessary was to increase the rate of saving and investment in order to stimulate more growth. The role of foreign assistance, according to this view, was to provide additional saving when the domestic saving rate was too low to achieve the desired rate of capital formation.

The emphasis on investment to promote economic development gave way to other theories when it became clear that capital alone was not in itself sufficient to generate satisfactory growth. Inappropriate exchange rates and factor prices often created severe distortions that interfered with growth in low-income countries. Economists argued, therefore, that getting prices right and avoiding interference with economic incentives is at least as important as a high rate of capital formation. This "new orthodoxy," which achieved preeminence in the field of development, blames slow growth and poverty primarily on badly conceived government policies, which misallocate resources and lead to huge inefficiencies. According to this school of thought, the solution to economic development is to avoid government interference with the operation of markets.

The new orthodoxy has itself been found wanting in some recent development literature, mainly because it pays little attention to the role of culture, institutions, and values as sources of development and improved welfare. The impact of government varies greatly among countries and has not necessarily been an impediment to economic growth, particularly in countries in which government historically provided responsible leadership in social and economic affairs. Clearly, suggests Bruton, the right approach is to use all a country's resources—human and physical, public and private—to promote its development.

Although individual countries and international organizations devoted a large amount of money to aid for poor nations, the results have not, in Bruton's assessment, been encouraging. Those who provided the aid as well as those who received it greatly underestimated the complexities of designing and implementing an effective aid policy. In part, this poor record is the result of arrogance on the part of donors, who have preconceived notions on how to use the aid; typically the recipients' views and aspirations do not interest them.

Despite problems and doubts, there have been successful aid experiences. One study concluded that about one-third of aid-financed capital projects achieved their objectives, another third came reasonably close, and the remaining third were disappointments. The successes involved specific physical projects, such as roads, harbors and ports, schools, and other buildings. Viewing the history of aid more generally, the most important failure has been the inability to reduce poverty or to relieve it even in the most needy countries. Food aid has on some occasions helped nutritionally deprived people but frequently at the expense of the long-run development of a productive agricultural sector.

Bruton identifies two general approaches to improving foreign aid. The first is to build on present programs, while trying to make them work better. The second is to devise a substantially new approach. Although significant improvement might be possible on an incremental basis, Bruton shows great sympathy with the idea of more far-reaching change.

All parties could improve the present aid system if there were more cooperation among the aid agencies (such as The World Bank, The International Monetary Fund, regional development banks, and the U.S. Agency for International Development), if the recipient countries established effective procedures to coordinate the aid effort, and if there were genuine cooperation between donors and recipients. It is particularly important that aid donors should understand the culture and aspirations of the society receiving aid and should respect its values and institutions.

The new aid orientation should build on lessons learned from the successes and failures of previous aid programs. Essentially, Bruton argues, foreign aid should contribute to indigenous development and create an environment in which searching and learning by the aid recipient take place routinely, rather than seek to "displace" that economy with that existing in the developed countries. Although the particulars must vary depending on the history and circumstances of the receiving countries, a likely initial step is to push the economy hard by a major devaluation of its currency, which will create new opportunities for replacement of imports by locally produced goods and will encourage the development of new exports. These opportunities will not only increase employment and output, they will also increase learning by managers and workers and impart to the private sector a capacity to move resources from one activity to another with only modest loss of productivity. In other words, in Bruton's view, aid should foster independence and self-reliance and lay the foundation for change in an orderly and efficient manner.

Bruton suggests a variety of ways in which a U.S. aid effort oriented to this way of thinking about development could be more productive than existing U.S. programs. The United States should recognize, for example, that providing a market for developing country exports through reductions of trade restrictions may contribute importantly to development; spending to compensate domestic interests harmed by such expanded U.S. imports might usefully be construed as a form of foreign aid.

Although Bruton is far from satisfied with the level of U.S. efforts to help developing countries, he argues forcefully that more dollars without more thought will not guarantee improvement and may even make things worse.

BUDGETING AND SOCIAL EFFICIENCY

The papers on social policy identify at least three areas where greater social spending and new policy initiatives are strongly urged: health care, public schooling, and welfare. In other areas, including housing and foreign aid, redesigning programs to be more rational and effective would justify expanded spending. Only in the area of retirement do these authors judge our national policies to be reasonably adequate.

Yet, the nation's social programs have been shortchanged in recent years despite the evident need for government assistance. The poverty rate and housing costs have been rising since the early 1970s, yet income transfers and housing assistance to low-income households have been curtailed in the 1980s. Medicare and private health costs have risen dramatically and will continue to do so, but 15 percent of the population still lacks health insurance. Measures of educational attainment are low, particularly for children from low-income families. And many of the poorest countries languish.

Some people, confronted with such assessments, suggest that it is more important to address these social problems than to lower the deficit, but failure to reduce the deficit makes social problems worse, not better, in the long run. Lower saving causes lower investment and slower productivity growth; even if foreigners make up the saving shortfall, a larger share of future resources must be devoted to paying foreign investors for using their capital. In either case, the result is slower or negative future income growth, which has been correlated historically with both higher poverty rates and lower non-defense spending. Thus, the vital issue for budgetary policy becomes finding the resources to improve social policy while working to reduce the federal deficit. It is this challenging assignment that Ned Gramlich tackles in his paper.

Forecasts by the Congressional Budget Office show the federal deficit declining in 1990–94. Adjusting for the social security surpluses, however, the predicted decline is less than 1 percent of the GNP. These forecasts do not fully account for the cost of bailing out insolvent thrift institutions, rising health-care costs, and the costs of cleaning up nuclear weapons plants, all of which will raise future federal outlays. A more reasonable prediction, Gramlich concludes, is that the deficit will not change much as a percentage of the GNP unless the government raises taxes.

Although there is a political aversion to increasing taxes, it should be possible to agree on a menu of tax changes that would increase economic efficiency as well as raise additional revenue. Three such measures are eliminating tax loopholes, adding to the taxes on energy, and taxing private activities that impose costs on others. A fourth measure—child-support enforcement—is as efficient, even though it is not strictly a tax.

Most tax preferences distort economic behavior by benefiting certain classes of taxpayers or economic activities. Clearly, eliminating such preferences would improve both horizontal equity and economic efficiency. One example is the deduction for home-mortgage interest, which artificially increases housing investment. Another is the deductibility of interest but not of dividends, which encourages excessive use of debt financing in business. Other tax provisions that distort economic decisions are deductions for state and local taxes and the exclusion of employee fringe benefits from the tax base. The Congressional Budget Office estimates that eliminating fourteen such inefficient provisions would raise revenues by almost $140 billion or 2 percent of the GNP in 1994. Substantial revenues could be gained even if these provisions were only partially curtailed by imposing caps on the deductions, allowing only a share of certain business expenses to be deducted, increasing the standard deduction, and other methods.

Because it relies heavily on foreign oil, the United States is vulnerable to the kind of supply shocks that occurred in the 1970s. Gramlich argues that it would, therefore, be in the national interest to encourage conservation by adopting a tax on energy use. A general energy tax would avoid discriminating among energy sources and uses. As alternatives, introducing an oil-import fee on the relatively inelastic foreign oil supply or raising the gasoline tax might serve the same purpose.

Another type of tax that would improve economic efficiency is one that increases the cost of private activities that impose costs on others. These include drinking, smoking, and emissions of hazardous materials. It would be possible to raise at least $20 billion a year by increasing the taxes on alcohol and tobacco and introducing taxes on pollution activities.

While child support may appear to be strictly an equity issue, Gramlich makes an interesting case that requiring absent fathers to pay support for their children improves economic efficiency. The courts award child support to 60 percent of mothers eligible for Aid to Families with Dependent Children, but only half receive the full award and a quarter receive nothing. A fully effective child-support system would directly increase the resources of low-income families and reduce welfare costs. In addition, the transfer of funds from the absent father to the welfare mother reduces the average tax rate of the two parents because the tax on the earnings of the mother—that is, the benefit-reduction rate as earnings increase—is very high (on the order of 75 percent). This cut in the tax rate would increase the incentive of mothers to work and thus raise the supply of labor.

Improving the structure of federal grants to states and localities would also improve efficiency. Presently two types of grants exist: open-ended grants, where the government pays a predetermined share of the costs regardless of how much is spent; and close-ended grants, where the government pays a higher percentage of the costs but sets an upper limit to the amount of its aid. It is ironic, Gramlich notes, that the government uses close-ended grants where open-ended grants would make more sense and vice versa. For example, a switch of the highway grants from the present 90-percent close-ended grant to 30-percent open-ended grants would raise total highway spending by roughly 17 percent while it reduced federal outlays by about 30 percent, or $8 billion a year.

Similarly, switching the federal welfare grants from open-ended to close-ended would eliminate the incentive of poor people to migrate to high-benefit areas and also reduce the variability of state benefits. For example, the federal government might pay all welfare costs up to 60 percent of the poverty line, 75 percent of costs from 60 to 80 percent of the poverty line, and 50 percent of costs from 80 to 100 percent of the poverty line. This close-ended grant would cost the federal government an additional $7 billion a year, but it would raise benefits by 6 percent—all in low-benefit states.

In brief, Gramlich claims that it is possible to increase social spending, improve economic incentives, and reduce the federal deficit. A concentrated effort is needed to modify the federal tax and grant systems to improve economic efficiency. On the tax side, elimination of preferences and taxation of activities that impose heavy costs on society would raise revenue and eliminate economic distortions. Similarly, revision of the federal grant system could raise total government spending to socially optimal levels while lowering federal spending. The government should consider these measures at all times, but the measures are especially relevant in current conditions when there are such formidable obstacles to tax-rate increases.

THE POLITICS OF SOCIAL POLICY

Proposals for reform, both in taxes and in spending, must be considered in light of the political reality of a decade of political stalemate on social policy. In Paul Peterson's analysis, that stalemate has left the major social programs relatively unchanged. Although some cuts in smaller, less visible programs occurred as part of the Reagan effort to cut the size of the federal government, real expenditures for the major entitlements remained virtually the same (while expenditures in other parts of the federal budget including defense and interest grew). Also, the design of most programs has remained unchanged.

In Peterson's view, the primary cause of this stalemate is the division of power between a Republican president and a Democratic Congress. Since the political balance is not likely to change, the stalemate on social policy is likely to persist for some time to come.

In earlier years of U.S. history, presidents usually brought congressional majorities with them, thus avoiding a division of power between the two branches of government. Since the end of World War II, this has not been the case. By 1992 the Republicans will have controlled the White House for twenty of the preceding twenty-eight years and twenty-eight of the preceding forty years. During that same period, the Republicans will have controlled both houses of Congress for only two years.

The tendency of incumbents to be reelected facilitates Democratic control of Congress. In 1948, only 80 percent of congressional incumbents went undefeated; by 1986, the reelection rate was 98 percent. In addition, the average margin of victory of House incumbents increased from 59 percent in 1956 to 86 percent in 1986.

During this period, changes in the organization of Congress have given individual members great influence on policies in specific program areas. The number of committees and subcommittees increased from 130 in 1955 to 193 in 1980 in the House, and from 118 to 205 in the Senate. The proliferation of committees gave almost every member of the House and Senate a chance to be chairman or ranking minority member of some committee or subcommittee. The chairmen and ranking members built close alliances with the agencies they oversee and the special interest groups involved in the programs they legislated. These "iron triangles" of interest groups, congressional subcommittees, and executive agencies established tight control over program development and have secured steady increases in funding for the activities in which they had a special interest. Outlays of the federal programs most susceptible to the influence of the iron triangles increased from 2.5 percent to 5.6 percent of the GNP during the 1970s.

During the Reagan presidency, Peterson suggests, the influence of special interest groups declined while that of the congressional party leaders increased. The groundwork for the shift in power was laid in 1981, when President Reagan pushed through Congress a huge tax cut and a large increase in defense spending. The resulting deficit and the problems of getting an agreement on the budget between the President and Congress greatly weakened decentralized subcommittee-based decision-making. Congressional leaders and the White House negotiated legislation with significant fiscal implications and then combined the legislation into one omnibus bill at the end of a legislative session. Control over budgetary decisions shifted from the individual congressman to the party leaders, thus undermining the influence of the major participants in the iron triangles.

The stalemate on social programs is likely to continue into the 1990s because there are irreconcilable differences between Democrats and Republicans. The Democrats will struggle to defend the entitlement programs (including social security, education, Medicare, housing, and welfare) while the Republicans will continue to resist tax increases. Since 50 percent of the federal budget is either directly or indirectly indexed for inflation, there will be no room for expanding old programs or establishing new ones until an agreement on tax increases is reached.

In contrast, Peterson notes, policies at the state and local levels were less confrontational and more oriented toward problem solving. During the 1980s, when the federal government was reducing taxes, the state and local governments were increasing them to pay for some programs formerly financed by federal grants-in-aid. For example, total per-pupil expenditures in elementary and secondary schools increased, while federal aid was declining. State and local governments are also supporting other programs that promote economic development, including higher education, environmental control, transportation, and infrastructure.

States have been less willing to take up the slack in programs that are redistributive in nature, such as welfare, health care for the needy, and assistance to the homeless. They are reluctant to fund such programs adequately because they do not wish to invite a larger indigent population into their jurisdictions. The Washington stalemate on redistributional programs tends to be replicated at the state level because of interstate competition for productive labor and industry.

Small-scale, incremental policy innovations are still possible in this environment, as both Cuban's discussion of education and Bane's discussion of welfare reform in this volume illustrate. Although the nation may fail to adopt a comprehensive solution to the health-care problem in the next decade, controls to limit the increase in costs will be likely to be carried out. Nor, Peterson argues, will there be a comprehensive solution to the poverty problem, but the government might raise welfare benefits modestly, perhaps by establishing a national minimum standard. It may improve eduction and training programs to help prepare the poor to participate in a modern industrialized economy. It may well address in a fragmented and decentralized manner the problems of the homeless by increasing the number of shelters and providing more funds to institutionalize the mentally ill.

Social issues are likely to be addressed in this piecemeal and fragmented way in the 1990s. But, Peterson concludes, the creative urge in American politics will reassert itself sooner or later to solve the urgent problems on the social agenda. To inaugurate the new era, America will need new political mechanisms to break the stalemate between the conservative and progressive political forces in its society.

CONCLUSION

How can a volume of this kind contribute to improved social policy in the United States for the remainder of the 1990s and beyond? As of this writing, political stalemate continues, even as pressures for resolution of our economic difficulties mount. Certainly there is no magic in these pages that will demolish the roadblocks in the way of the nation's leaders' coming to grips seriously with these problems. Yet the problems continue to grow more, not less, urgent, and the folly of one-dimensional policy formulas that do not deal with worsening failures of social policy is becoming more apparent.

A common theme of the essays in this volume is that when and as the nation comes to grips with these problems—whether in incremental steps or on a more wholesale basis—the importance of sound policy analysis is substantial. It is necessary to distinguish areas of relative success, such as retirement policy, from areas of substantial failure, such as federal housing policy. Within specific policy areas, the nation needs clarity about goals and about the efficiency as well as the equity consequences of policy choices. Tensions between economic analysis and political realities are inescapable, although the analyses in this volume suggest that they are much more severe in some areas, such as housing policies, than in others, such as retirement. In certain policy areas, such as education and welfare reform, there may be scope for significant state and local initiatives. In other areas like health care and, obviously, foreign aid, substantial recasting of federal policies may be essential. The relative successes of such recent federal policy efforts as the Tax Reform Act of 1986, the Family Support Act discussed in Bane's essay on welfare, and the restructuring of the financing of Social Security in the early 1980s show the possibility of intelligent and effective design of federal policies. When the time is ripe for further serious action on the important social problems examined in these papers, the analyses presented here may help provide the basis for effective action.

1 Policies for Public Schooling in the 1990s

LARRY CUBAN

> When he first arrived in Yankee Stadium, [Yogi] Berra was a notorious bad-ball hitter. A Yankee coach, Charlie Dressen, told him, "Yogi, think when you're up there hitting."
>
> The next time up, Berra struck out without taking the bat off his shoulder. When he returned to the dugout, Dressen asked, "What happened?"
>
> Berra explained, "I can't think and hit at the same time." (Berkow 1988)

Berra's statement about thinking getting in the way of action well sums up my assessment of the last decade of policymaking involving schools. Much policymaking and little thought produced barren reforms that have had few positive effects beyond symbolic media victories while they ignored substantial issues that daily touch the vast majority of students. Yes, policymakers in the 1980s worked the system harder, squeezing schools to do a better job, but the system of schooling is now a dry sponge with not much left for the children who need help the most. This is the core of my argument. Specifically, I will make two claims and provide evidence for them. They are, first, that the school-reform policies of the 1980s demonstrated the futility of incrementalism, and, second, that unless otherwise influenced, federal, state, and local policymakers in the 1990s will continue to define the fundamental problems of public schooling in a barren manner, framing ill-defined problems and pushing trivial solutions.

I begin with the framing of problems because major policies are often cast as solutions to problems. Federal legislation in education, such as the National Defense Education Act (1958), was a policy solution to the problem of Soviet scientific advances in outer space outstripping those of the United States. In the 1980s, low levels of academic achievement got defined as the central problem of schooling, and a consensus rapidly formed over the causes of mediocre student performance: soft-as-mush standards inherited from the permissive 1960s and 1970s and little instructional time spent on academic tasks. Policy solutions came swiftly from statehouses and governors' offices. Laws that mandated higher graduation requirements, a longer school year, improved teacher salaries, and merit pay plans spilled forth from state capitals.

Why do I claim that unless the problems that were poorly framed in this decade are corrected, they will continue to lead to trivial solutions into the 1990s? By "trivial" I mean incremental, short-term solutions that go for flashy gains for certain groups of students while ignoring the grave shortcomings in schooling for the majority. Such shallow gains as improved test scores and increased enrollments in math and science courses may have only weak links to improved teaching or, of even more importance, to what students learn.

In making this argument, I will concentrate on examining how policymakers conceptualize problems and solutions. I will not blast schools as failures, nor will I point to teachers, administrators, or even college professors as villains. There have been enough of these sledgehammer attacks that miss the stake and smash the foot. Instead, I will ask about the ends sought for reforms and whether or not changes really materialize where they count: in classrooms and schools. I am guided by the wisdom of Georges Bernanos, the French writer and educator, who said "There is no worse lie than a problem poorly stated" (Bernanos 1955:153).

I will argue that the school-reform policies in the 1980s—the so-called excellence movement—were barren because they benefited only those students preparing for college. These reforms failed largely those labeled "average," and worse yet, those in the bottom half, putting the nation further at risk in schooling than it was in 1983 when the report by that name was published (*A Nation at Risk* 1983). The reform policies of the 1980s worsened the schooling the urban poor received and thus contributed even more to the two-tiered society of haves and have-nots of which the Kerner Commission (1968) warned the nation.

(1). The reforms of the 1980s helped a minority of motivated, college-bound students but failed to work for the majority of students.

On the fifth anniversary of the *Nation at Risk* report, then U.S. secretary of education William Bennett reported to the president that while schools raised academic standards and students showed modest increases in achievement, still, "too many students do not graduate from our high schools and too many of those who do graduate have been poorly educated. Our students know too little and their command of essential skills is too slight" (*San Jose Mercury News* 1988).

To quote the abrasive former cabinet member is insufficient to support the claim. Harder evidence is needed, and it comes from the very data that reformers relish: numbers. For the last decade or so, low test scores on standardized achievement tests have been used as markers of dry rot in the schools. State-by-state comparisons, begun by former U.S. secretary of education Terrell Bell and continued by Bennett, his successor, hung on a wall chart, and both secretaries frequently cited the comparisons to show gains and losses in national academic performance and by inference the fruits of school reforms.

Let me update some of the test-score data. Instead of the Scholastic Aptitude Test (SAT) scores and other measures used in those wall charts, which are inappropriate in assessing performance, since they do not measure what is taught in schools, I will use the National Assessment of Educational Progress (NAEP) results for 9, 13, and 17-year-olds in math and science, two areas of particular emphasis since 1983 when state-driven mandates and federal interest accelerated.

Both NAEP reports measured achievement in 1986. At first glance, the news is welcome. They reported gains in average performance at different age levels and the equally important gains that black and Hispanic students made in partially closing the large gaps between themselves and white students. Also, more students were taking science and math, and teachers assigned more homework (Mullis and Jenkins 1988; Dossey et al. 1988).

There is also unwelcome news. Test-score gains were in what the reports called lower-order skills, such as adding and subtracting in math and knowledge about everyday facts and simple principles in science. Between 40 and 50 percent of 17-year-olds who took the math and science tests could perform moderately complex math reasoning and analyze scientific procedures; the rest could not. At the highest level of complex problem solving in math and integrating principles in science, only 7 percent of the eleventh graders displayed skills. Usually, colleges recruit science and math majors from this student pool. Furthermore, comparisons in achievement with other countries continued to place American students at the level of children from Third World nations (Dossey et al. 1988:32; Mullis and Jenkins 1988:39).

These results show an unfavorable picture of student achievement in the early years of 1980s school reform. What darkens the picture considerably is the persistence and growth of functional illiteracy among high school graduates and the substantial percentage of students who fail to complete school. The U.S. military continues to report high failure rates among high school graduates who take tests to enlist in the armed services. In the late 1970s, New York Telephone gave a basic exam for entry-level jobs to 23,000 people; 84 percent failed. Businesses continue to provide basic skills training to employees who hold a high school diploma. Community colleges continue to offer remedial work to high school graduates who have limited reading and writing skills. Far too many students who exit proudly from auditoriums waving their diplomas learn quickly in the military, corporate world, and community colleges that they are ill equipped—diploma and all (Perry 1988).

One can guess how much worse it is for their classmates who leave school before graduation. On the average, one out of every four students leaves high school without a diploma. While many of these dropouts will secure a certificate by returning to school or taking a special test within five to ten years of leaving school, the national dropout average of 25 percent remains high. For big cities, the numbers soar to 40 and 50 percent, especially in those schools enrolling large numbers of low-income ethnic students (Hammack 1987; Wehlage and Rutter 1987).

What may drive these numbers up is the stress on higher academic standards, which usually gets translated into setting higher hurdles for promotion from one grade to another. These get-tough standards are viewed as benchmarks of excellence. Hidden beneath the surface, however, is the personal price paid by the growing number of students retained—that is, those who flunk the grade or course. Students left behind two or three times in elementary or junior high school are prime candidates for dropping out (Gottfredson 1988).

It is probably too early to say with much confidence whether the current reforms requiring more time in school, more courses, and more tests push students out of school. Yet, among the ethnic poor, the number leaving school before graduation probably will not decrease. Moreover, the figures still remain at intolerably high levels for a society that prizes equal educational opportunity. The so-called excellence movement has yet to make a dent in those dropout statistics (McDill, Natriello, and Pallas 1987; Koretz 1988).

For the top quarter of students, however, there appear to have been some benefits. Many minority students with their sights set on attending college have responded to the increased demands of tougher graduation requirements and similarly elevated college-admission standards. Higher test scores and larger numbers of students taking advanced placement and the SAT courses are other examples of successes about which policymakers can crow. These results, however, touch only one of three to four students. Worse yet, such apparent successes blanket growing criticism of the type of learning these students display: they recall facts but have little understanding of concepts; they are winners in playing the game "Trivial Pursuit" but losers in applying knowledge in unfamiliar settings; they are responsive to grades and external rewards but evince little interest in learning difficult subjects on their own (Schrag 1988).

The impact of higher academic standards on teaching is far less clear. How much has really changed in classrooms during the period of these reforms? More students are taking an academic core of subjects, but are they doing more reasoning and problem solving as promised by the cheerleaders for reform? Are teachers teaching differently? What evidence there is suggests little change in the classrooms of college-bound students and even less change in instructional practices for those students who struggle with academics (Dossey et al. 1988; Mullis and Jenkins 1988; Eisner 1985).

A word of caution before I leave this part of my argument: When I assert that the reform policies of the 1980s have largely failed most students, I recognize and applaud those many instances of teachers and administrators who over the years have slowly and carefully constructed islands of effectiveness and intellectual engagement. Such places exist. These schools exist in spite of inhospitable conditions and provide witness to what extraordinary individuals can do collectively when faced with extreme adversity (Carnegie Foundation 1988; Corcoran, Walker, and White 1988).

(2). Reform policies of the 1980s worsened the schooling of the urban poor, further widening the gap between educational haves and have-nots.

Rather than cite test scores that improve, then plateau and turn downward, huge gaps in achievement between white and minority students, dropout statistics, and the culture of "cutting classes" that are the daily fare in urban schools, let me mention briefly recent reports from corporate executives, college presidents, school practitioners, researchers, journalists, and parents based on visits to schools. The Carnegie Foundation for the Advancement of Teaching bluntly stated: "We are deeply troubled that a reform movement launched to upgrade the education of *all* students is irrelevant to many children—largely black and Hispanic in our urban schools. In almost every big city, dropout rates are high, morale is low, facilities often are old and unattractive, and school leadership is crippled by a web of regulations" (Carnegie Foundation 1988:xi; Grant Commission 1988). The titles of some of these works tell it all: "Withered Hopes, Stillborn Dreams: The Dismal Panorama of Urban Schools" and "The Imperiled Generation" (Maeroff 1988; Carnegie Foundation 1988).

If titles and quotations are unconvincing, demographic data on shifts in poverty and on the intensification of poverty among children compel attention: The infants and toddlers who are counted and analyzed by researchers and policymakers in the 1980s are the elementary and secondary school students of the 1990s and the next century; and poverty and school failure are highly correlated.

- The number of children in poverty has increased by about one-third from the mid-1970s to the late 1980s, growing from 14 percent to more than 20 percent.
- Single female-parent families, nearly 54 percent of whom live in poverty, have increased to almost 10 percent of all households with children since 1970.
- The number of homes where English is not spoken has grown at about 4 percent per year, twice the population-growth rate for the nation (Sawhill 1988).

With all the data on poverty, haven't federal and state programs that pour billions of dollars into schools, such as Chapter 1 of the Education Consolidation and Improvement Act (1981), the successor to Title I of the Elementary and Secondary Education Act (1965), made a difference? After a quarter century, the answer is "maybe." Chapter 1 targets mostly low-income elementary school students who perform poorly in academic skills. There have been test-score gains in reading and math as long as students remain in the program; once they leave, however, gains evaporate.

Research and policymakers are divided over how much of the gains can be attributed to the targeted funds, staffing, and special programs provided by Chapter 1. Congress, remaining committed to this program, has authorized further studies of the impact of Chapter 1 on placing students in special education, leaving school before graduation, and promoting or retaining them a grade. While not the silver arrow to fulfill promises made by poverty warriors in the mid-1960s, Chapter 1 remains an ambiguous but important weapon in an almost empty quiver (Kennedy, Birman, and Demaline 1986).

Such statistics and conclusions often produce a vocabulary of crises and hopeless shrugs. Even with the steadfastness of individual gifted teachers and principals—heroes in the basic sense of the word—few informed citizens or educators can muster a language of optimism about the future of urban schools in the 1990s. Persistent poverty and institutional racism with their corrosive effects on individuals, families, and neighborhoods spill over onto the schools, further shrinking professionals' hopes (Wilson 1987; Ogbu 1978). The consequences of an inadequate schooling appear in statistics on adult illiteracy, unemployment, dependency on the dole, severe health problems, and crime. The result is a statistical portrait of a deeply riven society of haves and have-nots.

For these urban schools, the reform fever of the 1980s, driven initially by top-down mandates, swiftly became a movement for curricular and instructional uniformity. Specialists write scripts for teachers to use in classrooms. Additional refinements in labeling students and grouping by ability further segregated students. The symbols of getting academically tough with students wave like flags: more testing (and earlier testing even in kindergarten and the first grade); more homework; more failures in each grade; more tracking; more crackdowns on cutting and absenteeism. Mounting dropout rates, sinking morale among educators, and desperate cries for help from parents and public officials reveal the hollowness of squeezing the existing system (Hess et al. 1986; Olson and Rodman 1988; Maeroff 1988).

If the gap between an inner-city school and a suburban one is enormous now, few would argue privately or publicly that it has narrowed over the years. District policymakers, desperate to join the reform movement in the 1980s, willy-nilly grafted onto already beleaguered, cash-poor, and understaffed systems solutions mis-matched to the magnitude, much less the complexity, of the demographic problems they faced. Recall former Harvard University president James B. Conant's description of urban schools. He called them "slum" schools in 1961:

> I am convinced we are allowing social dynamite to accumulate in our large cities. I am not nearly so concerned about the plight of suburban parents whose offspring are having difficulty finding places in prestigious colleges as I am about the plight of parents in the slums whose children either drop out or graduate from school without prospects of either further education or employment. In some slum neighborhoods I have no doubt that over half of the boys between sixteen and twenty-one are out of school and out of work. Leaving aside human tragedies, I submit that a continuation of this situation is a menace to the social and political health of the large cities. (Conant 1961:2).

Schools may do a seemingly adequate job of preparing the one-quarter to one-third of students bound for colleges and universities. Reforms in the 1980s have indeed tightened up performance expectations that cater nicely to those who see the role of the school in narrow academic terms. For those in the bottom half, however, those who seldom apply to college, these reforms, if anything, have yet to show any positive gains. These are a substantial portion of the very students who corporate leaders, college presidents, researchers, and informed citizens say are the future workers, the very people who will be supporting retirees in the early decades of the twenty-first century. Discouragingly, there is even evidence that these academically driven, incremental reforms may violate the educator's Hippocratic oath: Do no harm.

The rising percentages of retentions in elementary schools and large numbers of low-income youth who leave schools before graduating suggest that things may be getting worse, not better. Also, there is harm in linking improved test scores with learning, since it misleads the public. Over time, scores improve due to better coaching, to a closer fit between what is taught and what is tested, and to other factors, including the age cohort taking the test; scores do not necessarily rise because students are learning more. Few educators and media reports make that essential point to the public. Unintentionally, students who leave high school with diplomas also mislead the public into believing that they can solve problems, perform basic skills, and display the responsibility, flexibility, and persistence so highly prized by employers. Well-intended policies and good-hearted people forge these misleading linkages that at their core misinform the public and pose additional harm to the majority of students who are compelled to attend school (Koretz 1988).

That is my argument, combining criticism of the reform of the 1980s with analysis of policy solutions and their consequences. In looking toward the 1990s, what policy direction do I propose? Even though policymakers are severely constrained in what they can and cannot do about teaching practices or what students must learn, there are promising directions to pursue. Before suggesting policy direction and illustrating the limits available to policymakers in changing practices, I need to give some background to the enterprise of school reform in the nation over the last century and a half.

KINDS OF SCHOOL REFORM

All school reform falls into one of two categories: incremental or fundamental. These planned changes are solutions to problems that policymakers define. To make clear the distinction between two kinds of change and the problems they attempt to solve, I will use the tragic destruction of the spacecraft Challenger in 1986 as an example.

The National Aeronautics and Space Administration (NASA) soared with the successes of lunar landings, shuttle flights, and space walks but staggered to a halt with the deaths of seven astronauts and two rocket failures. With the public aware of a complete collapse in NASA's performance, a presidential commission investigated the disaster and had to define the problems clearly. In engineering terms, the commission had to determine whether the Challenger accident was a design problem, a lapse in quality control, or some mixture of the two. Defining the problem accurately was crucial, since the definition could mean changes in NASA's goals, structure, and relationships with government contractors and Congress, and beyond that, the future of shuttle launches and the safety of the astronauts.

Similarly, for issues facing schools, there is a need to determine whether problems should be seen as a design issue, a quality-control issue, or some combination of the two.

For schools, solutions to what engineers call quality-control problems—improving the efficiency and effectiveness of what is done—are incremental changes. Incremental changes in schools include recruiting better teachers and administrators, raising salaries, allocating resources equitably, selecting better textbooks, adding (or deleting) content and coursework, scheduling people and activities more efficiently, and introducing new versions of evaluation and training (Watzlawick, Weakland, and Fisch 1974; Cuban 1988).

Incremental changes try to make what already exists more efficient and more effective without disturbing the basic organizational features, without substantially altering the ways in which adults and children perform their roles. Those who propose incremental changes believe that the existing goals and structures of schooling are both adequate and desirable.

What engineers call solutions to design problems, I call fundamental changes. Fundamental changes seek to alter the basic ways in which organizations are put together. They reflect major dissatisfactions with present arrangements. Fundamental changes introduce new goals, structures, and roles that transform familiar ways of doing things into new ways of responding to persistent problems.

One example of fundamental change is the introduction of the graded school in the mid-nineteenth century, which did away with the one-room schoolhouse. The graded school—at both the elementary and secondary levels—revolutionized curriculum, instruction, organization, and governance of schools. More recent proposals for fundamental change in school structures are the open classroom, vouchers, teacher-run schools, and schools in which the local community has authority to make budgetary and curricular decisions.

Although in this century most changes in school operations have been incremental, on occasion, particular fundamental reforms have been attempted in an uncoordinated fashion. Such innovations as schools without grade levels, team teaching, and open-space architecture have been tried but have had little enduring effect.

The last three decades, however, offer many more examples of incremental changes enacted by state and federal laws. The National Defense Education Act (1958), the Elementary and Secondary Education Act (1965), and the Education for All Handicapped Children Act (1975) spent billions of dollars to change schools. These changes altered existing rules, modified school practices, and led to the hiring of specialized staff members. These changes were not trivial. Expanding access and opportunity for children who had been poorly served by the schools, for example, was a massive task that was consistent with the goals of a democratic society.

In the 1980s, activist state governments replaced federal intervention. State after state introduced reform bills aimed at getting teachers and students to work harder in classrooms. Most of these state reforms aimed for quality control. They sought to make the existing system more productive, not to disturb staff roles or the governance of schools. After three decades of federal and state reforms, the historic design of public schooling instituted in mid-nineteenth century graded schools remains essentially intact.

Schools, then, indeed changed in this century, but the incremental nature of most of these changes means that they have barely touched what occurs daily in classrooms. Within the tradition of incremental change, the state-driven reform movement for academic excellence in the 1980s intensified and enhanced the existing structures of schooling without substantially altering school and classroom practices.

Comparing school changes in the 1980s and those needed for the 1990s with the shift from piston-driven to jet-powered airplanes may make clear the differences between incremental and fundamental reforms. Designers must consider three factors when they produce an aircraft: speed, weight, and range. For any mission, these three factors must be traded off against one another. It is most difficult, if not impossible, to maximize all three factors at the same time. To make it possible to fly further, load or speed must be compromised. In satisfying these factors, the operation and design of piston-powered aircraft engines probably went as far as they could by World War II (Branson 1988).

What broke the barriers on how far, how fast, and with what payload an aircraft could fly were not further refinements and enhancements of the piston-driven engine but the introduction of jet power. A completely new engine design—a fundamental change—permitted designers to reconsider speed, payload, and range. Trade-offs continue in refining the design and operation of jet-powered aircraft but in ways vastly different from those made in piston-driven machines.

What is the connection with public schooling? The piston-driven engine is the graded school. Invented in the mid-nineteenth century at a time of expanding industrialism and mushrooming immigration, and equipped to accommodate efficiently large numbers of students, the graded school was designed to turn students of different abilities and backgrounds into literate citizens and workers. To accomplish this, such schools were composed of classrooms, each with a teacher assigned to a group of students. For each grade and each subject, there was a specific body of knowledge and skills to teach every year; students had a clear expectation that promotion to the next grade, or even graduation, depended upon completion of the assigned work. The graded school was thus well suited to the needs of a rapidly expanding industrial democracy. If the late nineteenth- and early twentieth-century factory was a prized symbol of the economic engine for capitalism, the graded school was its prized counterpart for a democracy (Kaestle 1973; Tyack 1974; Katz 1987).

This mid-nineteenth-century invention—later enhanced by trained teachers, bigger buildings, scientifically designed tests for grouping students, and thicker textbooks to impart academic content—has about reached its upper limits in schooling masses of students in the closing decades of the twentieth century. Historically, for universal schooling to survive, school reform after reform responded to social and economic pressures by trading off key variables in educating children. At different times, external pressures for reform have forced incremental changes in the graded school, in terms of changing content, placing teachers in self-contained classrooms, and setting up multiple goals. Against the standard of equipping millions of students with a basic, no-nonsense literacy, the graded school has achieved a remarkable goal in the history of tax-supported, compulsory schooling. Other nations have copied the American example.

But standards and expectations have changed. In the closing decades of the twentieth century, the public demands of public schooling far more than basic literacy. The public, including the corporate sector, expects a much higher level of literacy and reasoning power. The statistics cited earlier on dropouts, unskilled entry-level workers, and test scores reveal low levels of knowledge and inadequate levels of reasoning and problem solving among high school graduates. The persistence of these numbers suggests that further squeezing of the system of schooling may produce only tiny gains from large efforts. The unrelenting failures of large numbers of students are unmasking the fundamental inadequacies in the entire system. No longer can "those" students be blamed for failing. Something is gravely wrong with the system itself.

The 1980s binge of state-driven reforms to secure academic excellence was a last-gasp try to extract higher performance out of a piston-driven system already stretched beyond what it can reasonably do for children and society as the twentieth century comes to a close.

Is there a jet engine for schooling in the 1990s? None has yet emerged, but the ferment for invention is rich. There is a growing awareness that previous formulations of the problems in terms of bashing teachers, principals, school boards, and superintendents are a futile search for villains. The inherent problems of public schooling in this society are being seen more and more in structural terms, rather than as the failings of particular people or of limited resources.

A new rationale grounded in practical realities of schooling is emerging. Just as the altered consciousness of the U.S. Congress produced a new law reforming the national system of welfare—really a flawed but partial fundamental change—there is a new awareness developing among school reformers. One message of welfare reform is clear: No more incremental change; no more tinkering. A system that can get people off the dole and into jobs is better not only for those individuals but for the American economy. A basic change in awareness is also apparent among advocates for school reform. Exactly what the jet engine for schooling will be, however, is unclear; but the conditions for its development are promising.

EMERGENT POLICY STRATEGIES FOR THE 1990s

At least three strategies promising fundamental change in schooling emerged in the late 1980s: restructuring, choice, and the school as a center of integrated social services (Kirst 1988). Those who advocate one of these approaches often draw upon elements of the other two.

Restructuring

Stripped of its slogans and hype, this policy strategy assumes that those who actually deliver a service are in the best position to make operational decisions. This strategy would drive decisions often made by state and district administrators and school boards to the individual school where the principal and teachers would determine what should be done. Restructuring, then, is overhauling the governance of schools and shifting power away from the state and district office to the school.

Two impulses have brought together an unusual coalition of corporate executives, governors, foundation officials, and union leaders to endorse this approach. One impulse came from examples of lean, smart, customer-driven businesses that innovated their way out of obsolescence and convinced many corporate leaders, in particular, that schools could profit from a similar dose of bottom-up decision making. David Kearns, then Xerox chairman and chief executive officer, and now Assistant Secretary of Education, wants schools managed by the principal and teachers. According to Kearns, "They would decide what lab equipment they need, which textbooks to use, and where to buy services. They'd design their own curricula, set their own specialties and compete with other schools. . . . In this scheme, what would district office administrators do? Kearns's answer is brief: "District offices would become service centers—helping schools, instead of dictating to them" (Kearns 1988).

A second impulse, which brings other groups to this coalition, is the strong desire to strengthen teaching as a profession. Slogans such as "empowering teachers" stud proposals for restructuring. The assumption is that teachers who make key schoolwide decisions are acting as other professionals who exercise their independent judgment about the nature of the work they do. Moreover, when teachers are responsible for the consequences of their schoolwide decisions, they will be more creative and sharper classroom teachers from whom students will learn more and work harder (David 1988; Carnegie Forum 1986; National Governors Association 1986; Conley, Schmidle, and Shedd, in press).

Although partisans of restructuring agree that major decisions should occur at the school site, they disagree over which major decisions should be made there, which ones should be made at the district office, and what is the proper role of the principal. While a consensus exists that judgments about subject matter and methods belong to the school staff, there is little agreement about who should decide such issues as spending, staffing, and school organization.

Talk is cheap. Is restructuring happening anywhere? Yes, a few districts and schools have begun the journey to restructure school governance and increase teacher professionalism. Much variation, however, exists among those ventures. Jefferson County, Kentucky (the metropolitan Louisville area), Poway, California (outside San Diego), District No. 4 in Manhattan's East Harlem, and Dade County, Florida, are pioneering districts in restructuring. The Coalition of Essential Schools, with its network of 56 high schools across the country, is an instance of a national effort (David 1988; *Innovation in Education* 1988; Coalition of Essential Schools 1988).

Dade County, for example, began with altering governance in 33 of their 276 schools. These schools receive their budgets in lump sums, thus allowing the principal and staff discretion in deciding how to allocate 90 per cent of their monies. If schools wish to spend more or less on items that may break school-board rules, the union contract, or state-department regulations, they can request a waiver from a special county committee. Schools can develop any form of governance they choose, as long as teachers are deeply involved in planning and making decisions (David 1988).

While talk of restructuring still outstrips action, it is much too early to assess whether the changes in these districts penetrated classrooms and produced the gains in teacher self-respect or student productivity the strategy promised.

Choice among Schools

The assumption that drives this strategy is that schools are a "failed monopoly," and a strong dose of marketplace competition will raise the quality of schooling out of its slough of mediocrity. While open support for vouchers—that is, giving parents checks to take to any school they wish their children to attend—appears to have vanished, variations of the concept have reappeared as plans for open enrollment, magnet schools, and alternative programs. With parents exercising choice beyond the neighborhood school their children would ordinarily be required to attend, the belief is that bad schools will starve for students and close, while imaginative, strong schools will flourish (Kearns 1988:567; Raywid 1985).

Open-enrollment proposals seek to abolish attendance boundaries that require children to go to certain schools. At the state level, Minnesota is the pacesetter, introducing both a tuition-tax subsidy and open enrollment. Since 1955, some form of tax credit has been available to Minnesota parents who wanted their children to attend non-public schools. While voucher bills failed in the legislature in 1985, Governor Rudy Perpich—embracing a report issued by the heads of the state's largest corporations—endorsed open enrollment throughout the state for eleventh and twelfth graders. Each family could send its teenager to any public school. While the initiative never made it through the legislature, what did survive in that session was an option that eleventh and twelfth graders could take a course from any eligible public or private college or university at taxpayers' expense and receive dual academic credit. In 1986, about 3500 students (3% of eligible students) exercised the choice (Mazzoni 1987).

At the district level, New York City's Community District No. 4 in East Harlem began in 1974 with two alternative programs; in 1988, it had thirty. These programs range in size from 80 to 250 students. Teachers created one, and each is housed in buildings containing other schools-within-a-school. Two teachers lead each program; they provide direction and teach within it. Parents in the district choose from among these programs for their children (David 1988).

Again, it is premature to judge this reform strategy's overall effectiveness and impact upon teacher performance and self-esteem, much less student learning.

The School as a Center for Integrated Social Services

The assumption buried within this reform strategy is that children who come to school hungry, poorly clothed, ill, abused, and neglected will learn little unless someone addresses those needs. The concept of the school as a place that cares for more than the mind goes back well over a century to the progressive movement, when reformers made the school the institution of last resort. These reformers claimed that the school must do for the child what the family, church, and community either could no longer do or failed to do (Cremin 1961). A corollary to this assumption is that while social services for children may be available, their existence in separate bureaucracies divided by turf struggles and narrow specialties bounces children from caregiver to caregiver. The strategy is to make the school a hub for child and family services to complement the usual academic and extracurricular programs.

Early twentieth-century schools, imbued with beliefs in the necessity of caring for the whole child, established lunchrooms, gyms, nursery and kindergarten suites, and space for medical exams and hired vocational counselors and social workers. Since then, even with surges of interest in academic concentration, such as those during the Sputnik years of the mid-1950s, the concept of the public school as a place interested in more than the mind persisted. Project Head Start, introduced almost a quarter of a century ago for low-income 4- and 5-year-olds, built upon the progressive tradition of reshaping schools in the early decades of this century.

Now, even with the pursuit of academic excellence in state-driven reforms, high schools in various cities have established programs staffed by nurses, social workers, teachers, and job developers, aimed at getting at-risk students through high school. Soaring rates of infant mortality, teen pregnancies, and family disintegration prompt this strategy of comprehensive social services centered in schools. It is less a strategy for improving schooling directly than it is a strategy for saving children so that they will do well in school (Schorr 1988).

These three strategies, often blended together in proposals, aim to alter fundamentally the ways schools operate. Blending occurs because the three strategies share a common faith in applying to schools the model of successful businesses. Nevertheless, what drives the debate on strategies is largely an economic imperative. The rationale for fundamental change is anchored in schools being social instruments for invigorating the economy. Where moral imperatives drove an earlier generation to improve schooling for the disadvantaged, the marginal, and those outside the pale, little moral language infused the policy debate in the 1980s.

What's Missing from These Strategies?

Because they raise serious questions about assumptions embedded in those earlier policies, these new approaches—even lacking as they are in a moral vocabulary about the future of the nation—offer some hope to policymakers willing to depart from the barren policies of the 1980s. They offer hope because the basic ingredient transforming policy talk into concrete programs is political clout; coalitions of citizens and professionals have begun lobbying local, state, and federal officials for new policies and programs. Finally, these approaches promise improvement for *all* students, not just those bound for college. Supportive as I am of these strategies, however, I do have some reservations.

First, champions of these approaches have their eyes fixed too closely on the strategy itself and not upon what the strategy aims to achieve or how the strategy will produce the desired ends. Restructuring schools, providing more parental choice, and integrating social services to students sound fine, but toward what ends? What are the vision and goals? Are the products of schooling to be skilled workers, wise citizens, and youth of sterling character? If they are, then advocates of these strategies will need to make the connection directly and lay out explicit goals.

What is missing is a vision, a picture of what schools can be—an ought-to-be of larger moral intentions than skilled workers and a Gross National Product growth rate of 5 percent. What is needed is a description of what kind of places these changed schools will be for both children and adults who work there. What is needed are visions, not blueprints, that will be compelling enough to bond citizens, parents, educators, and students. Without such pictures of schools as they might be, assessing the impact of these strategies will be very difficult. How can we compare the existing policies, structures, and practices and find them to be a proper or improper fit, unless we know what they ought to be? Without clear goals, grand strategies will decay into using illusionary silver-tipped arrows such as limited enrollment plans, hollow school-based management programs, and nurse-staffed clinics to dispense birth control pills.

Will restructured schools and more choice directly produce skilled workers and caring citizens? Hardly. These strategies are macro-tools, albeit very important ones, but tools nonetheless. To clear off an old building from a lot, a bulldozer is a useful tool. But once a construction company clears the lot, it needs other tools. Bulldozers and hammers are improvements over crowbars, but the larger question is: What are we building on the lot? Uncritical enthusiasts for these strategies risk converting a means into an end.

As an analogy, consider the environmental problem of air pollution. Studies show the decay of air quality in major cities and across the continent and the impact of decay upon individual health, plants, and animals. These macro-level studies have helped policy-makers frame the problems and define the targets: cleaner air that reduces health and environmental risk. Translating those macro-goals into concrete middle- and micro-level strategies has produced an array of specific policies that touch both the public and private sectors of the economy, international relations, and individual behavior, for example, Environmental Protection Agency regulations on industrial and automobile emissions, carpooling to reduce auto use, Canadian-U.S. negotiations over acid rain, and restrictions on what fuels can be used in the home and in the car. Aside from the inevitable loud political noises from contending interest groups that accompany such policies, at the very least the problems and desired goals are clear. Specific policies and programs that connect individual and organizational behaviors to the macro-goals mark how to get from here to there, from polluted to clean air. Clear vision, goals, strategies, and programs linked to individuals are necessary. Grand strategies are insufficient.

Missing from discussion of the strategies is a feel for the complexity of schooling, especially a sense for the potency of a school's culture. As promising as the three approaches are for reforming schools, they are narrowly conceived when they ignore the beliefs, norms, ceremonies, and relationships that combine to make up a school's inner life. In doing so, these reformers neglect those very factors that spell the difference between a strategy's having an impact or completely missing the desired end.

A vision of what schools can be, goals, linkages that show the directions parents, students, teachers, and administrators should pursue to attain desired goals are absent from current policy discussions on improving schools. An earlier generation of reformers in the 1960s also tried restructuring schools. They filled in the gaps between vision and goals with a host of recommended changes in organizational practices. They lacked a strategy of change and political muscle to secure those reforms. But at least they avoided the sin of policymaker hubris: thinking that once they designed a strategy, everything else would fall into place (Miller and Riessman 1965).

There are many possible visions of schools as they ought to be and the strategic linkages that bring those visions to life in schools and classrooms. Let me offer one example that is consistent with the beliefs and rationale of all three reform strategies. Woven into the fabric of virtually all proposals for fundamental change in schooling is a portrayal of the problems of students emerging after twelve years, unprepared to take on the complex responsibility of work and citizenship. All proposals take for granted that schools should be places where children learn to raise questions, try out new ideas, solve problems, and, in general, think for themselves while caring for the community in which they live. Corporate leaders, college presidents, state and national policymakers, educators, and the general public want schools to promote and inculcate habits of thinking. The problem of schooling is that these outcomes are difficult to produce. The solution is framed as altering what occurs in schools and classrooms to reach those goals.

When students leave a school as thoughtful, reflective individuals able to function well in the workplace and carry out basic duties of a citizen, the implication is that the adults who work in that school are (or at least should be) models of what is desired in the children. This vision also implies that the school is a place deliberately constructed to provide sufficient time for students to act as thinkers, to experience thoughtfulness, and to practice service in the community. For the vision to be more than fine words, then, schools must be settings for cultivating reason, inquiry, and caring among both children and adults (Resnick 1987; Schrag 1988; Schaefer 1967).

The vision, however, is out of sync with schools as they are currently organized. Presently, schools have gone as far as they can in providing basic literacy to a substantial minority of students, but they have compiled a lackluster record in equipping the bottom half with minimum knowledge and skills. If we believe the chorus of complaints about high school graduates that escalated in volume in the 1980s, schools have yet to produce graduates who can reason, solve real-life problems, respond flexibly to new situations, and demonstrate concern for their community.

Even if the shrillest critics are half-right about schools failing to produce thoughtfulness and problem solvers, the sources for that failure would be anchored deeply in the ways schools are organized and operated. Routine practices of instructing, organizing the curriculum, grouping students, scheduling time, and dealing with similar commonplaces of schooling are geared to prevent, even inhibit, thoughtfulness (Schrag 1988; Cuban 1984). Well-intended, decent teachers and administrators, more often than not, try their best, but the daily practices render them impotent by undermining the development of thoughtfulness. Such an alternative vision, one of many, is necessary not only to bring together a coalition of citizens and educators who endorse this direction but also to assess whether what exists fits what ought to be.

Just as vision is necessary, so is political will. What makes these three approaches hopeful for the 1990s is the recognition within various states that political coalitions and bargaining are necessary ingredients for fundamental reforms to occur within schools and classrooms. Based upon the 1988 election, however, I have little confidence now that either a middle-range vision or any of the above promising strategies will be picked up, much less endorsed, at the federal level. For President George Bush, intractable budget deficits harnessed to a peanut-sized program concentrating upon the Pledge of Allegiance, merit schools that receive cash for high test scores, and rewards for teacher improvement leave little hope for the 1990s to be any different from the 1980s insofar as federal leadership is concerned. That reform initiatives will remain at the state level is a safe bet (Bush 1988).

The states will play a critical role because governors and legislatures are in a familiar position to generate visions and strategies, fund both, and get reforms underway. But the sad lesson of the 1980s is that state mandates aimed at reforming schools and classrooms are outsized pliers used to repair delicate watches. States can establish frameworks for reform, provide resources, mobilize support, and hold districts accountable, even though they cannot alter what happens in schools and classrooms. Were even the states' modest but important outcomes to materialize, I would be less critical of the strategies and more optimistic about the 1990s.

A Final Word

So, what is the point? Policymakers in the 1980s framed the complex problems of public schooling as an inefficient and ineffective system in need of tightening up, that is, in need of higher standards, more resources, better staffing, and accountability. To paraphrase the commercial of the Ford Motor Company: The task was to make quality schooling Job No. 1.

The incremental improvements that occurred over the decade of the 1980s and the rising expectations of what literate high school graduates should accomplish nonetheless left the majority of students ill served and ill equipped by the reforms of the so-called excellence movement. Growing numbers of professionals and informed citizens have become aware that the system of schooling, not the people within it, needs transforming. They have come to see the entire system as a piston-drive engine overpowered by jet-engine expectations.

Policymakers in the 1990s should shake free from an obsolete and harmful way of framing problems and consider how to rearrange schooling so that children and the adults who work with them can learn, be productive, and enter a society where both give as much as they get. Such a reframed problem points no fingers of blame at interest groups, occupations, or nameless forces. It suggests no easy prescription as a solution; it can generate a broad range of options policymakers can investigate before arriving at what should be done. This is no academic exercise suitable for after-dinner sherry and relaxed conversation. How frequently have policymakers generated solutions hastily for ill-conceived problems, acted, and later smacked their foreheads in dismay over the bad fit between the problem and its solution? If anyone has the obligation of figuring out what the problems are, with care and sensitivity to consequences before rushing toward action, it is those who make school policy: governors, legislators, judges, school-board members, superintendents, and other public officials.

The reform strategies that emerged in the closing years of the 1980s need close scrutiny before they freeze into unexamined, hastily implemented programs. They are promising approaches, but they need a vision of what schools can be, and they need middle- and micro-level policies and programs that link the vision to classroom practices. We can no longer afford to have blurred visions, one for the top half of our students and another for those who fail in school.

Beyond vision, political clout is required. The apparent absence of political will at the federal level to seek fundamental changes in schooling during the Bush administration again, as in the Reagan administration, shifts attention to the states. Within the Bush administration there remains a consensus that the federal role is to cheerlead for national exams, parental choice, gather data, and continue limited funding for special programs while letting the states do the rest. Whether governors and state legislatures can reframe the problems of schooling, construct visions that schools can enact by pursuing these emerging strategies of change, and still mobilize the necessary resources to implement reforms, are questions that I cannot now answer. Fundamental reform of the entire system of public schooling is necessary in the face of its inability to provide the levels of literacy called for today. The game for the early 1990s will be played in the states' backyard. Given the high social stakes riding on better schools for all children, pray that state policymakers do not pursue the barren policies of the 1980s. Pray that they can do what Yogi Berra had trouble doing: Think and hit at the same time.

REFERENCES

Berkow, Ira. (1988). "The Science of Socking It." *The New York Times.* May 30:29.

Bernanos, G. 1955. *Last Essays of Georges Bernanos.* New York: Henry Regnery.

Branson, R. 1988. "Why the Schools Can't Improve: The Upper Limit Hypothesis." *Journal of Instructional Development* 10:15–26.

Bush, George. 1988. "The Bush Strategy for Excellence in Education." *Phi Delta Kappan* 70:112, 114, 116.

Carnegie Forum on Education and the Economy. 1986. *A Nation Prepared: Teachers for the 21st Century.* New York: Carnegie Forum on Education and the Economy.

Carnegie Foundation for the Advancement of Teaching. 1988. *An Imperiled Generation.* New York: Carnegie Foundation.

Coalition of Essential Schools. 1988. "Program Information." Providence, R.I.: Brown University, Education Department.

Conant, James. 1961. *Slums and Suburbs.* New York: McGraw-Hill.

Conley, S., T. Schmidle, and J. Shedd. "Teacher Participation in the Management of School Systems." *Teachers College Record,* in press.

Corcoran, T., L. J. Walker and J. L. White. 1988. *Working in Urban Schools.* Washington, D.C.: Institute for Educational Leadership.

Cremin, L. 1961. *Transformation of the Schools.* New York: Anchor Press.

Cuban, Larry. 1984. "Policy and Research Dilemmas in the Teaching of Reasoning: Unplanned Designs." *Review of Educational Research* 54:655–681.

——. 1988. "Constancy and Change in Schools: 1880s to the Present." In P. Jackson, ed., *Contributing to Educational Change,* pp. 85–106. Calif.: McCutheon.

David, J. 1988. "Restructuring in Progress: Lessons from Pioneering Districts." Washington, D.C.: National Governors Association.

Dossey, J., I. Mullis, M. Lindquist, and D. Chambers. 1988. *The Mathematics Report Card: Are We Measuring Up?* Princeton N.J.: Educational Testing Service.

Eisner, E. 1985. "What High Schools Are Like." Stanford, Calif.: Stanford in the Schools Project.

Gottfredson, G. 1988. "You Get What You Measure, You Get What You Don't: Higher Standards, Higher Test Scores, More Retention in Grade." Baltimore: Johns Hopkins University, Center for Research on Elementary and Middle Schools.

Grant Commission. 1988. *The Forgotten Half: Pathways to Success for America's Youth and Young Females.* Washington, D.C.: William T. Grant Foundation.

Hammack, Floyd. 1987. "Large School Systems' Dropout Reports: An Analyses of Definitions, Procedures and Findings." In G. Natriello, ed., *School Dropouts,* pp. 20–37. New York: Teachers College Press.

Hess, A., E. Wells, C. Prindle, P. Leffman, and B. Kaplan. 1986. "Where's Room 185?" Chicago: Chicago Panel on Public School Policy and Finance.

Innovation in Education: A Progress Report on the JCPS/Gheens Professional Development Academy. 1988. Louisville, KY: The Gheens Foundation.

Kaestle, C. 1973. *The Evolution of an Urban School System.* Cambridge: Harvard University Press.

Katz, M. 1987. *Restructuring American Education.* Cambridge: Harvard University Press.

Kearns, D. 1988. "An Educational Recovery Plan for America." *Phi Delta Kappan* 69:565–570.

Kennedy, M., B. Birman, and R. Demaline. 1986. *Effectiveness of Compensatory Education Services.* Washington, D.C.: U.S. Government Printing Office.

Kirst, M. 1988. "Recent State Education Reform in the United States: Looking Backward and Forward." *Educational Administration Quarterly* 24:319–328.

Koretz, D. 1988. "Educational Practices, Trends in Achievement and the Potential of the Reform Movement." *Educational Administration Quarterly* 24:350–359.

Maeroff, G. 1988. "Withered Hopes, Stillborn Dreams: The Dismal Panorama of Urban Schools." *Phi Delta Kappan* 69:632–638.

Mazzoni, T. 1987. "The Politics of Educational Choice in Minnesota." *Politics of Education Association Yearbook,* pp. 217–230.

McDill, E., G. Natriello, and A. Pallas. 1987. "A Population at Risk: Potential Consequences of Tougher School Standards for Student Dropouts." In G. Natriello, ed., *School Dropouts,* pp. New York: Teachers College Press.

Miller, S., and F. Riessman. 1965. "The Search for an Educational Revolution." In R. Rist, ed., *Restructuring American Education,* pp. New Brunswick, N.J.: Transaction Books.

Mullis, V. S., and L. B. Jenkins. 1988. *The Science Report Card: Elements of Risk and Recovery.* Princeton, N.J.: Educational Testing Service.

National Governors Association. 1986. *Time for Results.* Washington, D.C.: Center for Policy Research and Analysis.

A Nation at Risk. 1983. Washington, D.C.: National Commission on Excellence in Education.

Ogbu, J. 1978. *Minority Education and Caste: The American in Cross-Cultural Perspective.* New York: Academic Press.

Olson, L., and B. Rodman. 1988. "In the Urban Crucible." *Education Week,* June 20:27–32.

Perry, N. 1988. "Saving the Schools: How Business Can Help." *Fortune,* November 7:42–56.

Raywid, M. 1985. "Family Choice Arrangements in Public Schools: A Review of the Literature." *Review of Educational Research* 55:435–467.

Resnick, L. 1987. *Education and Learning to Think*. Washington, D.C.: National Academy Press.

San Jose Mercury News. 1988. "Bennett Criticizes Progress of Schools." April 25:1.

Sawhill, I. 1988. "Poverty in the U.S.: Why Is It So Persistent?" *Journal of Economic Literature* 26:1073–1117.

Schaefer, R. 1967. *The School as a Center of Inquiry*. New York: Harper and Row.

Schorr, L. 1988. *Within Our Reach*. New York: Anchor Press.

Schrag, F. 1988. *Thinking in Society*. New York: Routledge.

Tyack, D. 1974. *One Best System*. Cambridge: Harvard University Press.

Watzlawick, P., J. Weakland, and R. Fisch. 1974. *Change: Principles of Problem Formation and Problem Resolution*. New York: W. W. Norton.

Wehlage, G., and R. Rutter. 1987. "Dropping Out: How Much Do Schools Contribute to the Problem?" In G. Natriello, ed., *School Dropouts: Patterns and Policies*. New York: Teachers College Press.

Wilson, W. 1987. *The Truly Disadvantaged*. Chicago: University of Chicago Press.

2 American Health Care at the Crossroads

Uwe E. Reinhardt

The American health-care system currently finds itself in an odd position. It claims a much larger share of Gross National Product (GNP) than does the health system of any other industrialized nation. It boasts an abundance of hospital beds in most places and, in some, an outright excess. There is widespread anxiety, particularly among physicians, over a developing surplus of physicians. Yet in the very face of this abundance, many acutely ill Americans of low-income households find it difficult to gain access to critically needed health care, because they cannot afford it. These Americans suffer, and sometimes die, within sight of under-used health-care facilities whose managers desperately seek to attract paying "customers" with fancy atriums and with marketing campaigns that add billions annually to the nation's health-care bill.

What circumstances led a nation that thinks of itself as "the most generous people on earth" and that regularly boasts of having "the best health system in the world" to deny critically ill, poor patients access to resources of which it claims to have too many? That paradox has no counterpart elsewhere in the industrialized world; it is uniquely American.

To set the stage, the discussion begins with an overview of the system by which the American health-care system is currently financed. That system has been carefully constructed to prevent the amassing of significant market power on the demand side, consisting of those who seek or pay for health-care services. It has thereby become a major contributor to the high cost of American health care and, thus, to the high price of being one's sick and poor neighbor's keeper.

In the second section the discussion shifts to methods of cost control in health care. Other nations typically pursue that objective either by nationalizing the supply side of the health-care market or by converting the health-care market into a privately owned, publicly regulated utility whose capacity is constrained by health-sector planning and whose revenue stream is controlled with the aid of highly centralized market power on the demand side. The United States, by contrast, wavers between regulatory and market approaches to cost control, without much success in either mode. Worse still, while our current love affair with the market has not reduced the growth in health expenditures, it has eroded the hidden cross-subsidies by which health care for the nation's millions of uninsured have traditionally been financed in this country.

The final section will review a number of proposals for solving the twin problems of rising health-care cost and lack of access to health care by the uninsured poor. That section will end with the proposal of one particular solution tailored to this country's cultural norms: a two-track health-insurance system, with a voluntary, privately financed system for the bulk of employed or well-to-do Americans and a publicly financed, fail-safe system for everybody else.

An Overview of the American Health-Care System

Like any other sector in the economy, the health-care sector plays a dual social role: It provides goods and services to a clientele and an income to those who surrender real resources in the production of those goods and services.

Precisely how many Americans currently derive their income directly or indirectly from providing health care is not known. According to the *Statistical Abstract of the United States* (1987), "employed persons in the health occupations" numbered 5.7 million in 1985. This total, however, includes only persons directly working in patient care. It does not include the millions of employees and entrepreneurs who indirectly support these direct health workers—for example, persons employed in the manufacture and distribution of pharmaceuticals, medical supplies, and equipment; the financial advisors who help health-care entrepreneurs and facilities raise funds in the capital markets; and the growing number of management consultants who assist health-care providers to market themselves profitably and to extract the maximum reimbursements for health care from insurance carriers or the government.

If one defines *health workers* as "persons who directly or indirectly derive the bulk of their income from the process of health care in the form of wages, salaries, fees, or profits," then the total number of American health workers probably exceeds 10 million. The majority of these health workers are employees of health-care facilities, insurance companies, or manufacturers. Fewer than 1 million are self-employed, professional entrepreneurs, among them some 500,000 physicians, 130,000 dentists, and 170,000 pharmacists.

National associations of health-care facilities or professionals, whose chief objective is to enhance their members' economic status, represent all these health workers, whether employed by others or self-employed, in the political arena. By the power accorded them under our system of governance, and by the force of their financial strength, these associations have become the prime shapers of our national health policy.

Health-Care Expenditures: Sources and Uses

In 1987, the most recent year for which fairly precise data on health expenditures are available, Americans collectively allocated $500 billion or 11.1 percent of their GNP to this armada of health workers in return for whatever *real* resources these workers surrendered that year to health care. Figure 2-1 illustrates how that allocation has changed over time.

Patients paid directly at point of service, about 25 percent of total national health expenditures in 1987. The close to one thousand independent, private health-insurance companies and plans that sell health-insurance policies, chiefly group health-insurance policies purchased by business firms for their employees, paid about 32 percent (Levit and Freeman 1988: Exhibit 3). Private philanthropy and other private sources accounted for only about 2 percent of total health spending.

Government at all levels accounted for 41 percent of total national health expenditures. These expenditures flowed through the Medicare program for the aged, the Medicaid program for the poor, and other government programs, including some $10 billion of medical and hospital care for veterans.

Figure 2-1.   Health-care expenditures as percentage of the GNP, United States, 1975–87

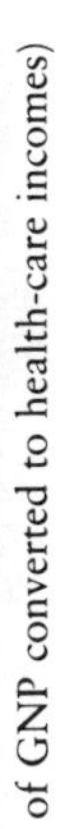

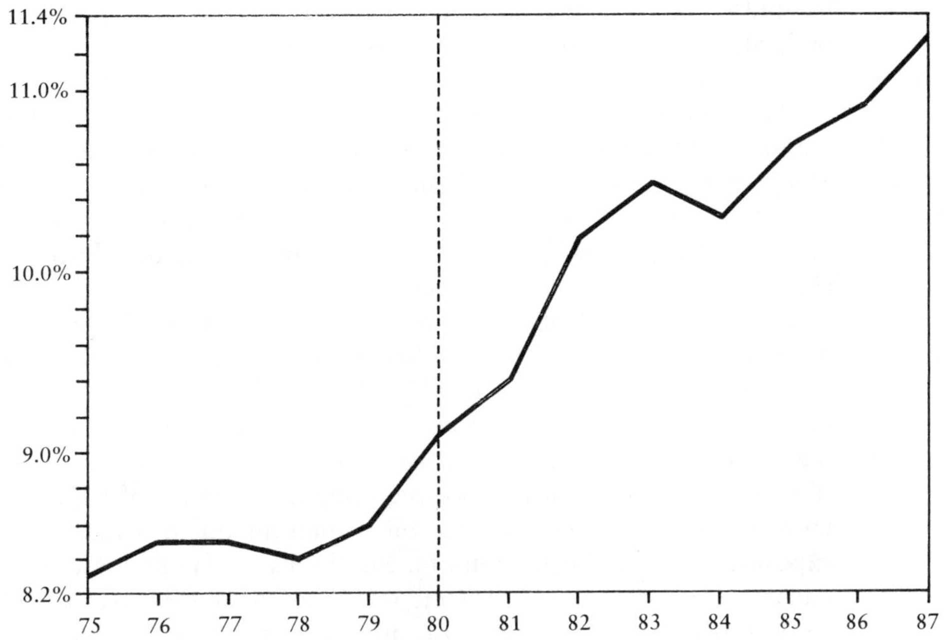

Source: Health Care Financing Administration, *HCFA Review,* various issues.

The hospital sector absorbed 39 percent of total national health expenditures in 1987, and physicians another 21 percent for services rendered in their offices or in the hospital. The remainder covered dental care (close to 7%), nursing-home care (8%), and all other professional services or supplies (27%).

Health Insurance Coverage

In 1987, roughly 85 percent of Americans had some form of private or public health-insurance coverage for at least some health services, and that coverage was not always comprehensive. Deductibles, coinsurance (a percentage, usually 20, paid by patients directly at point of service), and gaps in the range of services covered can still visit high annual out-of-pocket health expenditures even on families with health insurance. In 1987, for example, an estimated 15.3 percent of all families with health insurance spent more than 5 percent of their family income on health services, in addition to their outlays on health-insurance premiums. In that year, 3.7 percent of insured families spent more than 25 percent of their family income on health services (Congressional Research Service 1988a:4).

The Uninsured.   An estimated 35 million, or 17 percent of the population under age 65, had no health-insurance coverage at all in 1987. In 1979, the comparable number was 14.6 percent. Close to half of the currently uninsured are working adults, about 18 percent of the uninsured are nonworking adults and about one-third are children under age 18 (see Chollet 1988:11).

Roughly one-third of the uninsured live in families with income below the official federal poverty line (currently about $11,700 for a family of four), and another third live in households within 100 percent to 200 percent of the poverty line (ibid.:12). For families, if they were not plagued by preexisting illness or chronic disease, a standard health-insurance policy requiring a deductible of $250 per family member and coinsurance of 20 percent up to a maximum exposure—that is, the amount of medical bills the family must accumulate before it receives full reimbursement—of somewhere around $3,000 per family, would cost anywhere between $2,000 and $3,500 a year, depending upon the insurance carrier and the family's location. Should one or more family member be chronically ill, the policy would be commensurately more expensive, even if available. In short, the purchase of a private health-insurance policy would be a truly staggering financial burden for many uninsured, low-income families.

Medicare.   The federal Medicare program, set up in 1965, covers some 30 million Americans over the age of 65 and certain categories of disabled. It pays for the cost of physician services, hospital care, and a limited number of days in skilled nursing facilities. Until 1988, it did not cover prescription drugs, dental care, and a variety of other services, and it always required cost sharing by the aged through deductibles, coinsurance, and extra billings by physician above the fees allowed by Medicare.

Total spending on the Medicare program in 1987 amounted to $83 billion, or close to 17 percent of total national health expenditures. It is now one of the most rapidly rising components of the federal budget. Even so, unbeknownst probably to the majority of

Table 2-1. Average individual liability for medical care for the
noninstitutionalized elderly, 1984

Per-capita income (in 1984 dollars)	Percentage of Medicare enrollees	Total per-capita individual liability[a] (in dollars)	Liability as a percent of per-capita income
$ 5,000 and less	25.6	758	21.5[b]
$ 5,001–$10,000	39.6	901	12.7
$10,001–$15,000	15.8	1,053	8.6
$15,001–$20,000	11.2	1,194	3.1
$20,001 and above	7.8	1,009	5.9
All noninstitutionalized elderly enrollees	100	930	8.2

Source: Simulations by Marily Moon using the National Medical Care Expenditure Survey. Cited in Holahan and Palmer (1987:Table 6).

[a]Individual liability is the sum of out-of-pocket expenditures on medical care and per-capita insurance premiums (paid by the family) averaged across enrollees.

[b]This amount is net of the contribution that Medicaid makes for these low-income families.

American taxpayers, Medicare now covers less than half of the total health-care expenditures incurred by the aged. Medicaid pays another 13 percent, mainly for nursing-home care for very old and pauperized Medicare beneficiaries. The aged themselves, however, still cover an average of close to one-third of their own health-care expenditures with their own resources, either through private Medigap insurance coverage or out of pocket at time of service. Because the out-of-pocket expenditures borne by the aged are not income-related, their incidence is highly regressive. They constitute a serious burden on the already meager budgets of the low-income elderly, as is apparent from Table 2-1.

With the passage of the Medicare Catastrophic Coverage Act of 1988, Congress sought to limit the maximum out-of-pocket payments Medicare enrollees face annually for covered services, and it added partial coverage of prescription drugs in excess of an annual deductible of $500. The maximum risk exposure however, was not income-related, and it applied only to needed health services and equipment covered by Medicare. Furthermore, because the cost of the new benefits was apportioned solely to the aged in high-income groups through income-related premiums, a fierce opposition is now growing to the new law among the well-to-do aged who, it appears, are not inclined to finance any redistribution of economic privilege within their own age cohorts and would have preferred to have the added benefits financed with a further intergenerational transfer from the young as a group to the aged as a group.

Medicaid. Medicaid is a joint federal-state program that currently covers some 24 million low-income Americans of all ages, among them 3.5 million of pauperized aged and 3.4 million blind and disabled persons. The federal government pays for 56 percent of total program costs and the state government the remainder. Under the federal law, the states participating in the Medicaid program have a mandate to provide first-dollar coverage for hospital and physician services and care in skilled nursing facilities. Many states, however, opt to offer additional benefits, including prescription drugs.

The Medicaid program is remarkably generous in the range of benefits it covers, although it is much less so in its standards for eligibility. Since its inception in 1966, the program has been means-tested. Eligibility for the program is closely linked to the criteria for eligibility to the states' welfare programs. Because the latter vary enormously among the states, there are vast disparities in the level of income at which entitlement to Medicaid coverage sets in. In Alabama, Medicaid covers only about 15 percent of persons below the federal poverty level. In Michigan and Massachusetts, the ratio is about 70 percent. Overall, in 1986 Medicaid actually covered only 41 percent of Americans with incomes below the federal poverty threshold, while 24 percent of those with Medicaid coverage had family incomes above the poverty level (Congressional Research Service 1988b:269). The relatively low rates at which Medicaid compensates the providers of health care is a further limit of the program. At those low rates, many providers are reluctant to accept Medicaid patients for treatment, especially if there is an ample supply of better-paying patients.

The Compensation of Health-Care Providers

In any health sector, such as the population over age 65, that is embedded in a wider market economy, the upper and lower bounds set by market forces constrain the amount of money society transfers to the providers of health care per unit of real health-care resources—the fees, charges, or prices. This is so even in Great Britain, whose central government owns and operates the bulk of health-care facilities, and it is certainly so in the much more pluralistic American health-care system.

But even in the American context, the market for health services does not work in quite the manner envisaged by the textbook model of perfectly price-competitive markets. As a rule of thumb, only about 10 percent of the population account for over 70 percent of total health-care expenditures in any given year.[1] These individuals are likely to be seriously ill at the time they receive health care. They are likely to receive services they had never experienced before, and they are likely to experience them repeatedly again. No evidence suggests that patients in those circumstances shop around for low-priced or cost-effective care; in fact, there is evidence to the contrary (see, for example, Marquis 1984). Furthermore for these serious conditions these patients are also likely to be well relatively covered by third-party payment, which would blunt their or their anxious relatives' interest in the relative cost of alternative treatments in any event.

Even if patients were not well insured, however, they or their anxious relatives would typically not possess the technical knowledge to pass rational judgment on the medical and economic merits of alternative treatments. Instead, they must rely on highly trained professionals as their medical and economic agents. This asymmetry in information about the commodity being exchanged gives providers, particularly physicians, a natural advantage in the market for most health care. How physicians use that advantage—that is, how faithfully they perform their role as the patient's agent, especially when they stand to profit personally from the advice they give and when their income comes under pressure should fees be cut or the physician-population ratio rise—remains the subject of a lively controversy among health-services researchers, as does the degree to which the markets for health care do or could be made to approximate the textbook model of competitive markets (see, for example, Pauly 1978; Reinhardt 1985a; Sloan and Feldman 1988).

Because the American health-care sector nourishes itself from so many independent sources of funds, each individual doctor, hospital, nursing home, or other provider is likely to render services under a great variety of distinct contractual arrangements, so that even the same provider is likely to render the same good or service to different clients at different prices. In what follows, these methods will be described synoptically, mainly to expose the highly bureaucratic nature of the American health system. To describe these payment methods at any but the most superficial level would call for a lengthy paper devoted solely to that subject.

Private Payers.   Private payers—patients of their private insurance carriers—typically pay physicians, hospitals, and other providers of health-care fees or charges that the individual provider sets, subject to whatever limits the market may place upon the provider's discretion. Roughly 60 percent of all health expenditures flows to providers through this so-called free market, "free" in the sense that it is not directly regulated by government. For repetitively purchased, routine, well-patient care—for example, annual check-ups or well-baby care—these prices are likely to approximate those of a monopolistically competitive market (see McCarthy 1985). For crisis interventions, such as the removal of a brain tumor or trauma care, the limits on prices set by the market are less well understood.

Medicare.   Until 1983, Medicare reimbursed hospitals *retrospectively* for all costs demonstrably incurred in treating Medicare patients. That reimbursement covered all fixed operating costs, including depreciation on equipment, and also the cost of financing fixed assets. For investor-owned, for-profit hospitals, the reimbursement also included a guaranteed rate of return to shareholders' equity.

The retrospective, full-cost reimbursement of hospitals was widely believed to encourage waste in the hospital sector, among them excessively resource-intensive treatments and excessive lengths of stays in the hospital. To provide hospitals with incentives to minimize the cost of treatments, the Medicare program in 1983 switched to a system of *prospectively* set fees per case, with distinct fees for some 500 Diagnostically Related Groupings (DRGs) of medical cases. The federal government, however, unilaterally set the fees under this system, which is by now fully phased in. They are the subject of bargaining only indirectly, through the lobbying efforts of the national hospital associations. The new method of payment appears to have helped constrain Medicare expenditures for hospitals, in part by reducing the average length of stay, and also by using ancillary services per stay (Altman and Rodwin 1988).

Since its inception, Medicare has paid physicians on the basis of "customary, prevailing, and reasonable" (CPR) fees. Under that system, physicians are paid the lower of their "customary" charge (defined as the median of that physician's fees for the procedure in question during the previous year) or the "prevailing" fee in the physician's market area (defined as the fee at the 75th percentile of the fees charged by physicians in the physician's market area for that procedure in 1975, adjusted for the growth in a medical practice-cost index since 1975). This method is a cumbersome attempt to adapt Medicare's fees to the "market," although for many procedures mainly received by the aged—for example, cataract surgery, hip replacements, coronary bypasses—Medicare effectively represents almost all of that "market."

Not surprisingly, this system of compensation generates a pattern of fees that varies rather capriciously across regions and among similar providers within regions in ways that appeal to either the relative costs or the relative quality of services cannot reasonably justify. The system is no longer viewed as equitable; it is much in need of reform. One reform currently under discussion is the replacement of the CPR system by a relative-value scale (RVS) that is based on carefully estimated relative resource costs of performing a set of well-defined procedures in a nationwide, standard fee schedule. Once all health-care providers agree upon such an RVS, a monetary-conversion factor can be either set or negotiated with physicians to convert the RVS into a monetary-fee schedule. Most other nations that pay physicians on a fee-for-service basis have used this approach for many years.

Medicaid. Although the federal government pays for over half of the Medicaid program, it leaves the states great leeway in establishing the methods by which to compensate providers.

Most states now pay hospitals and nursing homes under the program a prospectively set amount per day or per case, although in some states the Medicaid program has simply joined an all-payer system under which every private or public payer has agreed to a single method of payment (every payer pays according to a fee schedule common to all payers) and a single charge or fee schedule.

For physicians and other self-employed health professionals, the state Medicaid programs pay on an established fee schedule, on the lesser of the provider's actual charge, or on a maximum allowable charge established by the state.

For prescription drugs, the states typically pay the pharmacist's cost plus a fixed fee, where the allowable "cost" is meant to be that of the drug that costs the least within a group of equivalent drugs. This cost clearly biases the system toward the use of generic drugs.

Compared with Medicare, the compensation of providers under Medicaid is relatively simpler. In most states, however, the rates of compensation Medicaid pays are unilaterally set by the state government and far below the rates Medicare pays, which in turn tends to pay less than do the private insurance carriers. This cleavage between Medicaid and other payers has led many providers, particularly physicians, to shun Medicaid patients altogether. The precise magnitude of the refusal rate is not known, but the available evidence suggests that the problem is significant and pervasive (Congressional Research Service 1988b:444–446).

The Virtue and Vice of Pluralistic Health Care

The preceding synopsis should clearly shows that the enormous annual flow of funds allocated to the American health-care system reaches the system through a myriad of independent and uncoordinated pipes, few of which are sufficiently large to grant those controlling the input valves any significant degree of power in the market for health services. The major exceptions to this pattern (in terms of their size) are the federal Medicare program, which now controls an average of 27 percent of the monetary flow into the hospital sector and an average of 22 percent of the gross revenue of physicians, and the state-administered Medicaid programs, which may constitute a major source of revenue for particular hospitals and medical practices.

But even these programs have found it difficult to exert countervailing power on the price of health care, for at least two reasons. First, against the backdrop of the much higher prices the private sector typically allows, attempts by Medicare or Medicaid to exert downward pressure on their prices tend to elicit from both the beneficiaries of these programs and the providers serving these beneficiaries cries of "two-tier health care" as these providers begin to avoid treating Medicare and Medicaid patients. Second, because health care is a natural context for price discrimination, private payers always suspect that Medicare and Medicaid, in attempts to control their own costs, will inevitably shift the overhead costs of their pro-

Table 2-2.   Total health expenditure as a percentage of gross domestic products, 1960–86

	1960	1970	1980	1985	1986
Australia	4.6	5.0	6.6	6.8	6.8
Austria	4.6	5.4	7.9	8.2	8.0
Belgium	3.4	4.0	6.6	7.2	7.1
Canada	5.5	7.2	7.4	8.4	8.5
Denmark	3.6	6.1	6.8	6.1	6.1
Finland	4.2	5.6	6.3	7.3	7.5
France	4.2	5.6	7.4	8.4	8.5
Germany	4.7	5.5	7.9	8.2	8.1
Greece	2.9	4.0	4.2	4.2	3.9
Italy	3.3	4.8	6.8	6.7	6.7
Japan	3.0	4.6	6.6	6.6	6.7
Netherlands	3.9	6.0	8.2	8.3	8.3
Spain	2.3	4.1	5.9	6.0	6.0
Sweden	4.7	7.2	9.5	9.4	9.1
Switzerland	3.3	5.2	7.2	7.9	8.0
United Kingdom	3.9	4.5	5.8	6.1	6.2
United States	5.2	7.4	9.2	10.7	11.1
Mean	4.1	5.4	7.1	7.3	7.2

Source: Schieber and Poullier (1988:106, exhibit).

grams to the private sector by extracting higher prices from it. For that reason, particularly the leaders of American business tend to decry attempts at cost control by the Medicare and Medicaid programs, although these executives also, of course, tend to decry high government expenditures and taxes.

The development of this highly decentralized financing system is not an accident begotten by inattentive policymakers. On the contrary, policymakers carefully designed that structure to deny any one payer—patient, private insurer, or government—a high degree of market power on the demand side of the market, of the sort typically enjoyed by payers under the more centralized national health-insurance systems abroad. These nations tend to allocate a much smaller percentage of their financial resources to their providers of health care than does the United States, as is readily apparent in Table 2-2.

Particularly noteworthy in Table 2-2 are the data for neighboring Canada, whose economic structure and cultural norms are relatively close to ours. Since 1970, Canada has had a comprehensive and universal health-insurance system administered through independent hospital and medical insurance plans by the country's provincial governments, albeit with heavy federal cost sharing. To qualify for federal cost sharing, the design of provincial plans must observe federal guidelines. For example, the provinces may not impose any deductibles, coinsurance, or extra billing by providers upon patients. Their plans must be universally available to all residents of the province, with financing based effectively on the ability to pay rather than upon actuarial standards that take the insured's health status into account. All the plans must cover necessary hospital and physician services, although not prescription drugs or dental care, which is covered only for defined categories of low-income families.

For the most part, the Canadian hospital sector consists of private, not-for-profit institutions, and Canadian physicians are self-employed professional entrepreneurs, like their American counterparts. Canadian hospitals are financed with prospectively set global budgets negotiated annually by each hospital with the provincial governments. The provincial governments pay Canadian physicians on fee schedules that the physicians negotiate annually with the provincial government. Patients in Canada have completely free choice of physician and hospital and, as noted, do not share in the cost of their health care at point of service.

Canada's success in controlling its health-care expenditures rests substantially in the amassing of monopsonistic market power in the hands of the provincial governments. That power affords the payer substantial influence over the capacity it wishes to finance and over the prices it pays providers although, clearly, that power is not absolute. The negotiations over capacity and prices cannot for long violate the outer boundaries set by the market, which includes the ready access many Canadian patients and physicians have to the health system in the United States.

Just how important the monopsonistic market power of the Canadian health-insurance plans is one may infer from the comparative data on physician fees shown in Table 2-3. Subtle differences in coding the procedures listed there—for example, by the inclusion or exclusion of pre- and post-operative services—may slightly distort the data. Even after such adjustments, however, the central point of the table would remain: Rightly or wrongly and for better or for worse, compared with the United States, Canadian society is able to

Table 2-3. Comparison of medical fees, United States and Canada, 1984

| | United States | | Ontario, Canada | |
Procedure	Prevailing fees under Medicare	Median fees	Cdn. $s	U.S. equivalent[a]
Electrocardiogram[b]	$ 40	$ 35	$ 7	$ 6
Insertion of pacemaker	1,815	1,200	334	296
Appendectomy	734	600	259	229
Extraction of lens	1,314	N.A.	368	326
Hysterectomy	1,393	901	503	445
Coronary artery bypass	5,200	N.A.	1,300	1,150

Source: Reinhardt (1985b:372 Table 2); Organization for Economic Co-Operation and Development (1986:117).
N.A. means "not available."
[a]Purchasing power parity, $1.13 Canadian per $1 U.S.
[b]Professional component only.

procure medical care from their physicians at a lower transfer of money per unit of real resource.

The comparative data on costs raise the question of precisely what extras American patients enjoy relative to their counterparts in countries with tighter control over health-care expenditures. Unfortunately, research on that issue has only just begun. On the traditional, crude health-status indicators, such as age-specific mortality rates or relative life expectancy, the United States does not rank particularly high, but these indicators are functions of so many variables completely outside of the health sector's control that citing them would be meaningless. Ideally, one should approach the question by tracing the health-care experience of large random samples of patients with well-defined episodes of illness through their respective health systems to observe what real resources (i.e., services) the patients absorb in the process, what monetary transfers they trigger to the providers of these real resources, and what incremental impact their contact with the system ultimately had on their health status.

A start down that path was recently made by Newhouse, Anderson, and Roos (1988), who explored differences between Canada and the United States in the use of acute-care hospitals. The authors observed that in the early 1980s the United States spent nearly 50 percent more per person on hospital services than did Canada, and they examine "what, if anything, the United States bought for the additional expenditure" (Newhouse, Anderson, and Roos 1988:12). They found that admission rates to hospitals and the case mix were quite similar in the two countries and thus could not explain the difference in per-capita spending on hospitals. In the end, they concluded that "patients at U.S. hospitals appear to use either more inputs [e.g., physicians, machines] or more highly paid inputs (or both) than do patients at Canadian hospitals" (ibid., 1988:15). Unfortunately, these findings, important as they are, leave open the question of just what additional benefits were bought with these additional inputs or outlays on them. That question can be answered only after careful study of outcomes in the longer run.

Until very recently, the pluralistic approach to health-care financing in the United States appears to have enjoyed the enthusiastic support not only of the providers of health care—who clearly benefit from the greater money transfers triggered by that approach—but also of broad segments of the American public who saw in pluralism the driving force behind the technical progress and organizational innovation that to the American mind has been a unique feature of the American health system.

There is now mounting evidence of increasing disenchantment with that approach, however, as the cost of the system continues to soar, and as both the private and the public insurance systems embroil American patients and providers in a mounting paper war. That paper war has no rival anywhere in the world. It has made ours without question the most bureaucratic health system anywhere.[2]

In a recent set of sample surveys, researchers asked citizens in Canada, Great Britain, and the United States to rate their own health system relative to that in the other two countries (Blendon 1989). British and Canadian respondents expressed a higher regard for their own health system than Americans expressed for their own. About 7.5 percent of American respondents (representing about 18 million individuals) reported that they did not receive needed health care because of financial reasons, while less than 1 percent of the British and Canadian respondents made that claim. Close to 90 percent of American respondents believed that their health system needs either "fundamental change" (60 percent) or a "complete rebuilding" (29 percent). The comparable figures for Canada were 38 percent and 5 percent respectively, and for Great Britain 52 percent and

17 percent respectively. Finally, 61 percent of the American respondents would prefer a system like Canada's for the United States, while only 3 percent of Canadian's would prefer the American health system for Canada. Even in Great Britain, whose government constrains the health system to a very low budget and where queuing for elective surgery is commonplace, only 12 percent of the respondents expressed a preference for the American system, while 80 percent preferred their own system, although 28 percent would prefer the Canadian system.

Generally, respondents in surveys of this sort tend to express a preference for their own system, which they know, to a less familiar alternative system. The surprising feature of this survey was the high dissatisfaction American respondents expressed with their own system. One must wonder whether the proverbial man or women in America's streets still shares the belief, still widely professed by the providers of American health care, that "ours is the very best health system anywhere in the world."

The Problem of Cost Control in Health Care

Physicians and other providers of health care often wonder why the percentage of the GNP going to health care attracts such fascination among policymakers when no one seems to care what percentage of the GNP is spent on other goods and services in the economy. The answer to that question is straightforward: For ordinary consumer goods, analysts subject every single expenditure to a benefit-cost assessment that they can generally judge to be well informed and rational. For reasons already enumerated above, analysts cannot perform that benefit-cost calculus for the bulk of the transactions that determine health expenditures. Yet some limit must be placed on the size of the slice the providers of health services are permitted to carve out for themselves from the proverbial national pie, the GNP.

"Regulation" vs. "Market"

The preferred approach to the task of cost containments hinges substantially on one's perception of the commodity "health care." If one thinks of health care as essentially a private consumption good whose financing is, primarily, the individual's responsibility, then the task of cost containment properly belongs on the shoulders of individual patients or private groupings of patients. On the other hand, if one thinks of health care as essentially a social good that should be available to all citizens on equal terms, regardless of ability to pay, then the task of cost containment ultimately falls to the authority that effects the implied redistribution of health-care resources—the government (as is the case in Canada) or private entities endowed with some governmental powers (as in the case in many Western European countries).

Most industrialized societies appear to view all but the most elective forms of health care—for example, purely cosmetic surgery—as a "social good." In its position paper on that issue, for example, even the Conservative government of Canada proclaimed in 1983: "The government of Canada believes that a civilized and wealthy nation, such as ours, should not make the sick bear the financial burden of health care. . . . The misfortune of illness, which at some time touches each of us, is burden enough: the cost of care should be borne by society as a whole" (Government of Canada 1983:7). It is a safe bet that a query to the government of any Western European nation could easily elicit a similar affirmation of health care as a social good.

Nations beholden to this distributional ethic for health care implement it through universal national health-insurance systems that provide comprehensive coverage for a broad range of services and that are financed with payroll or general taxes completely divorced from actuarial principle. Over 90 percent of the population share these systems on equal terms. The remainder buy out through self-insurance or private insurance coverage.

As already noted earlier, the favored instruments for cost control in these systems are (1) regulatory limits on the capacity of the health sector through formal planning, (2) curbs on the monopoly power thus created through price controls and prospective budgets, and (3) the entrusting of the equitable distribution of the available health-care resources to the planners and the professional norms of health-care professionals. In short, these systems seek to purchase both equity and cost control by infringing on the providers' economic freedom to configure their capacity and to price their services as they see fit. Their relative success at cost containment can be inferred from Tables 2-2 and 2-3 above.

Just like people in the other industrialized nations, the representative American citizens appear to view health care as essentially a social good. In survey after survey, Americans declare that health care should be available to all, at the same level of quality, regardless of ability to pay.[3] But neither the American providers of health care nor, indeed, the American public has even been willing to countenance the regulatory interventions routinely used elsewhere in the industrialized world to achieve an equitable distribution of health care. Unwilling to accept either the regulation implied by perfect egalitarianism in health care or the inequities implied by rationing health care through price and the individual's ability to pay, Americans have pursued a health policy since World War II that is perfectly well described, in the words of Stuart Altman and Marc Rodwin, as "a political stalemate between halfway competitive markets and ineffective regulation" (Altman and Rodwin 1988:323).

The late 1960s and the entire 1970s can be described as the phase of half-hearted regulation. As health-care expenditures began their inexorable rise during that period, and as the public sector's share in these expenditures steadily grew, timid attempts were made to pursue some of the regulatory supply-side strategies adopted elsewhere in the industrialized world.

The Nixon administration's Economic Stabilization Program (ESP) in 1971–74 froze prices in the health-care sector along with prices elsewhere in the economy. Although the administration aimed that strategy solely at prices, leaving utilization uncontrolled, the program did succeed in limiting health spending temporarily. Spending resumed its rapid growth, however, as soon as the government lifted price controls in 1974.

On the theory that in health care the available capacity will somehow always find a way to be profitably employed, Congress next sought to limit the acquisition of expensive capital equipment and structures by the hospital sector. To that end, a federal law in 1974 established the regional Health Systems Agencies (HSAs) from which hospitals had to secure Certificates of Need (CONs) for capital expenditures costing in excess of $150,000. Unfortunately, that law had two undesirable consequences. First, the HSAs had no responsibility whatsoever for financing their decisions. When in doubt, they tended to err on the side of permitting the hospital its expansion, for theirs was not the task of funding the operating cost of the new capacity. Second, when an HSA did refuse to permit the hospital to acquire expensive equipment, it offered on a platter the physicians affiliated with the hospital the profitable opportunity to provide that equipment with their own funds. The physicians did not need a CON to set up a profitable machine right next to the hospital. In one of the many ironies that attend government regulation, the government's half-hearted foray into health-sector planning during the 1970s actively encouraged the growth of venture capitalism among American physicians.

Legislative attempts late in the 1970s simply to cap hospital revenue were easily defeated by the hospital sector's promises to practice "voluntary restraint." When, predictably, the promise was kept in the breach during the late 1970s and early 1980s, there emerged a brief but fiercely fought national debate on the relative merits of "competitions vs. regulation." That debate was won by the proponents of the so-called pro-competitive market strategy, an approach that had gained respectability in the literature of mainstream, neoclassical economics and that was music to the ears of the incoming Reagan administration.

The Pro-Competitive Strategy

The pro-competitive strategy rested on the intuitively appealing premise that third-party payment is the chief cost driver in modern health care (as third-party payment increased, direct payment decreased). Although, as Newhouse (1988) observed, by itself the large postwar decline in direct payments by patients from an average of 66 percent in 1950 to 28 percent in 1984 can account for only a small portion of the postwar increase in real health-care expenditures. In place of the supply-side regulation practiced in other countries, the pro-competitive strategy called for the further *deregulation* of the supply side by granting American health-care professionals even greater clinical and economic freedom than they hitherto enjoyed to manage health care and to price their services as they saw fit. Furthermore, the strategy openly welcomed into the health sector the genius and energy of profit-seeking American entrepreneurship, including the latent energy of the financial markets, which soon discovered in health care a new and richly endowed economic frontier.

Today, the booths of venture capitalists are standard fixtures at conventions of hospitals and physicians, persuading both to join profitable joint ventures in imaging, laboratory testing, one-day surgery, and so on. Joint ventures effectively allow the physician to sell the cash flows sick Americans are likely to trigger. Although overt kickbacks for patient referrals are illegal under the Medicare and Medicaid programs, and for all patients in some states, ventures can easily circumvent that stricture by offering physicians who can supply the referrals—and only those physicians—direct investment opportunities in the facilities, at enticing annual rates of return.[4]

To constrain the push for added revenues (health-care expenditures) this entrepreneurial energy was likely to unleash, the pro-competitive strategy called for converting patients into more cost-conscious "consumers" of health care. Consumers would become more aware of costs by greater cost sharing at the point of service, a policy some economists (e.g., Baumol 1988) would extend even to the frail elderly. Next, the pro-competitive strategy envisaged the amassing of greater market power by private payers (self-insured business firms and insurance carriers) through selective contracting with a limited number of providers who promised to grant price discounts in return for having patients steered their way. Figure 2-2 illustrates both the strengths and the limitations of that approach.

Figure 2-2 depicts a set of hospitals in a hypothetical market area in terms of the two dimensions that matter in a price-competitive strategy: "quality" of the care rendered by each hospital and the associated "costliness." Only hospitals A, B, and C in the diagram are the relatively most economically efficient hospitals in this market, because each of them offers the maximum level of quality available in this market for the cost they incur. In a truly price-competitive market of this sort, all other hospitals would either fold or move towards the efficient frontier ABC.

Confronted with such a menu, a firm providing health insurance for its employees might settle on quality level B as the maximum it would be willing to cover fully, leaving employees who insist on hospital C to pay the additional cost associated with that hospital out of pocket and, perhaps, letting employees who opt for the cheaper hospital A to pocket much or all the cost savings thereby achieved. The firm might implement this incentive system by means of a so-called Preferred Provider Organization (PPO) that includes only hospitals A and B among the "preferred providers," whose charges the employer covers in full, or through a Health Maintenance Organization (HMO), whose prepaid capitation payments reflect hospital charges no higher than those of hospital B.

Figure 2-2.   Hypothetical menu of cost-quality combinations, hospital-market area: Hickville, U.S.A.

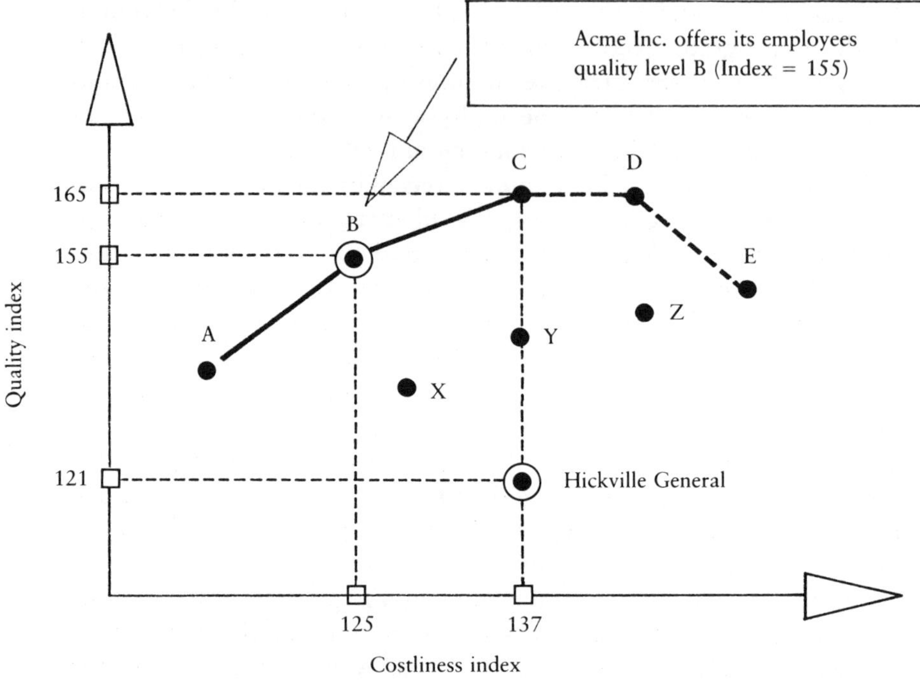

Source: Illustrative example constructed by author.

On its face, the strategy illustrated with Figure 2-2 may appear fundamentally "fair" and economically sound; but it has two major limitations.

First, its implementation presupposes the availability of reliable indices for "quality" and "costliness." These were not available in the early 1980s, and they are not available now—at least not at the stage of development that permits their widespread use by patients and third-party payers. In principle, such measurements ought to be no more complex than, say, the intelligence quotients this nation has shown no hesitancy to assign to its children. In the context of health care, however, where the flow of millions of revenue dollars may hinge on such numbers, the measurements would first have to withstand rigors of litigation by providers who might be assigned low-quality ratings. These ratings would next have to gain the trust of employees whose choice of provider would be limited by the indices. The latter consideration points to another difficulty associated with the pro-competitive strategy, namely, its tacit assumption that employed Americans will easily countenance a tiering of health care by income class. To be sure, the employer in our illustration could rightly argue that the firm is offering every employee, from the chief executive on down, the same health-insurance package and that employees were free to triage themselves into hospital A, B, or C. If employees perceived the levels of quality in the three hospitals to be significantly different, however, and the triage of employees perceptibly reflected their income class, the firm's management might have difficulty selling the scheme to its employees. In this connection it must be recalled that Americans continue to profess the notion that every American, regardless of ability to pay, should have access to the same quality of care.

The Footprints of the Pro-Competitive Strategy, So Far

The theoretical groundwork for the pro-competitive strategy was laid during the 1970s, largely in the writings of academic economists.[5] Associations of health-care providers actively promoted it in the political arena; they saw in it an effective shield against the more than half-hearted regulation they perceived on the horizon. Moreover, one suspects, they hoped that competition in health care would always take a form other than outright price competition.

As it turns out, there actually is little evidence that the health sector in recent years has been driven pervasively by more *price competition*, presumably, the objective of the pro-competitive cost-containment strategy. The government, which now pays for about 42 percent of national health expenditures, early on abandoned any hope of implementing a price-competitive strategy for its programs. Far from relying on competitively bid or even negotiated prices, it has generally imposed prices unilaterally, subject only to behind-the-scenes negotiation in the political arena. One would certainly not call this price competition as envisaged by the pro-competitive strategy. Although American firms have tried to make their employees shoulder more of the cost of their care at point of service and some of them have experimented with PPOs and greater reliance on HMOs, the available evidence indicates that at least so far, such efforts have been rather modest, and a broadening of covered benefits actually more than offsets them (Di Carlo and Gabel 1988; Jensen, Morissey, and Marcus 1987).

Figure 2-3. Index of health-care expenditures adjusted for inflation and population growth

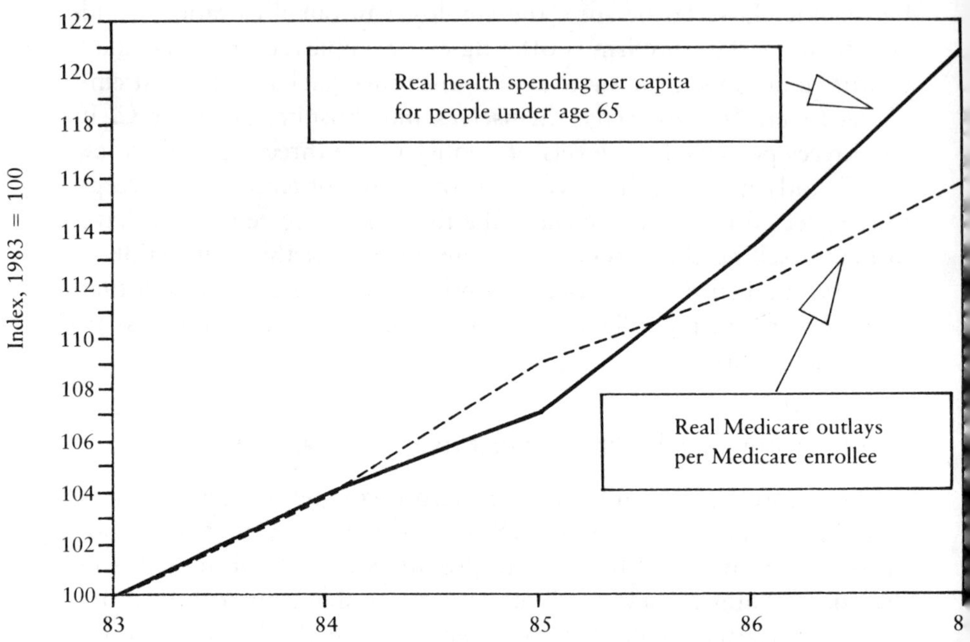

Source: Health Care Financing Administration, *HCFA Review,* various issues.

Nor has the growth of health-care expenditures abated during the deregulatory phase of the 1980s. On the contrary, that growth has turned out to be more rapid than it had been during the quasi-regulatory period of the 1970s. During the period 1980–86, overall real national health expenditures grew at an effective annual rate of 4.4 percent; during the period 1970–1980, they grew at only 3.8 percent (see Fuchs 1988). Ironically, only the strict price controls Medicare imposed on hospital compensation appear to have had the intended effect. Between 1976 and 1982, real inpatient revenues of hospitals grew at an effective annual rate of 9.5 percent; between 1982 and 1987, they grew at only 3.3 percent per year (Altman and Rodwin 1988:332, Table 1). But the triumph over cost growth in the Medicare program is hardly a vindication of market forces. It is a triumph of regulation!

In Figure 2-3, the trend in real personal health-care expenditures per capita for persons under age 65 is compared with the trend in real Medicare outlays per Medicare enrollee for the period 1983–87. Until 1985, the growth in per-capita outlays under the Medicare program actually outpaced that for per-capita outlays on persons under age 65. After 1985, with its case-based prospective payment method for hospitals firmly in place, the growth of Medicare outlays abates while the growth rate in per-capita outlays for persons under age 65 increases. Thus, it appears that the health sector has so far been able to shift at least some of the revenue losses suffered under the Medicare program to private payers. In any event, the premiums American business pays for private group health insurance have been rising in recent years at double-digit rates (Di Carlo and Gabel 1988). Insurers expect the payments to rise at an overall average of between 15 percent and 20 percent each year for the remainder of this decade.

There is little doubt that a market strategy based on more vigorous price competition could help constrain private-sector outlays on health care, if American business were prepared to limit its employees' freedom to choose providers more strictly than heretofore. That limitation would enable at least the larger business firms to extract price discounts and more conservative prescription of services from physicians and, in the process, to wring out of the system the excess capacity it now carries on its books and in its prices. Such a strategy, however, would have to overcome two major obstacles.

First, the American public would have to accept the implications for distributional equity of that strategy and also its potentially devastating impact on non-preferred neighborhood hospitals.

Second, a more vigorous pursuit of that strategy would eliminate still further the hidden cross-subsidies through which the nation has hitherto financed critically needed health care for uninsured, low-income Americans. As already noted, there are now some 35 million or so Americans without any health-insurance coverage whatsoever, a substantial rise from about 25 million during the 1970s. Under the regime of full-cost, retrospective reimbursement of hospitals customary during the 1970s, the uninsured could usually secure adequate hospital care when they fell seriously ill. To the extent that the hospital treating these patients failed to collect its bills directly from them, it could always pass on the cost of that treatment to well-insured patients.

The health system during the 1980s increasingly squeezed out these hidden cross-subsidies, partly in response to the price controls the Medicare and Medicaid programs imposed. But one also suspects that the system forced out these subsidies as the result of a subtle change in the ethical norms that drive the health-care system, after policymakers openly embraced the language and imagery of the new health-care "market" in which doctors and hospitals became "suppliers," patients became "consumers," and health services became "product lines" actively pushed by marketing consultants.

To avoid the cost of caring for poor, uninsured Americans, a fiscally beleaguered hospital merely needs to close its emergency and obstetrics departments, the traditional conduits of patients who are unable to pay for their own care. That trend has already set in some parts of the country, notably in Los Angeles. Before policymakers can give any thought to a more serious application of price-competition in health care, a workable alternative system must replace the traditional system of hidden taxation. Any such alternative will, of course, involve taxation, pure and simple.

SOLVING THE PROBLEM OF THE UNINSURED

As noted, many American citizens now seem willing at least to explore the merits of universal national health insurance on the Canadian model (see, for example, Blendon 1989; Himmelstein, Woolhandler, and the Writing Committee 1989). That strategy, however, would threaten the income of health-care providers and of the health-insurance industry, both of whom thrive under our more loosely structured, pluralistic system. They would likely vehemently oppose any serious attempt at universal national health insurance. There is the added question whether this country would ever be able to legislate a clean, workable national health-insurance scheme under our current system of governance. Countries with parliamentary systems ruled by party discipline find it much easier to legislate bold, coherent social programs. Finally, it is not at all clear that the American electorate would ultimately be willing to countenance the degree of government control such a system implies. For all these reasons, the United States is unlikely to move toward universal national health insurance soon, if ever.

This circumstance leaves the United States in the shorter run with a choice between two major classes of strategies, should there actually develop a widely shared desire to extend health-insurance coverage for at least a basic package of health-care services to all Americans. So far, no such desire exists.

First, the federal or state governments could mandate all firms to provide the requisite coverage to all their employees, with proper adjustments for part-time workers, and then sweep up the remaining uninsured into an expanded Medicaid program. Alternatively, the government could simply reform the Medicaid into a broader fail-safe insurance system into which every American not insured elsewhere would automatically fall and for which the government would charge enrollees a premium based strictly on their ability to pay. For purposes of cost control, either approach could embrace the idea of "managed competition" recently proposed by Enthoven (1988). Under managed competition, a network of private and public "sponsors" would create market power on the demand side. The sponsors would negotiate prices and other regulations with providers on behalf of enrollees who would be free to choose among competing sponsors. An HMO for example, would be one form of sponsor.

Mandated, Employer-Paid Health Insurance

Employer-mandated health insurance builds upon the American tradition to tie such coverage to the workplace. That approach has served millions of Americans well, albeit at an increasingly burdensome cost to employers. The extent of the burden, of course, raises the question how much longer American business will continue to support that approach enthusiastically, especially when the health sector presents to business the apparently staggering bill for unfunded and hitherto unacknowledged health-care benefits promised to retired workers. We shall learn more about the attitude of business after the Financial Accounting Standards Board (FASB) forces American business to report honestly to shareholders the magnitude of the liabilities already incurred on benefits. The FASB's attempt to mandate honesty in these matters may well sour the mood among America's business executives as they contemplate the virtue of employer-paid health benefits.

One can access the merits of mandated, employer-paid health insurance by means of a T-account, with a debit and a credit side, and then take an overall balance of the measure. The latter, of course, will inevitably be subjective.

The first point to the credit of the proposal is earned by virtue of its bipartisan origin. It is now fashionable among conservative politicians to decry employer-mandated health insurance as "outright socialism," because leading Democrats recently were its chief proponents. That labelling is ironic, because the proposal is actually an old Republican idea. It was the core of former president Richard Nixon's *Health Message to Congress*, dated February 18, 1971, which subsequently was translated into his Community Health Insurance Partnership (CHIP) proposal. Alas, a Democratic Congress that had its own ideas promptly shelved the proposal, which was truly generous by today's standards. As the general idea behind the Republican CHIP proposal—that employers should pay for health insurance—now does enjoy support among Democratic members of Congress as well, one must impute to it a fairly broad political base. One can decide the measure as "socialist" only by attaching that label implicitly also to former president Nixon. One can decry it as "inadequate"—as it was in the 1970s—only by questioning the commitment to the poor by today's leading Democrats.

A second major advantage of employer-mandated health insurance is the powerful sweep of the measure. If lawmakers extend the mandate to include the employees' dependents, with one stroke of the pen the measure would fold between two-thirds to three-quarters of the uninsured into mainstream American health insurance and health care.

A third credit mandated benefits earn, certainly in the eyes of politicians, must be that such mandates allow legislators to pursue preferred social goals without having to support them explicitly with added tax revenues. Because mandated benefits are *hidden taxes*, they are ideally suited to the current era in which honesty on the matter of taxation amounts demonstrably to political suicide. Even concerned and well-intentioned politicians who prefer honest, explicit taxation are therefore likely to support mandated benefits.

In his "Some Simple Economics of Mandated Benefits," Summers (1988) defends mandated benefits on grounds of economic efficiency. Some of his arguments center on the externalities in consumption inherent in so-called merit wants, of which health care is one. These arguments, however, merely make the case for mandating health insurance of some form, not necessarily for mandating employers to provide it. More compelling, however, is the argument that in the absence of the mandate the superior information job applicants have about their health status will leave firms that voluntarily offer generous health benefits with a relatively sicker, more expensive work force—that information asymmetry will lead employers in an unregulated, competitive market to underprovide health-insurance benefits.

Among responsible legislators, however, some of the deleterious side effects of mandated employer-paid benefits ought to temper its political allure. Mandated benefits are a special form of *payroll tax*, although, as Summers illustrates, the deadweight loss associated with them is likely to be smaller than would be the loss associated with an equivalent public insurance program that is purely payroll-tax financed.[6] Because the vast majority of uninsured workers are employed by small firms in low-paying jobs, employer-provided health insurance for these workers will mean a relatively large percentage increase in these firms' payroll expense. One cannot easily predict the ultimate effects of such an increase on employment, output, and prices. Therein lies the first debit to be lodged against the measure.

The owners of firms (be they proprietors or shareholders of corporations) may seek to reduce their own share of the tax burden simply by passing on the payroll tax to customers, in the form of higher prices. But customers' sensitivity to high prices may limit the degree of this forward shifting. If so, employers will seek to shift the tax backward to employees by substituting the mandated benefits for cash wages that would otherwise have been paid. In that case, the ultimate incidence of the tax will be quite regressive. One would effectively force even low-income wage earners to purchase government-mandated health-insurance benefits at a tax premium that does not vary by ability to pay but instead takes on the form of a head tax. It would burden substantially the very families one would like to help—reason enough to charge it with a second debit.

Third, minimum wage laws or other downward rigidities may make it impossible to shift the cost of mandated benefits backwards, and price sensitivity among the firm's customers may make it difficult to shift the cost forward. If those situations arise, then the long-run effect of the tax is likely to be that employers will substitute labor-saving capital equipment for the (now more expensive) labor or, worse still, simply reduce output and employment. Mandated benefits may thus transform some of the working uninsured into unemployed uninsured.

Fourth, as Summers (1988) readily concedes, to the extent that the mandates prohibit firms from varying the cash income of equally productive workers inversely with the fringe-benefits costs all workers trigger, a policy that mandates benefits may induce employers to discriminate against employees likely to trigger high health costs.

Finally, one must wonder whether it is wise to saddle particularly small firms with the bureaucratic burden of demonstrating compliance with the typically complex statutes our legislators pass. There would doubtless arise yet another class of consultants deriving their livelihood from interpreting the government's wishes to the laity. Mandated health insurance would also, of course, drive these small firms into the waiting arms of an insurance industry that has not traditionally distinguished itself in servicing small firms.

A Federal Fail-Safe System Financed by Income Taxes

Americans not afflicted with an instinctive aversion to honest federal taxation might contemplate an alternative, all-American approach, namely, a federal fail-safe health-insurance program primarily for the lower-income groups and financed substantially by earmarked federal income taxes.

Such a program, which would be available automatically to every American resident, would provide the insured with comprehensive health services, including specified preventive services for expectant mothers and for children. Managed-care systems such as an HMO or a PPO would deliver these services; under competitively bid or negotiated contracts with the fail-safe system, they would be, of course, under sustained external monitoring of the quality of care. The insured could procure emergency care everywhere at predetermined rates—perhaps those established under the federal Medicare program.

Because "actuarially fair" contributions to such a scheme would violate our professed social ethic—that unlucky sick individuals should not pay higher health-insurance premiums than lucky healthy ones—ability to pay would determine the financing of the proposed fail-safe system, as is customary virtually everywhere else in the world. One approach might be to include on the 1040 tax form a line calling for a health-insurance tax equal to X percent (say, 12 percent) of adjusted gross income above a low-income threshold. Taxpayers would have to pay that tax unless they clipped to the 1040 a copy of an equivalent or better private health-insurance policy, in which case taxpayers might be asked to contribute only a much smaller tax (less than 1 percent) earmarked for indigent care. It would be the individual's price for luxuriating in the social ethic prescribed in most religions that one be one's poor brethren's keeper. Any cost of the program not covered by these explicit tax rates would have to come from general revenue.

The tax rate X is an important policy parameter. It could be set, perhaps progressively, to discourage excessive reliance on the fail-safe system by the middle- and upper-income groups. In the impending era of the labor shortage, the majority of Americans could probably prevail upon their employers to provide health-insurance coverage, *but on a voluntary basis*, as before. Thus, the structure of the fail-safe approach could preserve the private-sector pluralism of which Americans are so fond and for which they have always been willing to pay a substantial premium above absolutely necessary health-care costs. The ability of citizens to opt out of the federal fail-safe program is an important design parameter in the American context because Americans harbor such a manifest distrust toward their government, and many Americans find it outright distasteful to deal with their government even when that government offers them a good proposition.

A federal fail-safe system would eliminate once and for all the providers' problem of "uncompensated care" and the attendant cost-shifting to commercial insurers and, thence, to the payroll accounts of firms. It would also remove from the uninsured the stigma of being "health-care beggars" forced, in case of illness, to cast about for the uncertain noblesse oblige of kindly providers of care. The system would be *federal* on the thesis that America is not just a place but a *genuine nation*, one whose government should set a floor beneath which no American is allowed to sink in health care.

There is no reason, however, to preclude state and local governments from administering and partially financing such a system. Many other nations—for example, Canada and West Germany—adopt that form of partnership in their health systems. Furthermore, there already exist at the state level the administrative agencies that manage the current Medicaid program. These agencies could have the task of procuring health services from providers at negotiated or competitively bid prices. They would also negotiate with providers all other regulations pertaining to the fail-safe program, all within the framework of the broader federal statute.

In 1986, the relatively comprehensive Medicaid program spent an average of $700 per child and about $1,100 per adult in the program. In that year, established HMOs charged annual premiums of $924 for individuals and $2,500 for families. Those rates would probably have been closer to $1,100 and $3,200, respectively, in 1988. Most of the uninsured are relatively young. As noted, one third of them are children under the age of 16. Had the proposed fail-safe system covered all 35 million uninsured Americans under age 65 in 1988, that system's total outlays might have been somewhere around $35 to $40 billion. Of course, one would assume that the 25 percent of uninsured with family incomes in excess of $30,000 (in 1987) would have opted out of the fail-safe system, because the income-related premium for that system would probably exceed the cost of a lean private health-insurance policy. On the other hand, some small firms might also attempt to dump into the fail-safe system low-income employees now covered by employer-paid insurance. The system, however, could devise incentives or strictures to discourage such dumping. In the end, the total outlays by the fail-safe system would probably not have exceeded $30 billion in 1988.

The total federal outlay of the fail-safe system would clearly not be a net addition to that year's total national health expenditures of about $550 billion. Current estimates suggest that on average the health spending per uninsured American is equal to somewhere between 50 percent and 70 percent of the spending of comparable groups of fully insured Americans. The uninsured themselves finance some of these outlays; the remainder represents some $8 to $10 billion of "uncompensated" care delivered by physicians and hospitals to critically ill, uninsured, and low-income Americans. Because the federal fail-safe system would pay for 100 percent of the care of the poor, the latter no longer would pay the share (approximately 60 percent) they now do out of pocket. The net additional expenditures induced by the fail-safe system's better insurance coverage probably would have been only about $15 billion or at most $20 billion in 1988—an increase of between 2 percent to 3 percent in total national health expenditures. It would not have been an intolerable extra burden upon the nation's economy.

Concluding Observations

Americans tend to take great pride in their cautious, incremental approach to domestic policy. But surely somewhere short of utter stalemate in policy formation that pride must give way to embarrassment. As should be apparent from the developments chronicled in this essay, the felicitous maxim that ours is the best health system in the world cannot any longer paper over the troublesome paradox born of this stalemate: the rationing of critically needed health care in the midst of enormous excess capacity and waste.

The options for our health policy at this time are stark and simple. First, the nation could muddle through as usual, exposing low-income Americans to even greater indignities and hardships than they already face. Alternatively, the nation could follow the path chosen by virtually all other industrialized nations and seek to combine equitable access to health care with cost control through a comprehensive, universal health-insurance system. Finally, the nation could develop an honest, two-track health-insurance system, with a relatively small track for publicly financed, low-income Americans and a private system for everybody else, leaving each of the two systems to cope with cost control as best it can.

Unfortunately, every single constructive idea on health policy in recent years has fallen hostage to the four major warring factions that control health policy in America:

The business sector, to the extent that it has articulated any coherent strategy at all, does not oppose broader health-insurance coverage, but it seeks cost control before any coverage is extended to the now uninsured.

The providers of health care, for their part, are forever ready to serve the now uninsured, if they receive "adequate" compensation for that purpose. In other words, the providers want insurance coverage first and discussions of cost control later.

The private health-insurance industry would like to see all the uninsured brought under coverage, as long as that could be achieved without a public program that might entice part of the industry's clientele into the public fold.

Finally, the nation's elected officials would like to see all Americans have the benefit of adequate health insurance and health care as long as that does not require additional public expenditures and taxes.

Alas, in the eye of such a stalemate, the exercise of policy analysis becomes an exercise of whistling in the wind.

NOTES

1.   See Berk, Monheit, and Hagan (1988:50, Exhibit 1). In 1963, 10 percent of the population accounted for 59 percent of all health expenditures. By 1970, the ratio had increased to 66 percent. In 1980, it stood at 70 percent.

2.   Himmelstein and Woolhandler (1986) have estimated that relative to the much simpler Canadian health-insurance system, the United States spends about 8 percent more on administrative costs. Using data for 1983, that percentage would have represented savings to the United States of about $30 billion. The equivalent number for 1987 would have been $40 billion.

3.   See, for example, "HMQ Survey: A Mandate for High-Quality Care" (1986).

4.   In this connection, see Bogdanovich and Waldholz (1989).

5.   See, for example, Greenberg (1978) and the collection of essays in a special issue of the *Journal of Health Politics, Policy and Law* (1988), which offers a ten-year retrospective on the market strategy.

6.   The reasoning is as follows: Under a payroll tax per se, the employers' demand for labor shifts downward, but labors' supply curve stays put. Under mandated benefits, labors' supply curve shifts down by an amount equal to the value labor imputes to the benefit. Thus, employment is reduced less than it would be under a pure payroll tax.

REFERENCES

Altman, Stuart H., and Marc A. Rodwin. 1988. "Halfway Competitive Markets and Ineffective Regulation: The American Health Care System." *Journal of Health Politics, Policy and Law* 13:323–340.

Baumol, William J. 1988. "Price Controls for Medical Services and the Medical Needs of the Elderly." Paper commissioned by the American Medical Association and presented to the Physician Payment Review Commission, March 11.

Berk, Marc L., Alan C. Monheit, and Michael M. Hagan. 1988. "How the U.S. Spent Its Health Care Dollar: 1929–1980." *Health Affairs* 7:46–60.

Blendon, Robert J. 1989. "Three Systems: A Comparative Survey." *Health Management Quarterly* 11:2–10.

Bogdanovich, Walt, and Michael Waldholz. 1989. "Warm Bodies: Doctor-Owned Labs Earn Lavish Profits in a Captive Market." *The Wall Street Journal* March 1, 1989:A1, A6.

Chollet, Deborah. 1988. *Uninsured in the United States: The Nonelderly Population without Health Insurance, 1986.* Washington, D.C.: Employee Benefit Research Institute.

Congressional Research Service, Library of Congress. 1988a. *Insuring the Uninsured: Options and Analysis.* Report prepared for the Subcommittee on Labor-Management Relations and the Subcommittee on Labor Standards of the Committee on Education and Labor and the Subcommittee on Health and the Environment of the Committee on Energy and Commerce, House of Representatives, and the Special Committee on Aging, United States Senate. Washington, D.C.: U.S. Government Printing Office, October.

Congressional Research Service, Library of Congress. 1988b. *Medicaid Source Book: Background Data and Analysis.* Report prepared for the Subcommittee on Health and the Environment of the Committee on Energy and Commerce, U.S. House of Representatives. Washington, D.C.: U.S. Government Printing Office, November.

Di Carlo, Steven and Jon Gabel. 1988. *Conventional Health Plans: A Decade Later.* Washington, D.C.: Health Insurance Association of America.

Enthoven, Alain. 1988. "Managed Competition of Alternative Delivery Systems." *Journal of Health Politics, Policy and Law* 13:305–322.

Fuchs, Victor R. 1988. "The 'Competition Revolution' in Health Care. *Health Affairs* 7:5–24.

Government of Canada. 1983. *Preserving Universal Medicare.* A Government of Canada Position Paper, Ottawa, Ontario, Canada.

Greenberg, Warren, ed. 1978. *Competition in the Health Care Sector: Past, Present, and Future.* Germantown, Md.: Aspen Systems.

Health Care Financing Administration. *HCFA Review,* various issues.

Health Message from the President of the United States Relative to Building a National Health Strategy. 1971. House Document No. 92-49, 92nd Congress, 1st session, Washington, D.C.: U.S. Government Printing Office, February 18.

Himmelstein, David U., and Steffie Woolhandler. 1986. "Cost Without Benefit: Administrative Waste in U.S. Health Care." *New England Journal of Medicine* 314:441–445.

Himmelstein, David U. 1989. Steffie Woolhandler, and the Writing Committee of the Working Group on Program Design. "A National Health Program for the United States: A Physicians' Proposal." *New England Journal of Medicine* 320:102–108.

"HMQ Survey: A Mandate for High-Quality Health Care." Unauthored paper in *Health Management Quarterly.* Fourth Quarter: 3–7.

Holahan, John, and John L. Palmer. 1987. "Medicare's Fiscal Problems: An Imperative for Reform." Mimeographed paper, November.

Jensen, Gail A., Michael A. Morrisey, and John W. Marcus. 1987. "Cost Sharing and the Changing Pattern of Employer-Sponsored Health Benefits." *The Milbank Quarterly* 65:521–550.

Journal of Health Politics, Policy, and Law. 1988. 13: entire issue.

Levit, Katharine R., and Mark S. Freeman. 1988. "Data Watch: National Medical Care Spending." *Health Affairs,* 7:124–136.

Marquis, M. Susan. 1984. *Cost Sharing and the Patient's Choice of Provider,* RAND Corporation Publication No. R-3126-HHS. Santa Monica, Calif.: RAND Corporation.

McCarthy, Thomas R. 1985. "The Competitive Nature of the Primary-Care Physician Services Market." *Journal of Health Economics* 4:93–117.

Newhouse, Joseph P. 1988. "Has the Erosion of the Medical Market Place Ended?" *Journal of Health Politics, Policy and Law* 13:263–278.

Newhouse, Joseph P., Geoffrey Anderson, and Leslie L. Roos. 1988. "Hospital Spending in the United States and Canada: A Comparison." *Health Affairs* 7:6–16.

Organization for Economic Co-Operation and Development. 1986. *National Accounts 1960–84,* Vol. I. Paris.

Pauly, Mark V. 1978. "Is Medical Care Different?" In Warren Greenberg, ed., *Competition in the Health Care Sector: Past, Present, and Future,* pp. 11–37. Germantown, Md.: Aspen Systems.

Reinhardt, Uwe E. 1985a. "The Theory of Physician-Induced Demand: Reflections After a Decade." *Journal of Health Economics* 4:187–193.

——. 1985b. "The Compensation of Physicians: Approaches Used in Foreign Countries." *Quality Review Bulletin* 11:366–377.

Schieber, George J., and Jean-Pierre Poullier. 1988. "Data Watch: International Health Spending and Utilization Trends." *Health Affairs* 7:105–112.

Sloan, Frank A., and Roger Feldman. 1988. "Competition Among Physicians." In Warren Greenberg, ed., *Competition in the American Health Care Sector: Past, Present, and Future,* pp. 45–102. Germantown, Md.: Aspen Systems.

Summers, Lawrence H. 1988. "Some Simple Economics of Mandated Benefits." Mimeographed paper, presented at the Annual Meeting of the American Economic Association, December.

U.S. Bureau of the Census. 1987. *Statistical Abstract of the United States: 1987* (107th ed.). Washington, D.C.

3 Housing for Low-Income Households: A Defense of Demand-Side Subsidies

JOHN F. KAIN

In 1982 I prepared a paper on housing policy entitled "America's Persistent Housing Crises: Errors in Analysis and Policy" for a special issue of *The Annals of the American Academy of Political and Social Science*. As the title suggests, the paper's theme was that the alleged housing crises were illusory or exaggerated, were the result of faulty analysis, and that, as a result, the wrong policies were being advanced to deal with them.

Since the publication of the *Annals* special issue, there has been surprisingly little debate about these questions. The disappearance of housing from the nation's policy agenda is explained by the Reagan administration's largely successful efforts to deemphasize domestic policy, particularly urban policy, and its success in sharply cutting taxes. A relatively slow growth in federal tax revenues, combined with a more rapid growth in spending, particularly defense spending, produced a rapid growth in federal deficits and discouraged costly new spending initiatives. More recently, the emergence of a highly visible homeless population, rising real rents, the explosive growth in house prices in several metropolitan housing markets, and the bankruptcy of a growing number of thrift institutions have caught the attention of the media, the public, and policymakers and have produced a boomlet in housing-policy analysis.

Congress, ever sensitive to the media and public opinion, established a National Housing Task Force in 1987. The commission's report, issued in March 1988, concludes that for too many families housing "is unavailable, unaffordable or unfit" and that "for millions of our families, we have not only fallen short but are losing ground."[1] The commission's report and the housing-policy literature identify dozens of housing problems. This paper discusses only one—the income/housing needs of low-income households, which I regard as one of two housing problems that deserves urgent attention. Housing-market discrimination, along with its widespread consequences, is the other pressing problem, which I have dealt extensively with elsewhere (Kain 1974, 1985, and 1986; Kain and Quigley 1975).

In my 1982 article, I discussed the nature of the low-income problem and appropriate policy responses, arguing that the most common mistake made by those concerned with the housing problems of poor households is to confuse the inability of many low-income households to obtain standard housing without spending an excessively high fraction of their incomes on rent with evidence of market failure.[2] The problem for most poor households is poverty, not inadequate housing, and I concluded that "while poverty, excess rent burdens, and inadequate housing remain serious problems for millions of Americans, there is no evidence that the problems have become more serious" (Kain 1982:145). In the same paper, I found:

> Previous studies of America's housing policy . . . uniformly conclude that (federal housing) programs tend to be both inequitable and inefficient. The inequity arises from the fact that government programs provide subsidies to only a small fraction of eligible households; while recipients obtain very large subsidies, most households receive no assistance whatsoever. The inefficiency results from the heavy emphasis on new construction programs. It is at least twice as expensive to build new units to assist poor households as it is to rent existing units. (Kain 1982:147)

On returning to the housing policy debate more than half a decade later, I find no reason to change my views concerning the nature of the nation's housing problems or the appropriate policy response. It remains true that most low-income households live in "standard" housing and have too little income to purchase adequate housing without spending an excessive fraction of their incomes. Yet there is some evidence that the income-housing problems of poor households may have worsened during the past decade as a result of increases in real rents and decreases in income and housing subsidies. Nonetheless, the well-intentioned proposals of the National Housing Task Force (1988), which, in spite of their vagueness and complexity, are arguments for an expanded government role in providing low-income housing and a return to large production programs, would be a step backward.

The emerging housing-policy debate tends to confuse, perhaps intentionally, two issues: (1) How much should governments spend to assist low-income households in obtaining better housing or to reduce their rent burdens; and (2) given a particular budget level, what programs and policies should the government use? Recent papers and reports dealing with housing policy tend to focus on one of the following three related, but still different, questions.

1. How adequate are governmental housing subsidies for low-income households? What has happened to the level of public support? What amount of federal, low-income subsidies should the government provide?
2. What is the nature of the low-income housing problem, how serious is it, and is it getting worse or better?
3. Given any level of government subsidies for low-income households, what is the most cost-effective means of spending these dollars to improve the housing conditions of low-income households?

The Adequacy of Housing Subsidies

The task of assessing the low-income housing problem is complicated by two distinct and largely uncoordinated sources of housing assistance for low-income households: The first is federal, state, and local subsidies for housing, and the second is housing payments under the welfare system. Newman and Schnare (1988) estimate that the Department of Housing and Urban Development (HUD) spent (circa 1988) around $10 billion a year on assisted housing and that the tax advantages associated with developing and rehabilitating low-income housing under the 1986 tax reform may produce an additional $2.7 billion of subsidies over the next five years. At the same time, they estimate that the welfare system—through the explicit and implicit shelter allowances provided under Aid to Families with Dependent Children (AFDC), Supplemental Security Income (SSI), and General Assistance (GA)—spends at least an additional $10 billion a year on housing assistance, or about as much as HUD.[3]

Using data from the Annual Housing Survey (AHS), Newman and Schnare (1988:5) estimate that about 8 million households received some form of income or housing assistance in 1983. Some households received both income and housing assistance: An estimated 4.6

Table 3-1. Number of assisted households, outstanding commitments, and total federal outlays for assisted housing in 1987 and FY 1988

Program	Thousands of households assisted end FY 1987	Thousands of committed units through FY 1988	Total outlays during FY 1987 (millions of $)
Rental assistance programs			
Section 8			
Existing housing			
Vouchers	82	184	81
Certificates	874	895	(a)
Loan management, property disposition, and conversions	414	438	3,819[a]
Moderate rehabilitation	76	126	244
Subtotal, existing housing	1,446	1,643	4,144
New construction/ substantial rehabilitation	794	868	3,981
Public housing	1,390	1,433	3,517[b]
Other HUD programs[c]	552	551	686
Section 515 rural rental assistance	349	394	853
Total rental assistance[d]	4,296	4,653	13,180
Homeownership assistance programs			
Section 235 mortgage interest subsidies	159	144	182
Section 502 rural housing loans	899	876	1,900
Total homeowners assistance	1,059	1,020	2,082

Source: Pedone 1988.

[a]Section 8 certificates are included in loan management, etc.

[b]Includes outlays for operating subsidies, for the up-front capital costs of new construction and modernization activities undertaken during 1987, and for debt service of activities undertaken before 1974.

[c]Includes currently inactive Section 236 and rent-supplement programs.

[d]The total does not equal the sum of the number of households assisted under the various programs; rather, it has been adjusted to avoid double-counting households receiving more than one subsidy.

million received only income assistance, 2.1 million received only housing assistance, and 1.3 million received both income and housing assistance.

A recent Congressional Budget Office (CBO) report estimates 4.3 million low-income renters and about one million low- to middle-income owners received federal housing subsidies in 1988 (Pedone, 1988). Commitments were made for an additional 357,000 rental units, the difference between commitments through 1988 and assisted households at the end of FY 1987. These data also show that HUD spent just over $13 billion on rental assistance programs in 1987 and just over $2 billion more on homeowners-assistance programs, exclusive of the upper-middle income tax expenditures under the internal revenue code (see Table 3-1). These expenditures consist of property tax and interest deductions for owner-occupied dwellings and the absence of taxes on imputed rent, that is, taxes on homeowner's equity.

The data in Table 3-1 indicate further that roughly two-thirds of those receiving rental assistance are living in units produced under costly supply-side programs, in spite of the Reagan administration's tilt toward more cost-effective demand-side subsidies since 1981. Pedone (1988:37) estimates that units in supply-side production programs accounted for 53 percent to 73 percent of all commitments between 1977 and 1983 but have accounted for only about a third between 1983 and 1988. The recent share of units in demand-side programs might have been much greater than two-thirds, except that the lags between the commitment to produce new units and completion for supply-side production programs are very long.

While the complexity of the housing-subsidy system makes it difficult to quantify precisely the exact levels of federal spending or the numbers of low-income households assisted, it appears, nonetheless, that the Reagan administration drastically reduced federal spending for housing assistance to low-income households. The impact of these cuts on the welfare of low-income households, however, was almost certainly less than the reduction in spending, because of a shift away from inefficient production programs in favor of demand-side subsidies.[4]

HAS THE PROBLEM GOTTEN WORSE?

Apgar (1988) contends real rents have risen substantially since 1974, and particularly since 1981. He argues, moreover, that nu-

Figure 3-1.   Bureau of Labor Statistics (BLS) and "corrected" indexes of real contract rents, 1967–87

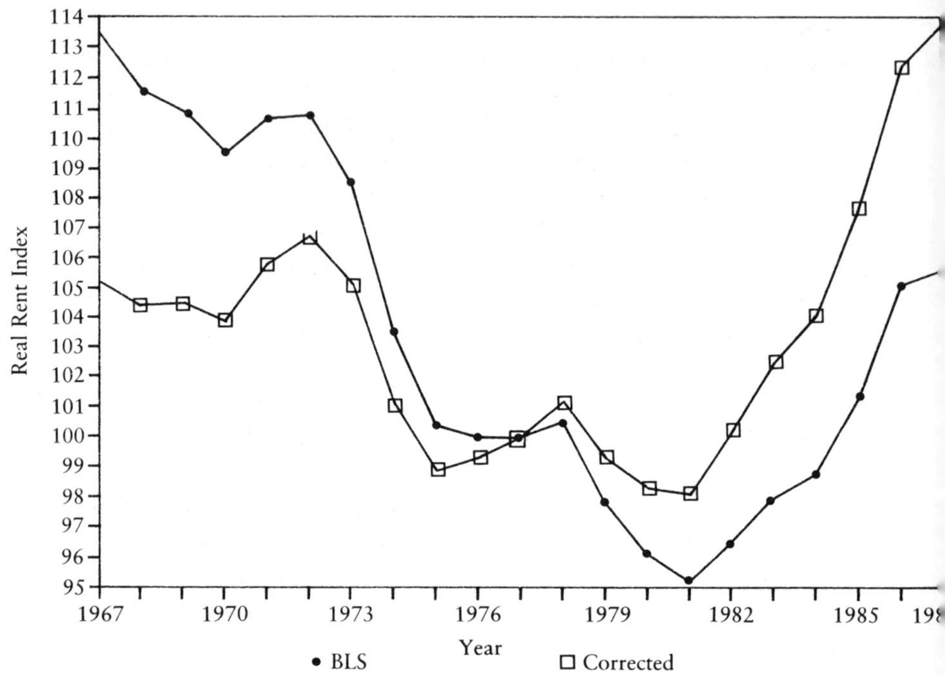

Source: Apgar 1988.

merous studies of housing trends over the past two decades, including my 1982 paper, underestimated the housing problems of low-income households by relying on the residential rent component of the Consumer Price Index (CPI) to measure real rents. (See Weicher, Villani, and Roistacher 1981 for a summary of these studies.) Apgar (1988:7) argues the CPI rent index presents an incorrect view of recent trends in rents, by failing to account for depreciation. Using corrections first suggested by Lowry (1982), Apgar obtains the "adjusted rental index" shown in Figure 3-1, along with the more familiar unadjusted index.

Apgar (1988, 1989) has also completed a recent analysis of the extent and nature of the low-income housing problem. His research, which the National Housing Task Force (1988) relied upon heavily, indicates that for the decade 1974–84 at least, the stock of low-rent housing has shrunk at the same time the number of low-income renters has grown.[5] Apgar's (1989) most recent estimates indicate the number of units renting for less than $300 per month (adjusted for inflation) fell by nearly 1.7 million between 1974 and 1985. The $300-per-month figure Apgar used is a weighted average of the amounts households of various types at the poverty threshold could pay for housing without devoting more than 30 percent of their incomes to housing. During the same period, the number of renters in poverty households increased by 2.8 million.

Apgar (1988:32) identifies several factors that contribute to the decline in the number of low-rent units, but he particularly emphasizes the role of upgrading, noting that the number of units with rents above $400 increased by 4.5 million during 1974–83. According to Apgar, the growing mismatch between the demand for rental housing by low-income households and the supply of low-rent rental housing is due principally to three factors: (1) the growth in the number of low-income renters, and particularly those with children; (2) abandonment of low-rent units; and (3) rapid rises in real rents. As I discuss below, these "losses" in low-rent units, whether by upgrading or real rent increases, could easily be compensated for in a demand-side subsidy program simply by increasing the rent levels used in defining subsidy levels. Analyses presented at a later point in this paper indicate that raising "Fair Market Rents" in existing demand-side programs by 10 percent would have added roughly 2.7 million units to the supply eligible for these programs in 1983.

Table 3-2 presents estimates, developed from data published by Apgar (1988), on the numbers and fractions of rental households who received federal housing subsidies in 1974 and 1987, as well as the percentage growth in recipients during the period.[6] Households with annual incomes below $5,000 per year roughly correspond to what are termed "very low income" households, those with incomes between $5,000 and $10,000 per year are what are usually termed "low-income" households, and $10,000 is approximately the income-eligibility cutoff for most low-income rental assistance programs.[7]

The data in Table 3-2 indicate that the percentage of very low and low-income households receiving housing subsidies rose sharply between 1974 and 1987, from 16.4 percent to 30.5 percent in the former, and from 16.0 percent to 23.7 percent in the latter. Indeed, the numbers of households with incomes below $10,000 receiving rental assistance grew by 141 percent. These estimates do *not* include

Table 3-2.   Number of rental households, number of housing-subsidy recipients, and participation rates by income class in 1974 and 1987 (percentage change, 1974 and 1987)

Income 1986 dollars (000s)	Number of renters (000s)		Number receiving subsidy (000s)		Percentage receiving subsidy		Percentage change, 1974–87		Number not receiving subsidy	
	1974	1987	1974	1987	1974	1987	assisted renters	all assisted	1974	1987
Under 5	2,691	4,560	441	1,391	16.4%	30.5%	69.4%	215.1%	2,250	3,169
5 to 10	4,491	5,942	719	1,408	16.0%	23.7%	32.3%	96.0%	3,773	4,534
10 to 17.5	5,283	7,372	507	774	9.6%	10.5%	39.5%	52.6%	4,776	6,598
17.5 to 25	4,606	5,225	327	256	7.1%	4.9%	13.4%	−21.7%	4,279	4,969
25 to 35	4,076	4,640	245	148	6.0%	3.2%	13.8%	−39.3%	3,831	4,491
35 to 50	2,491	2,935	0	0	0.0%	0.0%	17.8%	0.0%	2,491	2,935
50 plus	1,365	1,536	0	0	0.0%	0.0%	12.5%	0.0%	1,365	1,536
Less than $10,000	7,183	10,502	1,160	2,799	16.1%	26.7%	46.2%	141.3%	6,023	7,703
Total	45,668	57,266	2,239	3,978	4.9%	6.9%	25.4%	77.7%	22,765	28,232

Source: Apgar 1988:28 (exhibit 13) and 36 (exhibit 18).

households receiving housing subsidies through the income-maintenance system. If the estimates included these households (excluding those who receive both income and housing assistance), participation rates would be considerably higher in both years. At the same time, as the last two columns reveal, the growth in subsidized units has not kept up with the growth in eligible households. As a result, the number of "eligible" very low income households *not* receiving assistance grew by about .9 million and the numbers of "eligible" low-income households *not* receiving assistance grew by just under .8 million.

Annual data on assisted units by year and program, moreover, reveal that the growth in assisted units slowed markedly in the final years of the Reagan administration as units committed by previous administrations slowly made their way through the pipeline. Worse yet, Clay and Wallace (1988) point out that the number of low-income households receiving subsidies will soon begin to decline rapidly in the absence of a much larger federal commitment. They observe that the public housing inventory is wearing out and that subsidy agreements covering a significant fraction of subsidized units provided under earlier production programs will expire in a few years. Unless the federal government extends these agreements or replaces them with a comparable number of new demand-side program allocations, the number and fraction of low-income households receiving assistance is likely to fall.[8]

RENTAL HOUSING MARKETS AND DEMAND-SIDE SUBSIDIES

The answer to the question of how best to assist low-income households in obtaining adequate housing or to reduce their rent burdens seems clear to me: The majority, perhaps nearly all, of housing assistance to low-income households should take the form of some kind of demand-side subsidy to assist needy households in purchasing "adequate" housing in private housing markets. Exceptions might include dysfunctional individuals and families and other individuals and families with special problems; most, but not all, of the homeless fall into one of these categories.[9] Using existing housing units will usually, but not always, be the most cost-effective way of supplying these privately owned, but subsidized, units.

While demand-side programs—that is, rent supplements, Section 23 Existing, Section 8 Existing, Housing Allowances, and Vouchers—differ somewhat, their budgetary cost depends principally on: (a) income limits and other eligibility criteria; (b) the fraction of market rent paid by the subsidy (generally this fraction is determined by the difference in market rents and the household's contribution, usually a predetermined fraction of the household's income); and (c) the market rents of "standard" units.

The following questions are thus critical to any assessment of the cost-effectiveness of demand-side subsidies and of the desirability of relying on such programs as the principal way of assisting poor households.

1. How much does it cost per month to produce low-rent "standard" housing from the existing stock and from new construction?
2. What determines the level of rents in private housing markets, and is the recent rise in real rents likely to continue?
3. Do demand-side subsidies conserve the existing housing stock by encouraging landlords to maintain their units?
4. How would a significantly larger demand-side subsidy program affect market rents?

COST EFFECTIVENESS

Results from the Experimental Housing Allowance Program (EHAP)—discussed below—as well as those from earlier studies strongly indicate that cash subsidies for existing housing, whether leased housing, vouchers, or housing allowances, are about half as costly per assisted household as new construction or substantial rehabilitation programs (Mayo et al. 1979; Aaron 1972; de Leeuw 1971; Lowry 1971; Levine 1979; and Solomon 1972).

Martin Levine's (1979:43) Congressional Budget Office study of the long-term cost of federal lower-income housing-assistance programs is representative of the earlier studies. He found that "among current rental assistance programs, the Section 8 existing program is the least costly to the federal government." Analyzing six representative cases, based on a range of future increases in housing expenses and tenant incomes, Levine obtained the following projected average annual costs per unit in 1980 dollars. Section 8 NC/SR refers to Section 8 new construction/substantial rehabilitation:

Section 8 Existing: $1,560–1,750;
Section 8 NC/SR: $2,490–3,510;
Public Housing: $2,200–3,510.

Levine (1979:41) adds that "for subsidy commitments made in fiscal year 1980, starting Section 8 rents are likely to average about $3,000 per year in existing units and $5,000 in newly built or substantially rehabilitated projects, making it twice as costly at the outset to assist a typical lower-income household (one that pays about $1,000 per year toward its rent) in a newly built unit as it is to aid the same household in an existing unit." He cautions, however, that the gap in annual subsidy costs may narrow as the newly built projects age.

Demand-side subsidies typically use a definition of market rents to determine subsidy levels. Section 8 subsidies are based on Fair Market Rents (FMRs)—the cost of living in modest but decent housing in the local housing market.[10] Section 8 rents for existing units are set at a percentile of the distribution of rents for adequate housing within the local market aréa. Originally they were set at the median rent or the 50 percentile, but in 1984 the criterion was changed to the 45 percentile, excluding new construction, a change Weicher (1988:4) finds "has not noticeably changed the FMRs."

In 1983 the Reagan administration introduced a new demand-side subsidy program popularly known as the freestanding voucher. Section 8 Existing, EHAP, and the Voucher program all require participants to live in standard housing.[11] The most significant difference between the Section 8 Existing and Voucher programs is that in Section 8 the FMRs act as a ceiling for both rents and subsidies.

Tenants participating in the Section 8 program are not allowed to rent a unit costing more than the FMR. Lower rents (below FMR) in the Section 8 program translate into lower subsidies rather than lower tenant rental payments.[12] In the voucher program, however, participants can rent a more expensive unit and pay the additional amount from their own income. If they are able to find an "acceptable" unit that rents for less than the FMR, moreover, participants may keep the difference.

Demand Subsidies and Rent Levels

A common objection to expanding demand-side subsidies is that the resulting increases in demand by low-income households would cause unacceptable increases in rents for both participants and nonparticipants and cause program costs to rise. Concern about the impact of a full-scale housing allowance on private housing markets prompted Congress in 1970 to instruct HUD to carry out EHAP (Bradbury and Downs 1981; Struyk and Bendick 1981). EHAP consisted of three separate initiatives: (1) Housing Allowance Supply Experiment (HASE), conducted by the RAND Corporation, (2) the Demand and Administrative Records Experiments, conducted by ABT Associates, and (3) computer-simulation models, developed by the Urban Institute and the National Bureau of Economic Research (NBER).

The Supply Experiment, which RAND designed to evaluate the effects of a full-scale housing allowance program on rents and other marketwide impacts, implemented full-scale entitlement housing-allowance programs in two medium-size metropolitan areas, Brown County (Green Bay), Wisconsin, and St. Joseph's County (South Bend), Indiana, hereafter referred to as Green Bay and South Bend. Rydell, Neels, and Barnett (1982:vii), in discussing Supply Experiment findings about price effects, conclude, "Debates over the desirability of a nationwide housing allowance program can now shelve the issue of price increases and focus solely on whether the benefits to allowance recipients would be worth such a program's subsidy and administrative costs."

The Supply Experiment found that while average prices of rental housing services rose by 26 percent in Green Bay and 19 percent in South Bend during the first three years of the allowance program, these increases were due to inflation (ibid.:6–9). During the first three years of the Supply Experiment, the Consumer Price Index (CPI) rose by 27.4 percent in Green Bay and by 22.9 percent in South Bend. During the same period, the estimated cost of producing housing services rose 27.2 percent in Green Bay and 23.4 percent in South Bend. Rydell, Neels, and Barnett (ibid.:12) also found that "annual rent increases for dwellings occupied by program participants were only a few percentage points higher than those occupied by non-participants."

The principal reason the full-scale housing-allowance program tested in the Supply Experiment had so little effect on market rents in Green Bay and South Bend is that the program had almost no impact on demand.[13] As the data in Table 3-3 indicate, the housing-allowance program increased marketwide demand in Green Bay and

Table 3-3. Rental market demand shift caused by allowance program

Elements of demand shift	Green Bay	South Bend
Eligibility rate[a]	.257	.295
Participation rate[b]	.594	.498
Demand shift per recipient	7.8%	8.2%
Marketwide demand shift	1.19%	1.15%
Demand shift, recipient market	4.6%	5.6%
Demand shift, nonrecipient market	−6.0%	−3.5%

Source: Rydell, Neels, and Barnett (1982).

[a]Fraction of all renter households eligible for allowances.

[b]Fraction of eligible renter households receiving allowance payments at program equilibrium.

South Bend by about 1.2 percent. There was only a 5- to 6-percent increase in demand in the recipient submarket, which RAND analysts define as "the set of dwellings that recipients could afford and that either met program standards or could inexpensively be brought up to program standards." Demand in the nonrecipient submarket decreased by 4 to 6 percent, as recipients who previously lived in substandard units that could not easily be upgraded to satisfy program standards moved to the recipient submarket.[14]

Supply Experiment analysts explain the small increase in recipient submarket demand by the fact that only a fifth of the dwellings in the recipient submarket were occupied by recipients, and that most households entering the housing-allowance program were already spending nearly enough to pay for standard housing.[15] In addition, three-fourths of the allowance recipients who originally lived in substandard housing repaired their units rather than move to qualify for the allowance. Finally, the average low-income renter household in Green Bay and South Bend spent over half of its income on housing, in contrast to the average renter household, which spent only about a fourth. As a result of the factors listed above, demand had to rise by only a small amount (about 8 percent on average) for recipients to obtain housing that satisfied program requirements.

Supply Experiment analysts used the results to evaluate the probable impact of a full-scale allowance program in twenty-one other metropolitan housing markets (Rydell, Neels, and Burnett 1982). With the sole exception of Miami, with its large refugee population, RAND analysts found that a full-scale housing-allowance program similar to the one implemented in Green Bay and South Bend would induce rent increases and other marketwide outcomes similar to those caused by the experiment in Green Bay and South Bend.[16]

Rydell, Neels, and Barnett (1982:36) also review the experiences of other demand-side programs, referring in particular to reports of large rent increases induced by the Section 8 program. They argue that these increases occurred because landlords who were participating in the Section 8 program were able to raise rents toward the permitted ceiling (the administratively set "Fair Market Rent") without much opposition from their tenants. Section 8 program participants paid a fourth of their incomes for rent, regardless of the rent level, as long as the rent did not exceed the FMR.

Weicher (1988:19) reaches similar conclusions about the effects of existing demand-side program on rents. He asserts that "the findings are clear cut. Existing housing subsidies have not resulted in rent inflation." He points to the experience of EHAP and the findings of the Abt Section 8 Existing Housing Evaluation, which found rents for subsidized units were only 4 to 5 percent above the "expected" market rent, controlling for size, quality, and other unit characteristics (Kennedy and Finkel 1987:25). According to the Abt study, eliminating discounts received by households living in units owned by relatives caused these small differences. When these households joined the Section 8 program, their relatives typically, and understandably, raised the rents for these previously discounted units to market levels.

Weicher adds that a similar explanation most likely accounts for the very large increase in rents for households with extraordinarily low preprogram rents observed in an earlier Section 8 evaluation by Drury et al. (1978:66). Weicher (1988:19) claims that this study, which found that rents went up by an average of $100 per month for participants whose rents were initially less than $50, "is the only instance of apparent rent inflation in any of the program evaluations to date and it is obviously atypical and irrelevant for most households." Citing a study by Kennedy and Finkel (1987:70–74), Weicher (1988:19) adds that preliminary evidence from the freestanding voucher demonstration is that more than half the households that did not move incurred small increases or actual decreases in rent, but he notes that these rents were not adjusted for quality changes.

SUPPLY OF RENTAL UNITS

Virtually all studies of the market effects of demand-side subsidies on rents emphasize that nearly all potential participants in demand-side programs already reside in rental housing and that most of them occupy standard units. The most recent analysis of this kind by Carla Pedone (1988:116–117) found that 90 percent of very low income renters and 94 percent of low-income renters lived in "physically adequate" (standard and not crowded) housing in 1985.[17] In addition, Pedone determined that

a.   Only 8 percent of very low income and 5 percent of low-income households lived in physically inadequate housing;
b.   Only 2 percent of very low income and 3 percent of low-income households lived in physically inadequate housing and were crowded, that is, there was more than one person per room in the housing unit;
c.   57 percent of very low income households and 23 percent of low-income households paid more than 30 percent of their income for housing; and
d.   38 percent of very low income and 72 percent of low-income households experienced none of these problems (many of these households, however, lived in subsidized housing).

Another important aspect of the low-income housing question is demonstrated by Figure 3-2, which depicts the supply of rental housing in all United States metropolitan areas by rent level. Figure 3-2 should not be thought of as a supply curve in spite of its general appearance. It shows how the number of rental units varies with market rents, but contract rents are housing expenditures rather than constant quantity prices, since the units vary in terms of size, quality and location, as well as price.

The data shown in Figure 3-2 are, nonetheless, highly relevant to a discussion of demand-side programs, as they indicate how changes in FMRs would affect the supply of units available to participants in demand-side subsidy programs. The constant elasticity of supply for this "supply" curve is 1.7 over the entire range and 1.9 over the more relevant range, that is, $200 to $400 per month. If we use $315 as the average FMR in 1983, these data indicate that a 10-percent increase in FMRs would increase the supply of eligible units by nearly 2.7 million units. This would represent more than a two-thirds increase in the number of households that received housing subsidies in 1987 (Table 3-2).

The view implied by the "supply" curve shown in Figure 3-1 is, of course, a static and an exceedingly pessimistic one. While the technology for producing "standard," but modest, units from the existing housing inventory is still not well understood, it should be pos-

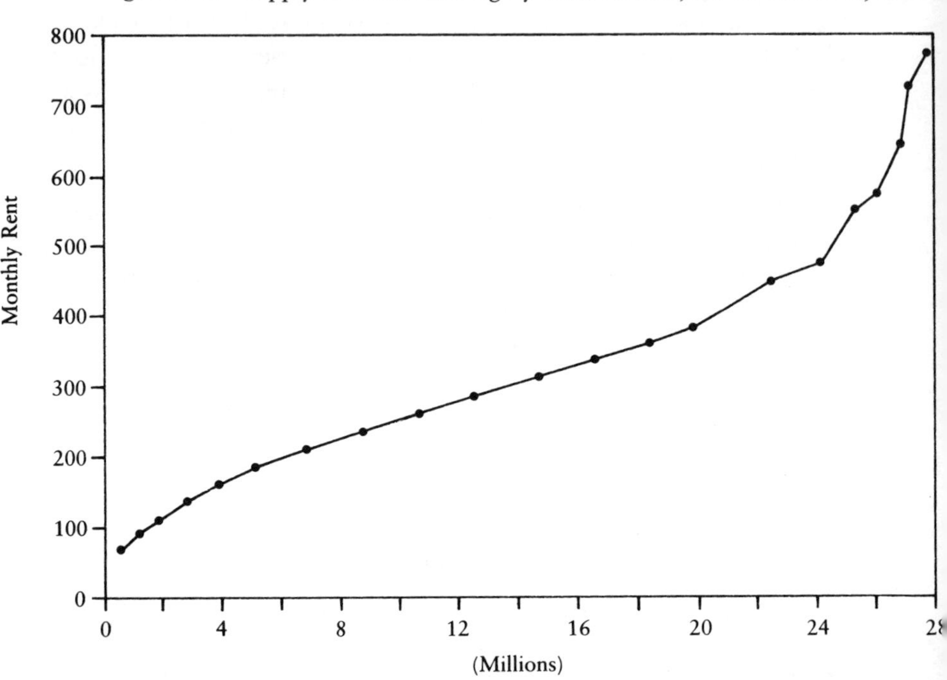

Figure 3-2.   Supply of rental housing by contract rent, all United States, 1983

Source: Calculated by author from Annual Housing Survey data for 1983.
Note: Data are for units in standard metropolitan statistical areas (SMSA).

sible, given sufficient time, to produce large, perhaps unlimited, numbers of "standard" units at or even below the FMR. A larger demand-side subsidy program would "produce" these units through some combination of preventing the deterioration and eventual loss of low-rent "standard" units and the upgrading of currently substandard units to the point where they meet program standards.

Apgar (1987:17), in his discussion of the declining supply of low-cost housing, points to the connection between rents and maintenance and the need for programs that prevent the loss of low-rent units from the inventory. Emphasizing the link between rent and maintenance, Apgar observes, "Many dwelling units were occupied in the 1970s and continue to be occupied today by households that are unable to pay a rent that is sufficient to cover the full costs of providing decent housing." He adds that $250 a month is a high rental payment for a household earning $10,000 a year (i.e., 30 per-

cent of income). Unfortunately, he notes, $250 a month is not suffi-
cient to cover the cost of operating and maintaining housing in most
metropolitan areas. "A rent of $250 is simply inadequate to cover
the costs of utilities, property tax, debt service and the like, let alone
provide property owners with sufficient resources to maintain their
dwelling units in good condition" (ibid.:17).

PUBLIC POLICY IMPLICATIONS

Growing awareness of the plight of the homeless and other
signs of distress have restored concerns about housing to the nation's policy agenda. In 1987, Congress, responding to growing media attention and public opinion, established the National Housing
Task Force. Its final report, released in March 1988, calls for an
expanded federal role in providing low-income housing, and particularly a return to large-scale production programs.

This paper argues that a greater emphasis on production programs would be a step backward and that if there is a decision to
raise federal expenditures for low-income housing, these additional
dollars should be devoted to demand-side subsidies. This conclusion
rests on the easily defended proposition that the principal housing
problem of nearly all low-income households is inadequate income
rather than inadequate housing. Only 8 percent of very low income
and 5 percent of low-income households lived in physically inadequate housing in 1985. In contrast, 57 percent of very low income
households and 23 percent of low income households paid more
than 30 percent of the meager incomes on housing.

This paper does not attempt to answer the question of how much
more the federal government should spend on housing assistance for
low-income households, since this is a complex issue that requires
consideration of a wide range of tradeoffs that are simply beyond
the scope of this paper. It does take the uncompromising position,
however, that virtually all new housing commitments should take
the form of demand-side programs rather than supply-side, that is,
production, programs. Demand-side programs cost only about half
as much per assisted household as production or supply-side programs. Thus, using more cost-effective demand-side programs, such
as Section 8 Existing or Freestanding Vouchers, would enable the
federal government to assist about twice as many deserving, low-

income households as it could help with production programs that cost the same amount.

In spite of the well-documented, clear-cut superiority of demand-side subsidies in terms of user benefits, costs, and other dimensions, supply-side, that is, production, programs continue to have strong political support. In particular, they are strongly supported by construction and real-estate interests who hope to benefit from participation in these programs. There appears to be no comparable constituency for vouchers. Many advocates of the poor, moreover, have knowingly supported the less cost-effective production programs on the grounds that they offer the best hope of enacting at least some sort of housing program that will provide some assistance to significant numbers of low-income households. Those advocating production programs for tactical reasons might ask whether the poor might not benefit more from a smaller, but more efficient, demand-side program than they would from a larger, but wasteful supply-side program.

Demand-side programs acutely raise the question of whether the federal government has any justification for being involved in housing assistance for low-income households at all. If poor housing is primarily the result of poverty, one can reasonably argue that the appropriate response would be to raise income support to low-income households. While I have considerable sympathy for this view, there is a reasonable argument for the broader society, whose tax payments are the source of subsidies to low-income households, deciding that expenditures for housing are more meritorious than expenditures for other goods and services. In addition, the cost of housing varies by large amounts from one area to another and accounts for most of the variation in living costs among areas. Housing allowances or vouchers may be a valuable tool to adjust for these differences in living costs within the context of a more general program of assistance to low-income households.

The Bush administration faces many difficult policy choices in trying to reduce the worrisome federal budget and trade deficits. Money for domestic programs is going to be scarce, even with the demise of the Soviet threat and President Bush's back peddling on his "no new taxes" pledge. It is thus essential that these dollars be spent wisely and in the most cost-effective way. The choice seems to me to be clear cut in the case of housing policy: demand-side subsidies provide roughly twice as much bang for the buck.

Notes

This paper benefited greatly from substantive and editorial comments by Sanjay Daniel, from suggestions by Langley Keyes, and particularly from extensive discussions with and data provided by William C. Apgar, Jr.

1.   National Housing Task Force 1988: Introduction. The National Housing Task Force, chaired by James W. Rouse, is the third blue-ribbon commission to examine issues of housing policy in the past 20 years. In contrast to the Kaiser Commission (1969) and the President's Commission on Housing (1982), which were presidential commissions, the National Housing Task Force was created by the Democrat-controlled Congress to help formulate a new national housing-policy agenda and to build political support for an expanded federal role in housing. While the commission's proposals acknowledge the current budget realities and endorse the continuation of demand-side subsidies, they nonetheless imply a greatly expanded federal role, significantly increased federal spending for housing, and a renewed emphasis on production programs.

In addition, President Nixon established an "in-house" National Housing Policy Review (1976) in conjunction with his call for a moratorium on housing-subsidy programs. This important and highly influential task force produced a significant amount of high-quality analysis, suggested that production programs be curtailed, and called for greater emphasis on demand-side strategies.

2.   This and most other discussions of housing policy emphasize the housing problems of low-income renters. This is not because the problems of low-income homeowners are unimportant. Instead, it is because the problems of low-income renters are much greater. Pedone (1988), for example, found that 72 percent of low-income homeowners, as opposed to 38 percent of low-income renters, are "problem free"—i.e., they live in standard units without crowding and pay less than 30 percent of their income in housing.

3.   Housing assistance provided under welfare programs is generally less generous than that provided under assisted housing programs. According to Newman and Schnare (1988:6–8), "AFDC shelter allowances covered less than 50 percent of the FMR (Fair Market Rent) in 34 states; SSI covered less than 50 percent of FMR in 13 states, and General Assistance covered less than 50 percent of the FMR in 17 states." On average, they found that "AFDC shelter payments represent only 49 percent of the applicable FMR, while SSI and GA allowances hover around 66 percent of the FMR."

4.   Pedone (1988:xiv), indicates that the "number of new commitments funded each year have decreased over the past twelve years" and that "the number of net new rental assistance commitments fell from 375,000 in 1977 to fewer than 108,00 in 1978." Thus, the number of assisted units has continued to increase, but at a slower rate than previously.

5.   Using Annual Housing Survey (AHS) data for 1983, Newman and Schnare (1988:3) conclude that more than 5.5 million additional low-income units would be needed to house adequately the poor. In proposing these estimates, they found that about 9.7 million renters nationwide had annual incomes of less than $8,000 in 1983. Using the standard definitions of affordability leads to the conclusion that these low-income renters could afford to pay

no more than $200 per month on housing. Only 5.3 million units had rents below $300 per month in 1983, and 20 percent of these units were in substandard condition. Some of the sound, inexpensive units, moreover, were occupied by higher income households.

6. Using somewhat different data and methods, Pedone (1988) obtains an estimate of the number of recipients in 1987 that is about eight percent higher than Apgar's. Pedone's estimates are presented in Table 3-1.

7. Income alone is a poor measure of the ability of households to secure adequate housing in the private nonsubsidized market. Federal poverty definitions define the income required by various types of households to consume adequate levels of housing, food, and other necessities. By this measure, only 2.1 million (or 28 percent) of the nation's 7.5 million poverty-level renter households lived in public housing or other subsidized rental housing last year. Among the near-poverty level (households with incomes above the poverty level, but less than two times that level), participation was only 19.8 percent (Apgar 1988:37).

8. The mere expiration of these agreements or the wearing out of the public housing inventory are not by themselves valid arguments for renegotiating these agreements or for making uneconomic expenditures to renovate public housing units. These actions should be taken only if it can be unambiguously shown that renewing the agreements or upgrading public housing would be cheaper than the per-unit subsidies under Section 8 existing or vouchers, or that the units serve populations with special needs that cannot be effectively served by more cost-effective demand-side programs. Stegman (1988) makes the latter argument for public housing.

9. While the characteristics and problems of the homeless stubbornly resist quantification, it appears that many, if not most, of the homeless population are dysfunctional individuals or individuals and families with special problems. A significant fraction of the homeless are, for example, individuals with mental health problems who were released from institutions with inadequate provisions made for them. A generous housing allowance would help many of these individuals, but other kinds of community health facilities and support facilities may be more important. For families who are homeless because they cannot find affordable housing, a housing allowance would obviously make a great difference. Keyes (1988) discusses these questions.

10. The Section 8 program actually has two market rents, one for new construction and one for existing units. Weicher (1987:4) observes that new construction FMRs, which are much higher than existing unit FMRs, are based as much on cost as on market rents.

11. Weicher (ibid.:6) concludes that "all the programs have set standards that are well above any of the commonly used measures of 'standard' or 'adequate' housing that analysts have developed from the broad national housing data bases."

12. In assessing these provisions, Weicher (ibid.:4) argues that removing the cap should make it easier for households to find satisfactory housing in the freestanding voucher program and that success rates should be higher. He adds that average rent/income ratios are likely to be higher in the voucher program as

some tenants are likely to choose to pay more than the FMR. At the same time, he notes that "if households take advantage of the voucher's 'shopping incentive' they will pay lower rents, but if rents reflect quality, they will live in lower quality housing." Weighing these offsetting factors, Weicher (ibid.:4) concludes that "it is likely that the removal of the ceiling will be more important than the shopping incentive, and on balance both rent burdens and housing quality will be higher in the demonstration than in Section 8 Existing Housing."

13.   Rydell, Neels, and Barnett (1982:vii) observe that "the housing allowance program caused only small price increases, even in the short run, for two reasons. First, it caused modest increases in the demand for housing services. Poverty dynamics kept participation in the program low, and households that participated used much of their allowance income to reduce their rent burden rather than increase their housing demand. Moreover, the demand increase that occurred was diffuse rather than focused on a narrow segment of the market; much substandard housing could readily be repaired to standard condition."

14.   This result was anticipated by the NBER housing policy simulations and accounts for the fall in average rents in those simulations. Rent increases in what Supply Experiment analysts refer to as "recipient sub-market" were more than offset by declines in other submarkets, particularly low quality units in the least desirable neighborhoods (Kain and Apgar 1977, 1985).

15.   The allowance simulations carried out using the Urban Institute and NBER models obtained somewhat larger increases in rents in "recipient submarkets," although the NBER simulations found rents fell on average (de Leeuw and Struyk 1975; Vanski and Ozanne 1978; Kain and Apgar 1977). RAND analysts used the larger rent increases obtained by the simulations to argue the "models were wrong" (Rydell, Neels, and Barnett 1982:22). The larger rent increases, however, arose principally because the Urban Institute and NBER simulations assumed higher participation rates than actually occurred in the experiments and tested housing-allowance programs that caused larger increases in housing expenditures than occurred in the *particular* housing program tested in Green Bay and South Bend. While the program tested in Green Bay has many attractive features, and while I do not fault the RAND analysts for "their" choice of housing standards, findings from the Demand Experiment indicate the use of alternative, although not necessarily preferable, housing standards would likely result in larger increases in housing expenditures by recipients. These issues are discussed in Kain (1981) and Kain and Apgar (1985). The argument that the difference in Supply Experiment outcomes and Urban Institute and NBER model predictions shows that the models are wrong appears in Rydell, Neels, and Barnett (1982), in Barnett (1979), and in Barnett and Lowry (1979).

16.   Rydell, Neels, and Barnett (1982:34–35) also refer to a HUD study of a "housing voucher" program's impact on rents in twenty other metropolitan areas in 1976 and 1977. Using parameters from the Supply Experiment, HUD analysts obtained program-induced price increases ranging from 0.6 to 4.8 percent for a program that the RAND analysts describe as only slightly different from the program tested in the Supply Experiment. The HUD study also found

that half of the projected participants already lived in standard housing and that they did so by spending a disproportionately large share of their incomes on housing. As a result, the HUD study anticipated that participants would use only a small part of the hypothetical allowance payment to increase their housing consumption. Most would use it to reduce rent burdens.

17.   The definitions of low-income and very low income households depend on family size and composition. A four-person household is classified as very low income if its income is less than or equal to 50 percent of the median family income of the area where it resides; it would be classified as low income if its income ranges from 51 percent to 80 percent of the area median (Pedone 1988:12).

References

Aaron, Henry J. 1972. *Shelter and Subsidies: Who benefits from Federal Housing Programs?* Washington, D.C.: Brookings Institution.

Apgar, William C., Jr. 1987. "The Declining Supply of Low-Cost Housing." Working Paper W87-6. Cambridge: Joint Center for Housing Studies of MIT and Harvard University.

———. 1988. "The Nation's Housing: A Review of Past Trends and Future Prospects for Housing in America." HP#1 (May). Cambridge: MIT Center for Real Estate Development.

———. 1989. "The State of the Nation's Housing: 1989: A Summary of Major Problems." Cambridge: Joint Center for Housing Studies, Harvard University.

Barnett, C. Lance. 1979. "Expected and Actual Effects of Housing Allowances on Housing Prices." *American Real Estate and Urban Economics Journal* 7:277–297.

Barnett, C. Lance, and Ira S. Lowry. 1978. *How Housing Allowances Affect Housing Prices.* R-2452-HUD. Santa Monica, Calif.: RAND Corporation.

Bradbury, Katherine L., and Anthony Downs. 1981. *Do Housing Allowances Work?* Washington, D.C.: Brookings Institution.

Clay, Phillip L., and James E. Wallace. 1988. "Preservation of the Existing Stock of Assisted Private Housing." HP#1. Cambridge: MIT Center for Real Estate Development.

de Leeuw, Frank. 1971. "The Cost of Leased Housing." House Banking and Currency Committee, Subcommittee on Housing, 92 Cong., 1 sess. Washington, D.C.: U.S. Government Printing Office.

de Leeuw, Frank, and Raymond Struyk. 1975. *The Web of Urban Housing: Analyzing Policy with a Market Simulation Model.* Washington, D.C.: Urban Institute.

Drury, Margaret et al. 1978. "Lower Income Housing Assistance Program (Section 8)." *Nationwide Evaluation of the Existing Housing Program.* Washington, D.C.: U.S. Government Printing Office.

Kain, John F. 1974. "What Should America's Housing Policy Be?" *The Journal of Finance* 29:683–698.

——. 1981. "A Universal Housing Allowance Program." In Katherine L. Bradbury and Anthony Downs, eds., *Do Housing Allowances Work?* pp. 339–373. Washington, D.C.: Brookings Institution.

——. 1982. "America's Persistent Housing Crisis: Errors in Analysis and Policy." *The Annals of the American Academy of Political and Social Science* January: 136–149.

——. 1985. "Black Suburbanization in the Eighties: A New Beginning or a False Hope?" In John M. Quigley and Danield L. Rubinfeld, eds., *American Domestic Priorities: An Economic Appraisal*, pp. 253–282. Berkeley: University of California Press.

——. 1986. "The influence of Race and Income on Racial Segregation and Policy." In John M. Goering, ed., *Housing Desegregation, Race, and Federal Policies*, pp. 99–119. Chapel Hill: University of North Carolina Press.

Kain, John F., and William C. Apgar, Jr. 1977. *Simulation of the Market Effects of Housing Allowances, Vol. 2: Baseline and Policy Simulations for Pittsburgh and Chicago.* Research Report R77-3. Cambridge: Department of City and Regional Planning, Harvard University.

——. 1985. *Housing and Neighborhood Dynamics: A Simulation Study.* Cambridge: Harvard University Press.

Kain, John F., and John M. Quigley. 1975. *Housing Markets and Racial Discrimination: A Micro-Economic Analysis.* New York: National Bureau of Economic Research.

Kennedy, Stephen D., and Meryl Finkel. 1987. *Report of the First Year Findings for the Freestanding Housing Voucher Demonstration.* Washington, D.C.: U.S. Department of Housing and Urban Development.

Levine, Martin D. 1979. "The Long-Term Costs of Lower-Income Housing Assistance Programs." Congress of the United States, Congressional Budget Office, Budget Issue Paper for Fiscal Year 1980. Washington, D.C.: U.S. Government Printing Office.

Lowry, Ira S. 1971. "Housing Assistance for Low-Income Urban Families: A Fresh Approach." House Committee on Banking and Currency, Subcommittee on Housing, 92 Cong., 1 sess. Washington, D.C.: U.S. Government Printing Office.

——. 1982. "Inflation Indexes for Rental Housing." Working Note N-1832-HUD. Santa Monica, Calif.: RAND Corporation.

Mayo, Stephen, Shirley Mansfield, David Warner, and Richard Zwetchkenbaum. 1979. "Draft Report on Housing Allowances and Other Rental Housing Allowance Programs—A Comparison Based on the Housing Allowance Demand Experiment. Part 2: Costs and Efficiency." Cambridge: Abt Associates.

National Housing Policy Review. 1976. *Housing in the Seventies.* Washington, D.C.: U.S. Government Printing Office.

National Housing Task Force. 1988. *A Decent Place to Live: The Report of the National Housing Task Force.* James W. Rouse, chair. (available from the task force, 1625 I Street, Washington, D.C.)

Newman, Sandra, and Ann Schnare. 1988. "Integrating Housing and Welfare Assistance." HP#12. Cambridge: MIT Center for Real Estate Development.

Pedone, Carla 1988. "Current Housing Problems and Possible Federal Responses." Congress of the United States, Congressional Budget Office. Washington, D.C.: U.S. Government Printing Office.

President's Committee on Urban Housing. 1969. *Report of the President's Committee on Urban Housing.* Edgar F. Kaiser, chair. Washington, D.C.: U.S. Government Printing Office.

———. 1982. *Report of the President's Committee on Urban Housing.* William F. McKenna, chair. Washington, D.C.: U.S. Government Printing Office.

Rydell, C. Peter, Kevin Neels, and C. Lance Barnett. 1982. *Price Effects of a Housing Allowance Program: A Final Report of the Housing Assistance Supply Project.* Santa Monica, Calif: The RAND Corporation.

Solomon, Arthur P. 1972. "Housing and Policy Analysis." *Public Policy* 20 (Summer): 443–472.

Stegman, Michael A. 1988. "The Role of Public Housing in a Revitalized National Housing Policy." HP#13. Cambridge: MIT Center for Real Estate Development.

Struyk, Raymond J., and Marc Bendick, Jr., eds. 1981. *Housing Vouchers for the Poor.* Washington, D.C.: Urban Institute.

Vanski, Jean, and Larry Ozanne. 1978. *Simulating the Housing Allowance Program in Green Bay and South Bend: A Comparison of the Urban Institute Model and the Supply Experiment,* 249–5. Washington, D.C.: Urban Institute.

Weicher, John C. 1988. "The Voucher/Production Debate." HP#13. Cambridge: MIT Center for Real Estate Development.

Weicher, John C., Kevin E. Villani, and Elizabeth A. Roistacher, eds. 1981. *Rental Housing: Is There a Crisis?* Washington, D.C.: Urban Institute.

4 Welfare Policy after Welfare Reform
Mary Jo Bane

In the fall of 1988, Congress passed and the president signed the most comprehensive welfare-reform bill since the Social Security Act of the 1930s. This bill, the Family Support Act, has as its purpose "to replace the existing AFDC [Aid to Families with Dependent Children] program with a new Family Support Program which emphasizes work, child support and need-based family support supplements . . . [and] to encourage and assist needy children and parents under the new program to obtain the education, training and employment needed to avoid long-term welfare dependency" (Conference Report on HR 1720).

Passing the Family Support Act was a long and tortuous process, involving politically difficult decisions and compromises. Congress can rightfully be proud of itself for taking an important step, and it no doubt feels that it is finished with welfare reform for the foreseeable future. Before concurring with that judgment, though, and leaving Congress to rest on its laurels, it is worth asking a few questions. What will be the likely accomplishments of welfare reform after the dust settles and the provisions of the new law are in place? Have the important policy changes now been made, with only implementation remaining as the policy challenge? Where should welfare policy go from here?

To begin answering these questions, I start with some description of the current welfare system, highlighting the "problems" seen by various parties to the policy debate. Critics from across the political and ideological spectrum can agree that welfare is a mess, but they generally do not agree on why. Liberals criticize the system because it covers too few among the poor, because benefits are too low, and because the system harasses and stigmatizes recipients. Conservatives criticize the system because it supports too many of the poor, because it costs too much, and because it encourages "dysfunctional" behavior. Critics on both sides agree that there are too many long-term welfare recipients and that the system is not effective in moving its clients into self-sufficient lives. In sketching a description of the current system, I will suggest the extent to which these various criticisms are on target.

I then turn to two important precursors of the Family Support Act: the Work Incentive Program (WIN) that added work programs and requirements to the AFDC program in the mid-1960s; and the work/welfare demonstration programs that many states operated in the 1980s. Experience with these two programs offers important insights on what may be possible and likely under the Family Support Act.

The third section of the paper discusses the Family Support Act. The act represents a political compromise and as such avoids taking positions on the more controversial among the problems of the current system; it is important for what it does not do as well as for what it does. Finally, I provide some analysis and suggestions of where we ought to go from here.

The analysis departs somewhat from the standard policy-analysis framework of problem, alternatives, assessment, and recommendations. Instead, the focus is on the characteristics and activities of clients and workers in the welfare system. This focus results from a conviction that the "welfare policy" that we ought to care about occurs on the streets and in the welfare offices, in what clients' lives are like, and in the progress they are making toward bettering their lives. "Welfare policy" in this sense is shaped and constrained, but not determined, by federal legislation. Although I return to questions of legislation at the end of the paper, I raise them in the context of their likely effect on life in the welfare system and on outcomes for clients.[1]

The Current System

Conversations and legislation about welfare and welfare reform usually focus on the AFDC program, and I will follow that convention. The AFDC program is a federal-state partnership, with both levels of government participating in funding the program and establishing its characteristics. There is a fair amount of state-to-state variation in how the program operates but enough commonality to be able to describe roughly how the system works.

The Clients

The AFDC program serves a subset of poor families with children. In 1987, about 5.5 million families with children had annual incomes below the census-defined poverty line (about $11,600 for a family of four). The AFDC system provided cash assistance to about 3.7 million families per month, a number that has been approximately stable since the early 1970s.[2]

What distinguishes families that receive welfare from other poor families and more generally from families with children? The most important distinguishing feature is defined by the original legislation that established AFDC for children "deprived of the support of a parent" through death, desertion, and (in twenty-eight states) unemployment. Applying this criterion has meant that more than 90 percent of the families eligible for welfare are composed of children and their mothers. By comparison, about 60 percent of poor families with children and about 20 percent of all families with children are not eligible for welfare. Poor, two-parent families with working adults—35 to 40 percent of all poor families with children—are not eligible for AFDC. Poor, two-parent families with an unemployed parent are not eligible for AFDC in twenty-two states that may contain a quarter to a third of all poor families.[3]

Welfare, therefore, is a program for single-parent families. But not all single-parent families receive welfare. About half of all single parents have incomes above the poverty line that are from nonwelfare sources: In most of these families, the single mother works full time at a job requiring at least some education and paying good wages. Yet another group of single parents are ineligible for welfare because they have incomes below the poverty line, but their incomes are still large enough that they are above their state's level for welfare eligibility; they may be working part time, or part year, or at low wages. Single parents are more likely to be on welfare in states with relatively generous eligibility levels.

What we have, then, is a welfare system that basically serves a group of poor, single-parent families. Who are these families on welfare? The typical welfare family in 1987 was made up of a never-married mother in her late twenties or early thirties with two children. About 40 percent of welfare recipients were white, 41 percent black, and 14 percent Hispanic. Most lived in metropolitan areas; about half lived in six large, highly urbanized states: California, New York, Illinois, Ohio, Michigan, and Pennsylvania. The typical welfare recipient did not finish high school and had relatively little previous work experience.

About a third of the welfare clients who come on the rolls will leave after one or two years, and about 30 percent will stay on welfare for eight or more years (Bane and Ellwood 1983; Ellwood 1986). Although there is a good deal of turnover on the rolls, long-term welfare recipients are heavily represented in the welfare caseload at any point in time. This occurs because long-termers appear on the rolls year after year, just as the beds in hospitals are disproportionately occupied by the chronically ill who stay a long time, even though most admissions to the hospital are for short-term illnesses. A substantial portion of the welfare caseload at any point in time is in the midst of a very long welfare spell. (This apparent paradox, by the way, can explain why the liberals can be right when they say that most people who come on welfare go off quickly, and the conservatives can also be right when they point to a substantial problem of long-term welfare receipt.)

Those who leave welfare are most likely to do so because they marry, reconcile, or remarry, or because some other adult joins the family or gets a job. It is not common for welfare mothers to "work their way" off the rolls; only about a fifth of those who leave welfare do so because their own earnings increased enough to obviate their need for welfare.

The difficulty of moving from welfare to economic self-sufficiency provides the impetus for much of the welfare-reform effort. It is worth asking, then, why the transition is so difficult. Two sorts of explanations are worth exploring: those related to the economics of the work/welfare tradeoff and those related to the sociology of life on welfare.

The Work/Welfare Tradeoff

Single mothers face a nearly impossible tradeoff when they consider the relative costs and benefits of staying on welfare versus going to work. Welfare benefits in most states are quite low—well below the poverty line. The maximum AFDC benefit in 1988 ranged from a low of $120 per month in Mississippi to a median of $359 per month to highs of $633 per month in California and $779 per month in Alaska, all for a family of three. In the median state (Pennsylvania is an example), the combination of AFDC and Food Stamps amounts to an income of about 74 percent of the federal poverty line. Work would seem to be a better choice.

But the costs of going to work and of losing benefits when income rises combine to negate this. In 1986, for example, a welfare recipient in the median state who did not work at all received disposable income from AFDC and Food Stamps of $6,284 per year and was also eligible for Medicaid. If she went to work half-time at the minimum wage and spent $1,000 per year for day care, her disposable income—AFDC, Food Stamps, and earnings—would be $7,156.[4] If she worked full time at $4 per hour, and if her day-care costs rose to $3,000, these increased costs, plus the reduction of AFDC and Food Stamps, would leave her with disposable income of just $6,795. If she managed to get a full-time job paying $5.00 per hour, she could increase her income to $7,798—but would lose Medicaid.[5]

Under these financial constraints, it makes no sense for a single mother to work part time or at a low-wage job. This is not to imply that these financial disincentives keep women on welfare who could be working full time at good jobs and earning enough to keep their families out of poverty. Welfare benefits are very low, and the stigma and harassment associated with welfare almost certainly make working at a good job preferable.[6]

The crux of the problem lies in the near impossibility for poorly educated single mothers with little work experience to work and earn enough to keep their families out of poverty. The 35 percent of all single mothers who work full time and earn above-poverty wages are overwhelmingly better educated and more experienced than welfare clients.[7]

Consider a few facts. First, it is hard for any family to make it with only one earner: 72 percent of families who have children and who have incomes above the poverty line have more than one worker. Second, it is hard for anyone to be both a full-time parent and a full-time worker. Only about 30 percent of married mothers work full year and full time, a recognition of the difficulties of holding two jobs. Third, it is not uncommon for young adult high school dropouts or even many high school graduates—male or female, welfare recipients_or not—to be unable to earn the $10,000 or so that is needed to keep a family of three above the poverty line. For example, 47 percent of male high school dropouts age 25 to 34 earn less than that amount.

Life on Welfare

The sociology of the welfare system and the interactions of clients with the system exacerbate the work/welfare dilemma. Despite some efforts to encourage work, welfare is perceived and operated as a program for women who do not work. Welfare workers give clients little help to make a staged transition, such as by taking on part-time work while still on welfare and then gradually increasing hours of work or wages. The system does not encourage combining work and welfare and thus reinforces the either/or character of the work/welfare dilemma.

Several features of the welfare system heighten this dilemma. The first is the general orientation of the program and its workers to issues of eligibility rather than self-support; an ironic corollary of this orientation is that the system becomes even more difficult for clients and workers to manage when they try to go to work. The second is the general difficulty of life on welfare, which makes it hard for clients to engage in the kind of activities that would lead to self-support.[8]

To apply for AFDC, the single mother in a typical state goes to the local welfare office, where she fills out an application form, typically 8 to 10 pages long, which asks for detailed information about family composition and income. At an interview with an eligibility worker, she must present documentation of the information on the form (birth certificates, pay stubs, and so on), which is then further checked through computer matches with records of banks, the social security system, and the tax system. After a month or six weeks, during which the worker checks information and does paperwork, the worker notifies the client of her eligibility status, and, if eligible, the client begins receiving checks.[9] The eligibility process focuses on determining that the applicant does not, in fact, have other available sources of income and that her household composition is what she says it is.

The welfare office requires the applicant to assign child-support rights to it and to assist it in locating the absent father. The office expects the client to notify it of any change in her family and financial status and, under certain circumstances, to fill out a reporting form every month. Federal or state auditors may occasionally audit the client as part of the system's quality-control procedures, designed to ensure that no one is receiving benefits to which he or she is not entitled.[10]

As part of the application process, if the applicant's youngest child is at least 6 years old, the applicant must register with the local employment service. This is normally the only part of the eligibility process oriented toward achieving self-support. In many welfare offices, this requirement simply reinforces the separation of welfare and work. Sometimes applicants can register by signing a form, which the welfare office sends to the employment office. The welfare and employment offices are usually physically separated and staffed by different workers. Many welfare workers treat employment registration as only another piece of paperwork to be completed. On the employment side, the workers often attempt to deal with welfare clients, whom they experience as difficult to serve, as quickly and with as little effort as possible.

While she is receiving welfare, the welfare worker typically asks the client to return to the office every four to six months to verify her eligibility status in an interview. The typical worker a client sees is an "eligibility specialist," who has a high school or college education (requirements vary by state) and who receives almost no further training. The time that a worker spends with a client usually focuses on questions of eligibility, structured by a set of forms. The worker sees her clients in tiny interviewing cubicles or in a large office shared with other workers, usually after the clients have spent a fair amount of time in an impersonal and often unpleasant waiting room. (States and cities are usually reluctant to provide anything other than minimal physical amenities for their welfare offices.) Many workers are sympathetic to their clients' plights and provide comfort and assurance. They are not expected, however, to elicit needs for other services or to do casework.[11] They typically do not visit clients' homes or see clients' children. They limit their interactions to establishing and continuing to verify financial eligibility. They do not have the time, the training, or the resources to become important people in their clients' lives.

Ironically, a client who has a job or wants to go to school means more time and trouble for the worker, since these situations require more documentation and checking. For the client, going to work means being reclassified in many instances as an "error-prone" case, a creation of the quality-control system designed to focus the efforts of workers on those cases most likely to be receiving excessive benefits. A working client is more "error-prone" because she has income that must be deducted in calculating benefits and because her income may fluctuate from month to month. The quality-control system sees these cases as requiring more checking because of the possible need to recalculate benefits each month. The welfare worker may ask such a client to submit more reporting forms and come in more often for eligibility interviews than clients who do not work. Thus, at precisely the time when a client is struggling to balance a job with her responsibilities as a parent, the system places additional burdens and requirements on her. This would seem to reinforce a perception among clients that they are not expected to work and that welfare is a system for those who do not work.

Other aspects of the welfare system make it hard for clients to look for work or training. The typical welfare family receives a check through the mail for about $350 per month in cash benefits and also receives about $200 worth of food-stamp benefits, which usually must be picked up in person once a month. Making ends meet for a family of three is not easy at these benefit levels, which represent about 75 percent of the poverty line and allow for about $4 per day per person to be spent on food. A welfare recipient spends much of her time acquiring the necessities of life for as little money as possible. Receiving AFDC also entitles a family to Medicaid, which in most states pays for all medical services. Obtaining medical care for the numerous illnesses and chronic conditions that are endemic in poor communities typically involves using a community health center or the emergency room of the local hospital, with long waiting times and numerous indignities.

Not surprisingly, given the disadvantages of a poor education and lack of work experience, the difficulties of life on welfare, and the messages implicit in the way the welfare system operates, very few welfare recipients (about 7 percent) work.[12] Only a tiny proportion are reported to be in school or training programs. Even a client's registration in the WIN program seldom involves more than having her name on record at the local employment service and showing up once every six months to prove that she is willing to take a job. On the whole, a lack of involvement in employment, school, or community activity characterizes life on welfare. As time goes on, it becomes even less likely that clients will be working or looking for work.

PRECURSORS OF THE FAMILY SUPPORT ACT

Efforts to change the welfare system's expectations about work have been made in the past and provide an interesting basis for thinking about the Family Support Act. Until 1981, the primary mechanism for encouraging work was a system of incentives that allowed recipients to keep a portion of their earnings, without having them deducted from their grants. In 1981, efforts to focus the program more on the "truly needy" led Congress to reduce these monetary incentives and remove many working clients from the rolls.[13] Clients were to make the transition to work by participating in employment activities including work experience (workfare), which Congress encouraged the states to require of recipients.

Employment programs were run under the WIN program, part of the AFDC law since 1967, which was established with some of the same expectations that now surround the Family Support Act. How the WIN program, generally considered to be a failure, operates gives some hints about potential pitfalls in implementing large-scale work programs. Nevertheless, a few states operate successful work/welfare programs.[14] The best known of these programs is the Massachusetts ET Choices program, which has been operating since 1983. Good information is also available on the programs in California, Maryland, West Virginia, Illinois, Arkansas, Maine, and Virginia that the Manpower Demonstration Research Corporation (MDRC) described and evaluated.[15]

WIN

WIN has been the basic program for assisting AFDC recipients to find work and leave the welfare rolls. The federal government required states to set up programs under their state employment services. AFDC recipients with no preschool children were required to register for the WIN program, to take advantage of employment services, and to accept jobs when offered.

In 1986, 1.6 million AFDC clients were registered for the WIN program. However, only about 220,000 were actually receiving any services, most of them "employment search," and most of them under the state demonstration programs, described below. Only 130,000 WIN registrants left welfare by "working their way" off the rolls, most of them without any help from the program.[16] The common judgment on WIN is that in most welfare offices it quickly became a paper-compliance process, with clients and workers going through the motions of WIN registration, followed by a tacit understanding that neither the client nor the employment service was required to do much more. (The most extreme version of this attitude is apparent in a number of states that automated their welfare-eligibility systems and programmed the computers to automatically register all welfare applications in WIN.) This lack of involvement of clients and workers in the WIN program came about partly because the WIN program never made enough resources available to do the job. In addition, the states seldom coordinated very effectively the welfare and employment programs. Welfare workers typically felt no obligation to require or encourage more active employment-directed activity. Employment-service workers found welfare clients difficult to place and saw no reason not to focus their activities on more promising clients.

There were, of course, exceptions to this general rule, offices where workers and clients were genuinely committed to preparing for and finding work. In general, however, the WIN program had little success in directing life on welfare toward a goal of self-support. Legislative mandates do not necessarily lead to effective action; complying with the mandate in ways that require minimal effort and thus generate minimal results is an equally possible outcome.

Work/Welfare Programs

Beginning in the early 1980s, a number of states established work/welfare programs aimed at correcting the shortcomings of WIN and at making serious efforts to prepare welfare clients for employment. In most cases, welfare departments rather than employment services, under federal waivers of some of the WIN rules, operated these programs. A number of the programs have operated long enough to become well established.

The well-known Massachusetts ET Choices program is a voluntary program that encourages clients to participate in education, training, and employment activities and that provides both work opportunities and supporting services, such as day care and transportation. ET appears to have brought about important changes in the lives of both workers and clients and to have changed the character of their interactions. The offices look and feel different: welfare applicants encounter job listings and recruiters in their first visit to a welfare office. After an initial and relatively streamlined eligibility interview, the offices assign clients to a case manager, who assists them in developing a Family Independence Plan aimed at self-sufficiency. The core of the plan is a set of activities directed at employment, which can include basic education, job-skills training, job search, or supported work. Child care and other services are provided as needed.

Although clients participate voluntarily, ET is successful in getting them to participate. A large portion of the caseload participate in some employment-related activity. Almost half of the participants are women with young children, and many are long-term welfare recipients. Management has made participation and placement, especially of long-term recipients, important goals for welfare workers and evaluates them on how well they "sell" the voluntary program. Welfare workers see the marketing of ET and placing their clients in employment as important parts of their jobs. It appears that both clients and workers now see movement to self-support as an important goal and view the system not as a means of providing income for people who do not work but as help for people making a transition to work. It also appears that the daily activities of clients have changed substantially under ET. Many more of them are going out for education or training, or are looking for work or actually working, than in the typical welfare system.

Work/welfare programs in other states have many features in common with ET. MDRC described and carefully evaluated seven of them in a well-designed, random-assignment demonstration project. The Baltimore Options Program, for example, has a number of components, including job search, education, training—on-the-job or in a classroom; and thirteen weeks of work experience.[17] ET and these other work/welfare programs, in contrast to WIN, show that under some circumstances, life on welfare can change dramatically.

Work/Welfare Results

One must ask whether the changes in the character of life on welfare that some work/welfare programs can bring about translate into shorter durations on welfare. The best results occurred in the Baltimore Options Program. Twenty-eight percent of its participants were off welfare in the fifth quarter after they came on the rolls, compared to 26 percent of the control group—a positive, though hardly earth-shattering, finding. The Options Program appears to be cost effective, under reasonable assumptions about costs and about the permanence of earnings gains. But the total net benefits amount to only about $600 per participant. These are modest gains, to say the least.[18]

ET has not been carefully evaluated, though its proponents claim large employment gains and welfare savings. Their claims could conceivably prove correct. But the Massachusetts caseload has gone down only 5 percent over the period of ET's existence, a drop comparable to that in other states without work/welfare programs—though also without the substantial welfare-benefit increases that occurred simultaneously with ET's enactment. Thus, a careful evaluation of ET might generate results similar to or only slightly better than the Baltimore Options Program.

THE FAMILY SUPPORT ACT

How much change is the Family Support Act likely to effect in the welfare system and the lives of clients? First, the act does not deal with and therefore will not change the politically controversial issues of basic eligibility requirements, state variability, and welfare-benefit levels.[19] It does not modify the quality-control system in any important ways and thus maintains the need for state welfare systems to devote much of their energy to determining eligibility and benefit levels. These omissions limit the law's potential for affecting who comes on welfare and some aspects of life on welfare. The law does include provisions related to child support, to work and training programs, and to transitional assistance. We can assess the potential impact of these provisions on the work/welfare dilemma and on the sociology of the welfare system.

Life on Welfare

The act's main vehicle for changing in some important ways other aspects of life on welfare and in welfare offices is the JOBS (Job

Opportunities and Basic Skills) program, which states are now required to establish. In contrast to WIN, the JOBS program requires recipients to participate, not just register. Moreover, the act extends the requirement to women whose youngest child is aged 3 or older. States must submit plans for operating programs that assess the education and training needs of clients, plus provide programs and services that will enable recipients to move toward self-support. Their programs must include basic skills, job-skills training, and job development and placement. The act expects the state to provide child care and other supportive services as needed. The goal of the program is to help clients move off welfare into jobs and to provide some transitional assistance as they establish themselves in employment.

If states design their JOBS programs in ways that change the expectations of workers and clients about work and welfare, and that provide education and training activities to restructure clients' daily lives, the experience of the most effective work/welfare programs could become more widespread. But many of the states most likely to implement effective programs—New York, New Jersey, California, and Illinois, among others—have already done so. These states are now mandated to expand their programs, and other states to establish them. Nonetheless, the most important progress in establishing work/welfare programs may already have been made.

Several characteristics of ET that seem to have been instrumental in its success may not be replicable in other states, even with the new legislation. ET was developed and implemented at the state level, with the solid backing of the governor and the fervent commitment of an inspired welfare commissioner; the federal government did not impose the program on the state. Management experience in both the public and private sectors suggests that decentralized programs that are responsive to local conditions and "owned" by participants are more likely to be successful than programs imposed from the top.

Because clients participate in ET activities voluntarily, workers must sell the program to clients and thus invest themselves in its success. Workers cannot get away with simply having clients fill out forms. Moreover, because the program is voluntary, clients are committed to their own success. They participate in the program because they believe it can help them; this seems to make them better able to work and learn and allows the training programs to maintain standards for attendance and participation. By contrast, because the Family Support Act requires participation by all clients whose youngest child is at least 3 years old, it is less likely to achieve the advantages possible in a voluntary program.[20]

Another feature of ET's success has to do with resources. At considerable cost, the state has been willing to appropriate substantial resources for child care, training, and other services. In addition, a large network of nonprofit providers of these services was already in place. The Family Support Act, in contrast, carries modest appropriations.[21] Finally, ET has operated in a Massachusetts economy of less than 4 percent unemployment and an effective minimum wage of over $5 per hour, almost ensuring successful placement for motivated clients willing to make some investments in themselves. These conditions do not obtain nationwide (nor, at this writing, in Massachusetts).

In summary, although the Family Support Act has the potential for bringing about important changes in the lives of welfare clients and workers, some of its features may make these changes difficult. The incremental changes, over what many states have already done, may be modest.

The Work/Welfare Dilemma

Let us suppose, however, that the Family Support Act were to bring about the establishment of ET-like programs in all states, with the attendant changes in what welfare workers and clients do. How likely are these changes to accompany substantial changes in the numbers of clients leaving welfare?

Untangling the work/welfare dilemma requires creating conditions under which welfare clients are able to support their families above poverty, through nonwelfare income. Improving their ability to get and hold jobs is obviously part of this. But the evaluations of the work/welfare demonstrations suggest that the improvements in earning power that education and training can bring about are modest: a not-surprising finding given the labor-market disadvantages of the typical welfare recipient.

An unintended result of expanded work programs may therefore be to transfer some welfare poor to the ranks of the working poor. This is not a satisfactory solution, not even a long-term one, since it seems likely that working poor families may soon be back on the welfare rolls. Thus, when the Family Support Act does not deal with the problems of the working poor, it makes a serious omission. The act does include provisions for temporarily extending Medicaid and child-care benefits for those who work their way off welfare. Because these are time-limited provisions, however, they do not address the fundamental difficulty of the working poor in obtaining health care and child care.

If welfare clients are not simply to become working poor, they almost certainly need to supplement their earnings, especially if parental responsibilities limit their ability to work full time. A logical source of supplemental income is child support. The act does include some new child-support enforcement measures, including standard guidelines for establishing awards and mandatory wage assignment. These provisions may enable some single mothers to obtain enough child support to keep their families off welfare, especially if the women themselves are able to work at least part time. Given the poor employment prospects of many young men, however, the large numbers of never-married women who go on welfare may not be helped much by the new child-support provisions.

Thus, the Family Support Act does almost nothing to make work potentially more profitable for single mothers, nor does it make available a reliable source of nonwelfare income to supplement work. In short, although the Family Support Act includes a number of potentially very important provisions, it does not deal in any fundamental way with the work/welfare dilemma that faces single mothers.

Where Do We Go From Here?

So what does all this imply for welfare policy after welfare reform? The welfare bill of 1988 built on an important group of state welfare initiatives that established a new focus on transitions to self-sufficiency and new conceptions of the purpose of welfare, the jobs of welfare workers, and the expectations of clients. It is an important reform that if effectively implemented has the potential for changing the character of life on welfare. This is worth doing. We should put our best efforts into making the massive management and attitudinal changes that are necessary for the reforms implicit in the Family Support Act to happen.

Such a reorientation of life on welfare is probably the best that can be expected from welfare reform. Anything more would be very hard to pass and very controversial, as the lengthy and sometimes rancorous debates over the Family Support Act illustrated. There is both public and political resistance to significant expansion of the welfare system, and reopening the welfare debate is probably impossible. This suggests that we should celebrate the reforms that occurred in 1988 and refrain from taking on new battles for additional welfare reform.

On the policy side, what is now needed are reforms to make it possible for working families to support themselves above the poverty level without welfare. No one believes that welfare should be a long-term way of life; it is degrading to recipients and irritating to society. We should not look to expansion of means-tested, welfare-like programs to solve the problems of the two-parent working poor. Moreover, we should find ways to provide financial security for single-parent families that do not involve long-term dependence on welfare.

These nonwelfare reforms include supports for two-parent working poor families as well as for single parents. I believe that the most important of these reforms for two-parent families are provision of health insurance and expansion of the Earned Income Tax Credit. The EITC, already part of the tax code, gives a refundable tax credit of 14 percent of the first $5,714 of earned income, up to $800 per year, for families who have children and whose earnings are between $5,714 and $9,000. Above that level, the credit is reduced by 10 cents for each dollar of earned income, and it phases out entirely when families reach $17,000.[22] The credit is related to earnings and administered through the tax system; it is an ideal mechanism for providing support to working families. If the credit were expanded and made to vary with family size (an expansion that might double the currently modest cost of the EITC), it could have an important impact on poverty rates. Other proposals suggested as supports for the working poor are raising the minimum wage and providing day-care assistance to working families.

The non-welfare reform of greatest potential importance to single-parent families is an expanded and guaranteed child-support system. Children are entitled to support by both their parents. Recent legislation has made great strides toward establishing fair child-support guidelines, increasing the number of awards, and improving enforcement. Legislation needs to continue these efforts. The most important next policy step is guaranteed child support, a minimum level that single parents can count on, guaranteed by the government. With a decent level of child support as an income base, single parents ought to be able to work and earn enough, at jobs they can plausibly get and hold, to support their families above poverty.[23]

These reforms will not make welfare obsolete. There will always be a need for a means-tested system that supports people through periods of hard times and that invests in the education, training, and services that they need to become self-sufficient. This is what welfare should be, and the 1988 welfare reform takes the system in that direction. I suggest we declare a victory for welfare reform and work hard to make the new system actually work. But welfare reform cannot fulfill its promise in any real sense without serious attention to the economic plight of working families, both single parent and two parent. That is the next task.

NOTES

1.   This approach borrows heavily from the literature on program implementation, especially from Elmore 1982:18–35.

2.   These statistics, and the statistics on poverty and welfare in the sections that follow, come from two sources. Poverty statistics are primarily from the publications of the Current Population Reports, P-60 Series, the most recent of which are U.S. Bureau of the Census, Current Population Reports, Series P-60, No. 160, *Poverty in the United States: 1986*, and No. 161, *Money Income and Poverty Status in the United States: 1987*. Welfare statistics and program data are primarily from the "Green Book"—*Background Material and Data on Programs within the Jurisdiction of the Committee on Ways and Means*, prepared for the use of the Committee on Ways and Means, U.S. House of Representatives, by its staff.

3.   States have the option of establishing AFDC-UP (unemployed parent) programs, which extend AFDC eligibility to families in which the principal breadwinner is unemployed. Twenty-eight states, including most of the large states, have such programs. The Family Support Act requires the establishment of AFDC-UP programs in all states, but the act allows them to be time-limited and requires recipients to participate in work programs.

4.   This amount includes a $229 earned income tax credit. Earnings this low do not incur federal taxes, though they are subject to the payroll taxes and, in some places, state income taxes. The earned income tax credit, which is refundable, was designed to mitigate the effect of the payroll tax on low-income workers.

5.   These estimates are from Ellwood 1988, based on data compiled and estimated by the House Ways and Means Committee. Their estimates are based

on benefit levels and estimated costs in Pennsylvania, the median state in terms of welfare benefits.

6.   The analysis in this section borrows heavily from Ellwood 1988.

7.   These statistics are drawn from the Current Population Reports on poverty, cited note 2, above.

8.   This section draws heavily on my observations and experience with the New York State Department of Social Services, as Executive Deputy Commissioner from 1984 to 1986. It also draws on observations in welfare offices in several states by students at the Kennedy School of Government, especially Thomas Kane.

9.   Because AFDC is a state-run system and in many states county-administered, specific procedures vary somewhat from place to place. The description here draws heavily on New York State experience but is relatively typical of many states.

10.   Federal legislation, passed at least partly in response to very high overpayment rates in many states, requires quality-control procedures. The system includes a mechanism to levy federal sanctions on the states if they exceed certain overpayment rates. The threat of sanctions led the states to focus seriously on the accuracy of payments and to institute a number of new procedural and documentation requirements. States are currently litigating the sanctions. Nonetheless, quality-control requirements continue to be extremely important influences on state behavior.

11.   Interestingly, this reluctance of welfare workers to get involved with the service needs of their clients came about at least partly as a result of another "reform" of the system in the earlier 1970s, which required states to establish separate offices and workers for income maintenance and services. The idea was to reduce the power and intrusiveness of the welfare system in the lives of clients. The result, however, may have been that the non-income needs of many clients, perhaps the most troubled, are virtually ignored by the system.

12.   The "Green Book" reports that in 1986 1.6 percent of AFDC recipients worked full time, and another 4.2 percent worked part time. The proportion working was higher before 1981, when changes made as part of the Omnibus Budget Reconciliation Act (OBRA) removed many working clients from the rolls because their incomes were "too high." In 1979, 13 percent of recipients worked. Even this pre-OBRA number, however, is not high enough to challenge the perception that welfare is a program for those who do not work.

13.   Before OBRA, the first $30 of earnings, plus one-third of the remainder, plus all work expenses, were disregarded in calculating AFDC benefits. OBRA limited work expenses to $75 per month and allowed the "thirty and a third" disregard for only four months. The states denied eligibility for benefits to families with a gross income greater than 150 percent of the state's standard of need, whatever the family's net income. The 1984 revisions loosened the restrictions somewhat, raising the gross income level to 185 percent of the standard of need and extending the $30 part of thirty-and-a-third for eight months beyond the four-month limit.

14.   States mostly operate these programs under the WIN demonstration authority established by OBRA. This legislation authorized the states to seek

waivers of a number of AFDC provisions, including the requirement that the employment service participate in WIN. The WIN Demo authority, as it is known, allows states to centralize work/welfare programs under the jurisdiction of the welfare deparment.

15. This section draws from my own observations, Kane (1989), Mead (1986), and Behn (1989). The evaluation data on state work/welfare programs comes from a series of reports from MDRC, especially Friedlander et al. (1985).

16. WIN program data come from Committee on Ways and Means, U.S. House of Representatives (1988).

17. A good summary of the programs and the evaluation results appears in Gueron (1986).

18. These results appear in MDRC's final report on the Baltimore Options Project (Friedlander et al. 1985).

19. The Family Support Act does make one important change in eligibility that is worth noting: It requires all states to establish AFDC-UP programs for unemployed parents. There is less to this requirement than meets the eye, however, since all the large states already have AFDC-UP programs and since it is a relatively small part of the caseload everywhere.

20. I have argued elsewhere (Bane 1989) that both voluntary and mandatory programs carry their own dangers and that both types of programs can be implemented successfully. The dangers of welfare workers falling into paper-compliance routines under a mandatory program, however, seem real to me.

21. Basically, the federal government will pay 90 percent of the costs of JOBS programs up to the amount of states' WIN appropriations, plus additional funding estimated at about $1 billion for JOBS-program personnel. The legislation is not clear about federal participation in the costs of child care; there are those who believe that an open-ended entitlement to reimbursement for child care has been established.

22. The Tax Reform bill of 1986 established the parameters of the EITC; they apply to 1987 and later years. Information on the EITC comes from the Committee on Ways and Means, U.S. House of Representatives (1988).

23. Ellwood (1988) treats in more detail many of these proposals. Irwin Garfield is a long-time advocate of guaranteed child-support programs (see Garfinkel and McLanahan 1986). Garfinkel's analyses suggest that a guaranteed child-support system would involve very modest, if any, additional costs, because of improved collections, increased work effort, and a substitution of guaranteed child support for much of AFDC.

REFERENCES

Bane, Mary Jo. 1989. "Welfare Reform and Mandatory versus Voluntary Work: Policy Issue or Management Problem?" *Journal of Policy Analysis and Management* 8:285–288.

Bane, Mary Jo, and David T. Ellwood. 1983. *The Dynamics of Dependence: The Routes to Self-Sufficiency*. Report prepared for the U.S. Department of Health and Human Services by Urban Systems Research and Engineering, Cambridge.

Behn, Robert D. 1989. "The Management of ET Choices in Massachusetts." Durham, N.C.: Institute of Policy Sciences and Public Affairs. Duke University.

Committee on Ways and Means, U.S. House of Representatives. 1988. *Background Material and Data on Programs within the Jurisdiction of the Committee on Ways and Means*. Washington, D.C.: Government Printing Office.

"Conference Report on HR 1720, The Family Support Act of 1988." *The Congressional Record*, September 28, 1988.

Ellwood, David T. 1986. *Targeting Would-Be Long-Term Recipients of AFDC*. Prepared for the U.S. Department of Health and Human Services by Mathematica Policy Research, Inc., Washington, D.C.

———. 1988. *Poor Support*. New York: Basic Books.

Elmore, Richard. 1982. "Backward Mapping: Implementation Research and Policy Decisions." In Walter Williams et al., *Studying Implementation*, pp. 18–35. Chatham, N.J.: Chatham House.

Friedlander, Daniel, et al. 1985. *Maryland: Demonstration of State Work/Welfare Initiatives, Final Report on the Employment Initiatives Evaluation*. New York: Manpower Demonstration Research Corporation.

Garfinkel, Irwin, and Sara S. McLanahan. 1986. *Single Mothers and their Children*. Washington, D.C.: Urban Institute.

Gueron, Judith M. 1986. *Work Initiatives for Welfare Recipients*. New York: Manpower Demonstration Research Corporation.

Kane, Thomas J. 1989. "The Caseworker-Client Relationship and Welfare Reform." Cambridge: Center for Health and Human Resources Policy, Kennedy School of Government.

Mead, Lawrence M. 1986. *Beyond Entitlement*. New York: Free Press.

U.S. Bureau of the Census. 1988. Current Population Reports, Series P-60, No. 160, *Poverty in the United States: 1986*, and No. 161, *Money Income and Poverty Status in the United States: 1987*. Washington, D.C.: U.S. Government Printing Office.

5 Silver Threads: Pension and Health Policy for an Aging Society

Henry J. Aaron

The extension of life is perhaps the most enduring goal of human beings. Rising incomes and the attendant improvements in diets and living conditions, the provision of clean water, and improvements in health care have made possible dramatic advances toward this goal in all developed industrial countries. Together with declining birth rates, now well below levels necessary to sustain population in several countries, the fall in mortality rates assures the gradual aging of the population of all developed countries. While continued high birth and death rates have forestalled similar trends in many poor countries, any successful effort to raise living standards will almost certainly cause the trends that industrial nations are now experiencing to be replicated elsewhere.

One can view societal aging either as a drop in the proportion of the population that is young or as a rise in the proportion that is old. Whether the aging of America is largely behind or ahead of us depends on the choice between these perspectives. Measured by the proportion that is young, the United States has been aging for at least a century.[1] The proportion of the U.S. population below age 19 has been falling since the mid-1800s, from about 70 percent in 1850 to 40 percent by the late 1980s. The "baby boom" between 1940 and 1960 represented a temporary, but rather small, interruption in the 140-year fall in this proportion (see Figure 5-1). Current projections indicate that over the next seven decades the proportion will drop to about 35 percent. The trend in the proportion of the population between ages 20 and 30 follows an almost identical pattern. The drop in the proportion of the population that is young is largely behind us.

Figure 5-1. Population 19 and under and population under 30 as percents of the total population, 1850–2060

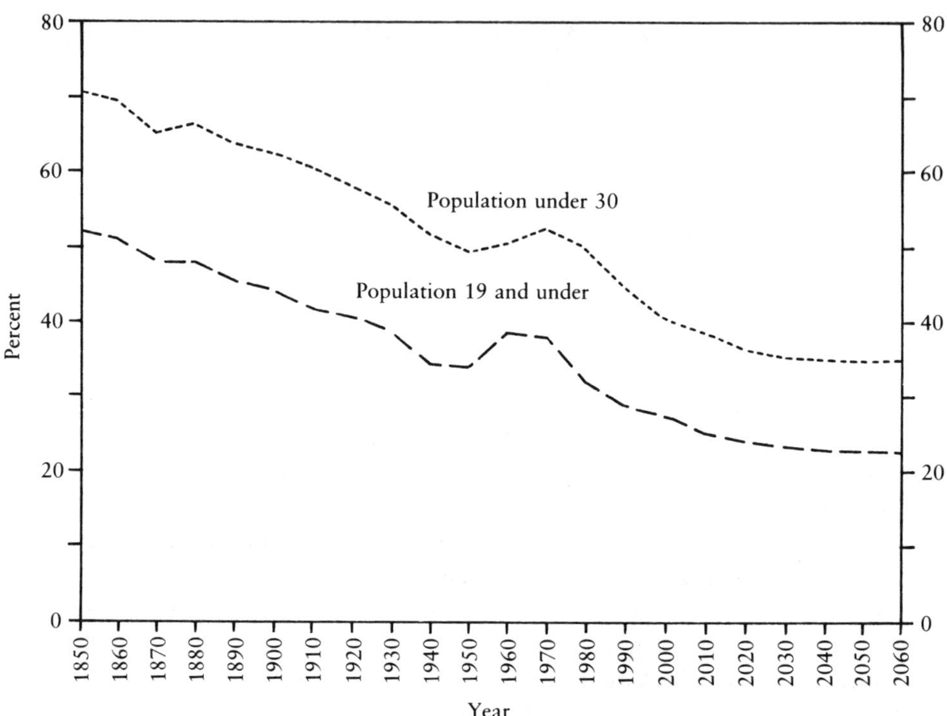

Sources: Data for 1850 to 1970 are from "Historical Statistics of the United States: Colonial Times to 1970," U.S. Dept. of Commerce, Bureau of the Census, p. 15. Data for 1980 to 2060 are, for population 19 and under, from "1991 Annual Report of OASI & DI Trust Fund," May 22, 1991, U.S. GPO, p. 103; and, for population 30 and under, from author's projections.

Measured by the proportion of the population that is old, however, the aging of American society is either well under way or barely begun, depending on one's definition of old age (see Figure 5-2). The proportion of the population 55 or older, which has been growing steadily for more than a century, has leveled off temporarily and will resume rapid growth only after the turn of the century. As recently as 1930, those aged 55 or over represented only about 11 percent of the population, the same proportion that those 65 or older constitute today. Measured by the proportion of the population that is very old, 75 or older and 85 or older, most of America's

Figure 5-2.   Older population as percents of the total population, 1850–2060

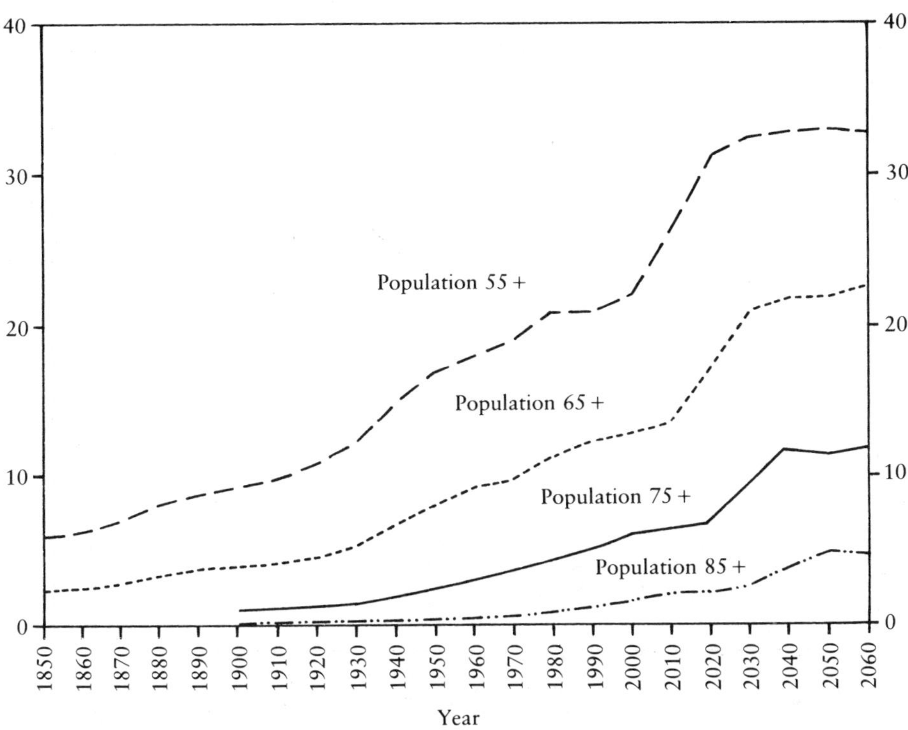

Sources: See Figure 5-1 sources.
Note: Population projections for 75 + were linearly interpolated for certain years; data for populations 75 + and 85 + could not be found for 1850–1890.

aging lies ahead. Half a century from now, those 75 or older will form about the same proportion as those aged 65 or older do today.

The increase in the proportion of the population that is old is not a temporary, baby-boom phenomenon. All baby boomers (defined as those born between 1950 and 1970) will have reached age 65 by the year 2035. Yet the proportion of the population in the older age brackets does not fall after that year. The share of the population age 65 or over remains relatively constant, because it depends on the relatively low birth and death rates that are presumed to persist indefinitely.

Despite the sharp increase in the proportion of the elderly, the share of the population in age brackets that supply most workers has varied little and will not vary much in the future. This is because

Figure 5-3.   Population aged 20 to 64 as a percent of the total population, 1850–2060

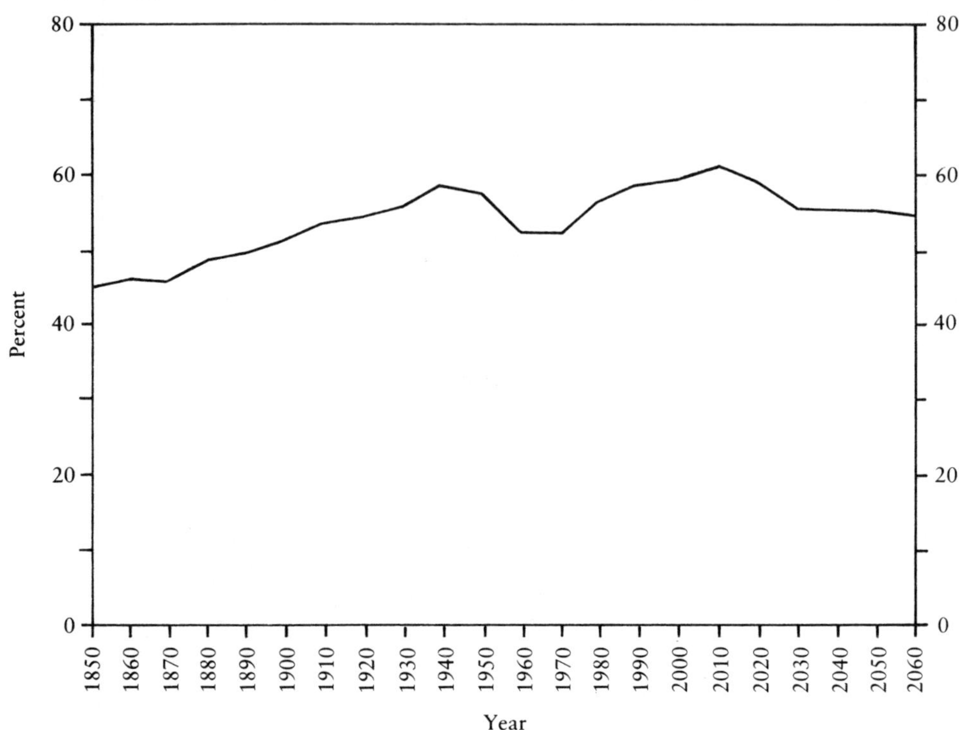

Sources: See Figure 5-1 sources.

the proportion of the population that is young moves in the opposite direction from the proportion that is old (see Figure 5-3). The proportion of the population age 20 through 64 in 1990 will be about the same as it was in 1940, modestly higher than it was in prior decades or will be in the future.

The trend in the ratio of labor force to total population follows a similar pattern. The relative size of various age cohorts not only influences the trend but also changes in labor-force participation rates (see Figure 5-4). The ratio of the labor force to the total population is now at an all-time high, reflecting not only the growth in the prime-age population but also the large increase in the labor-force participation of women that exceeds the drop in male labor-force participation. The proportion of the population in the labor force is projected to fall slightly starting in the year 2000, both for demographic reasons (the increase in the proportion of the popula-

Figure 5-4.   Labor force as a percent of the total population, 1850–2060

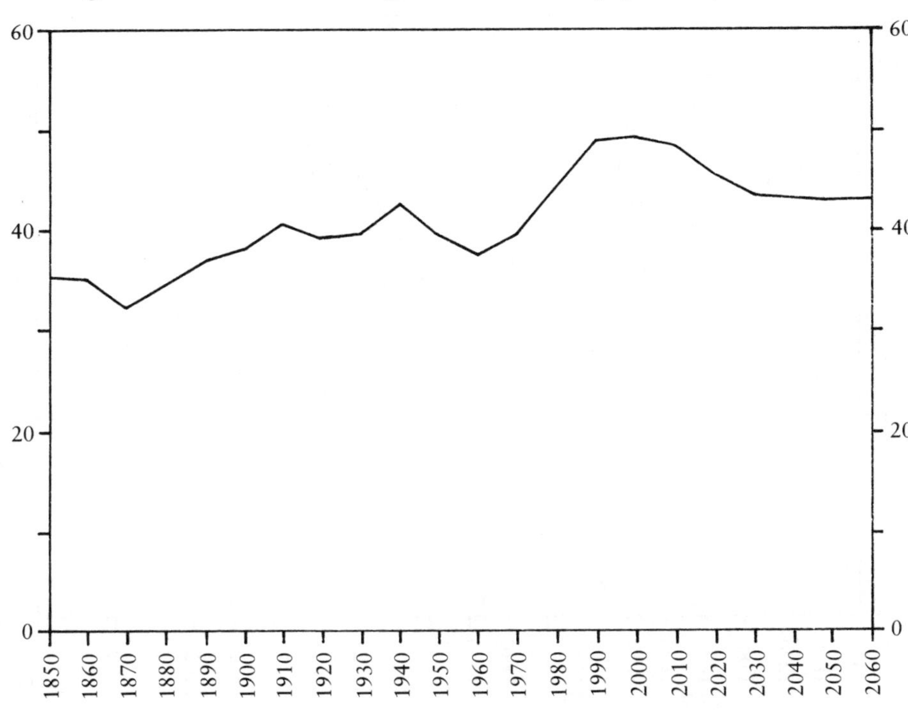

Sources: Data for 1850 to 1970 are from "Historical Statistics," pp. 139 and 127. Data for 1980 to 2060 are from "1991 Annual Report of OASI & DI," p. 103, and "Economic Projections from OASHDI Cost and Income Estimates: 1987," Actuarial Study #101 (SSA), Pub. No. 11-11548 (Social Security Administration, May 1988), U.S. Dept. of Health and Human Services.

tion that is elderly and retired will exceed the decrease in the proportion of the population that is too young to work) and for economic reasons (female labor-force participation rates should level off, while male participation will continue to decline).

The share of the population in the labor force conceals much more dramatic changes in the growth rates of the labor force (see Figure 5-5). The U.S. Labor force tripled over the last seventy years because of both immigration and natural increase. It will grow only 10 percent over the next twenty years, but not at all over the succeeding fifty.[2] This transformation represents a watershed in American economic and social history. Until now, the United States has always expanded, both geographically and demographically. The

Figure 5-5. Growth of the labor force by decades, 1850–2060

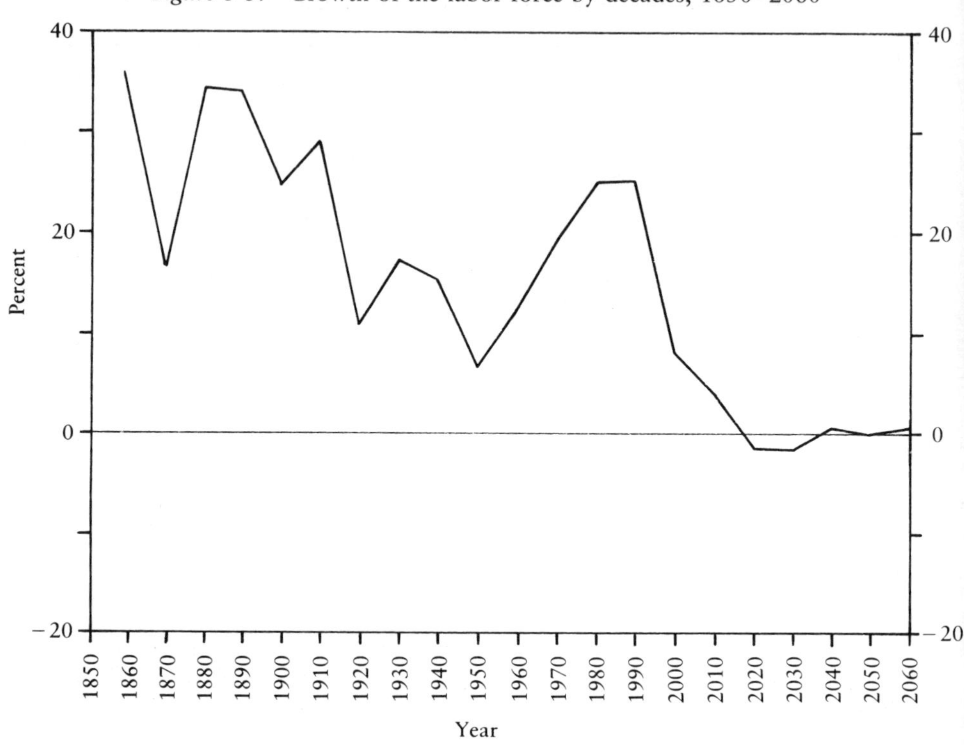

Sources: See Figure 5-4 sources.

geographical frontier closed a century ago. The era of demographic expansion is now ending.

The United States is not, of course, alone in experiencing these demographic changes. Declining birth and death rates (together with the bloodletting of war) determine the age distribution everywhere; only the timing differs (see Table 5-1). As measured by the fraction of the population aged 65 and over, the United States will not be aging as rapidly or as much as will many other countries. In the space of three decades, from 1990 to 2020, Japan, for example, will experience a larger increase in the proportion of its population that is 65 or over than the United States will experience in the next seventy years. Denmark, West Germany, Norway, Sweden, Switzerland, and the United Kingdom already have nearly the proportions of people aged 65 or older as the United States will have in 2020, almost midway through the retirement of the baby-boom generation.[3]

Table 5-1. Population aged 65 and over, 1980–2050,[a] as % of total population

	1980	1990	2000	2010	2020	2030	2040	2050
Australia	9.6	11.1	11.7	12.6	15.4	18.2	19.7	19.4
Austria	15.5	14.6	14.9	17.5	19.4	22.8	23.9	21.7
Belgiuim	14.4	14.2	14.7	15.9	17.7	20.8	21.9	20.8
Canada	9.5	11.4	12.8	14.6	18.6	22.4	22.5	21.3
Denmark	14.4	15.3	14.9	16.7	20.1	22.6	24.7	23.2
Finland	12.0	13.1	14.4	16.8	21.7	23.8	23.1	22.7
France	14.0	13.8	15.3	16.3	19.5	21.8	22.7	22.3
Germany	15.5	15.5	17.1	20.4	21.7	25.8	27.6	24.5
Greece	13.1	12.3	15.0	16.8	17.8	19.5	21.0	21.1
Iceland	9.9	10.3	10.8	11.1	14.3	18.1	20.1	21.1
Ireland	10.7	11.3	11.1	11.1	12.6	14.7	16.9	18.9
Italy	13.5	13.8	15.3	17.3	19.4	21.9	24.2	22.6
Japan	9.1	11.4	15.2	18.6	20.9	20.0	22.7	22.3
Luxembourg	13.5	14.6	16.7	18.1	20.2	22.4	22.0	20.3
Netherlands	11.5	12.7	13.5	15.1	18.9	23.0	24.8	22.6
New Zealand	9.7	10.8	11.1	12.0	15.3	19.4	21.9	21.3
Norway	14.8	16.2	15.2	15.1	18.2	20.7	22.8	21.9
Portugal	10.2	11.8	13.5	14.1	15.6	18.2	20.4	20.6
Spain	10.9	12.7	14.4	15.5	17.0	19.6	22.7	22.9
Sweden	16.3	17.7	16.6	17.5	20.8	21.7	22.5	21.4
Switzerland	13.8	14.8	16.7	20.5	24.4	27.3	28.3	26.3
Turkey	4.7	4.0	5.0	5.5	7.0	8.9	10.2	11.5
United Kingdom	14.9	15.1	14.5	14.6	16.3	19.2	20.4	18.7
United States	11.3	12.2	12.2	12.8	16.2	19.5	19.8	19.3
OECD average[b]	12.2	13.0	13.9	15.3	17.9	20.5	21.9	21.2

Source: Aging Populations: The Social Policy Implications (OECD: Paris, 1988), pp. 78–79.
[a]1980 actual; 1990 to 2050 projections.
[b]Unweighted.

The aging of the population now has and will continue to have profound effects on many aspects of life in the United States and elsewhere. It determines the number of elementary and secondary education students, influences the size of college and university enrollments, affects the rate of growth and the age distribution of the labor force, and influences the composition of demand for housing and other consumer durable goods.

Recently, scholars and journalists have focused on another consequence of aging—the sharp projected rises in the costs of pension and health benefits for the elderly. Many have questioned whether the United States will be able to afford fulfilling the promises embodied in current legislation, notably old-age, survivor's, and disability insurance and Medicare hospital and supplemental medical insurance (Boskin 1986; Longman 1987). These trends in program costs add an economic edge to the old and important question of what role the elderly should play in American life. In particular, should retirement some time during one's sixties continue to be the norm for most American workers? If not, what actions could society take to reverse the trend, evident throughout the twentieth century, toward retirement at progressively younger ages? How much support should society guarantee to the elderly through collectively assured pension and health benefits, and how much should be left to individuals to provide for themselves?

Can America Afford to Grow Old?

Before one can begin to think straight about the burden the elderly will impose on others, one has to be clear on the mechanism through which one person or one cohort can impose economic burdens on others. Children initially depend on adults for support. Eventually, most go on to work, parenthood, and retirement. In the course of its collective life, each cohort earns a certain amount of income. It pays a certain amount of taxes and benefits from publicly provided goods and services, including pensions and services in kind.

A cohort imposes burdens on others only *if its consumption in the course of its collective life exceeds what it earns.* Just because a cohort is elderly and is currently dependent in part on publicly financed pensions does not mean that this cohort is imposing burdens on others. Whether it is doing so or not depends, quite simply, on whether it has paid its dues.

The Ratio of Retirees to Active Workers

Some observers suggest that the sharp decrease in the ratio of active workers to social security beneficiaries that has occurred and that will continue is a good index of the burden the elderly will impose on the rest of the population. That the ratio is dropping is indisputable. The ratio of workers to beneficiaries fell from 13 to 1 in 1950 to 3 to 1 in 1990 and will continue to fall to 2 to 1 by 2035.

This measure is striking, but it gives almost no information about the economic burdens that the elderly impose on others, now or in the future.

To understand why, suppose that all income of every retired person comes exclusively from pensions financed by premiums previously paid by each retiree and by interest earnings on those pensions. Such pensions are nothing more than contractual savings accounts, the balance of which the worker uses at retirement to buy an annuity. These workers would receive no transfer payments from the government. Nevertheless, the ratio of retirees to active workers could take on any value. In particular, it could follow the pattern observed in the United States.

Whatever the ratio of retirees to active workers, in this situation the elderly would impose no economic burden on others. Every dollar they receive would come from the return of their own savings. This example makes clear that it is not the proportion of the population that is retired that determines whether the elderly impose burdens on others. Rather, it is the degree to which the elderly consume over their lives more than they have earned. Knowing only the ratio of the number of retirees to active workers gives no information whatsoever on this question of whether the elderly are imposing a burden on others.[4]

Measuring the Burden

Correctly measuring the burden that the elderly impose on active workers requires that one determine whether each cohort consumes more during its life than it earns (plus interest on its savings) and, if so, how much. Data to carry out such calculations with precision are unavailable, in part because the necessary information concerns future behavior. It is possible, however, to get a rough idea of whether a cohort will or will not impose burdens on others by isolating the principal channels through which such transfers could be imposed: child-parent transfers, pensions, health-care costs, and the federal budget. Rough calculations suggest that the baby-boom generation or its successors are likely to impose burdens on other generations through the last two of these channels. By contrast, most current retirees and those who will retire during the next two decades will benefit from an excess of public pension benefits over the present value of the taxes they and their employers paid.

Child-Parent Transfers.   Each cohort receives help from its parents and spends resources on its children. Factors that affect the resources available to the baby-boom generation at its retirement are the shrinking family size, the increasing participation by women in the labor force, and the rising divorce rate. The first of these trends means that children are growing up with fewer siblings, a development that provides each child with benefits from a larger proportion of family economic resources. The second trend implies that children are less likely than in the past to receive the attention of at least one parent who works at home full time. A result of the third trend is that children are more likely than in the past to have to rely on the relatively meager earnings of one female parent.

| Year | Children residing only with | | Children residing |
| | mother | father | with both parents |
		(millions)	
1960	3.96	0.52	46.95
1970	7.98	1.34	57.74
1987	13.42	1.65	46.01

If birth and divorce rates and the proportion of out-of-wedlock births remain at about their current levels and female labor-force participation rates continue to climb, the baby-boom generation will grow up in larger families than will later cohorts. The families of the baby-boom generation are more likely both to have included one nonworking parent and to have remained intact throughout their childhoods than the families of those born since 1970.

What this demographic fact means for resources devoted to children is debatable. On the one hand, the decline of family size means that the baby-boom generation benefited from greater *aggregate* expenditures than it is spending on its children. On the other hand, baby-boom children on the average received a smaller *proportion* of family resources than will their children. The baby boomers seem likely to have received more parental time than their children will, because their parents were less likely to divorce, separate, or have children as single parents than they are, and one parent was more likely to remain at home. How one should evaluate the differences is quite controversial. But it seems hard to argue that the baby-boom generation clearly will transfer more to its heirs than it received from its parents.

Pensions. The elderly currently receive pensions, both public and private, worth far more than they paid. This means that the rate of return explicitly or implicitly provided to pensioners on the premiums that they and their employers paid exceeds a fair market rate of return. This net transfer is projected to diminish and to vanish entirely early in the next century.

Social security currently provides to retirees pensions that contain a considerable net transfer. The reason for this transfer is that social security is a typical "defined benefit" pension plan. The distinguishing characteristic of such a plan is that benefits are based on earnings and years of service, not on premiums (or, in the case of social security, payroll taxes) paid. This feature permitted the payment of relatively generous benefits to workers soon after benefits were first paid in 1940. Current tax revenues were used to pay pensions to people only three years after payroll taxes were first imposed.

The alternative was to pay negligible benefits to those who became eligible soon after the government instituted the payroll tax and to pay full benefits only after the elapse of the thirty-five-year earning history used for calculating benefits. A side effect would have been the accumulation of large reserves. Government planners rejected this course, as did private managers who set up the defined-benefit pension plans covering most private workers who have pensions.

While it might seem that current beneficiaries, most of whom have spent nearly all their working lives in jobs covered by social security, would no longer benefit from this start-up transition, the program has been adjusted periodically, so that no cohort of retirees has spent its entire working life paying payroll taxes at rates necessary to sustain the program over the long run. That means that the implicit rate of return to current retirees is quite high—in the vicinity of 6 percent. But this rate of return will fall as retirees spend a larger portion of their working lives paying payroll taxes necessary to support the system under which they are claiming benefits.[5] Baby-boom cohorts, in particular, can expect to receive a real rate of return of about 2 percent on the payroll taxes that they pay directly and that their employers pay on their behalf.[6]

In short, the baby-boom generation will pay fully for the social security benefits it receives, imposing no burden on future workers for the social security benefits it will receive. The taxes it pays during its working life are projected under current law to exceed current social security costs, generate a reserve, and thereby add to national saving, the capital stock, and the productive capacity of the nation.[7] This addition to productive capacity almost exactly equals the additional social security pension costs that result because the baby-boom generation is larger than those before it (Aaron, Bosworth, and Burtless 1988).

No one has suggested that a retiree burdens anyone else when using up personal saving to pay for current consumption. Exactly the same line of reasoning applies to private pensions. The Employee Retirement Income Security Act (1974) requires private employers to maintain reserves adequate to support newly accruing pensions, should the employer cease operations. The act also requires firms to gradually build up reserves to support pensions accrued before the law's enactment. Standard economic theory suggests that employers base demand for labor on the total costs of workers' compensation. If employees place a value on pension accruals that is close to cost, employees pay for pensions through lower wages than they would otherwise enjoy. The accruing reserves add to national saving and productive capacity. When workers draw upon their pension when they retire, they are, in effect, simply receiving the wages they have previously foregone, plus accrued interest on their savings.

Health Care.   Health care is an unusual service in many ways. Among its special characteristics, I shall focus on only two. First, per capita spending, after adjusting for increases in the general price level, has risen sharply and continuously for a long time (see Figure 5-6). Official projections indicate that the proportion of the net national product spent on health care has risen from slightly under 5 percent in 1950 to roughly 14.4 percent in 1991, and is expected to absorb greater shares of NNP in the future. Only a small part of this rise reflects the increasing proportions of the population in the relatively costly over-65, and especially over-75 and over-85 age groups. In fact, projections suggest that outlays on hospital and physician care would rise only 10 percent over the next two decades because of all demographic changes, if per capita costs remained unchanged. Most of the projected rise in outlays is attributable to technological advances that will require more staff and costly equipment and that

Figure 5-6.   Health-care expenditures: per capita 1990 dollars, and as a percent of NNP, 1950–91

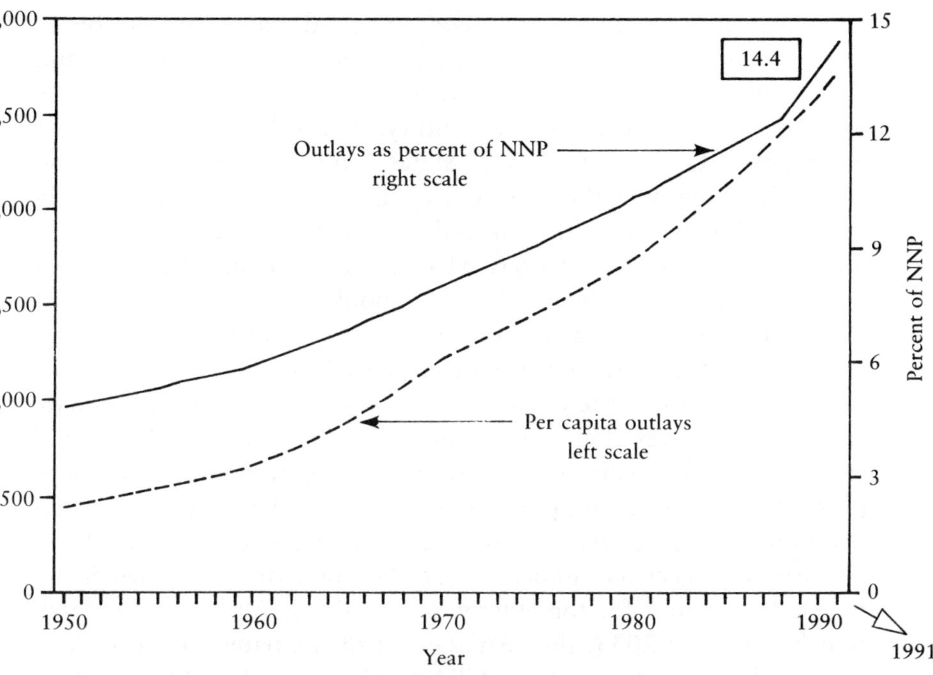

Sources: Katherine R. Levit et al., "National Health Care Spending, 1989," *Health Affairs,* 10 (Spring 1991), pp. 117–30; Katherine R. Levit, Mark S. Freeland, and Daniel R. Waldo, "National Health Care Spending Trends, 1988," *Health Affairs,* 9 (Summer 1990), pp. 171–84; Barbara S. Cooper, Nancy L. Worthington, and Mary F. McGee, "Compendium of National Health Expenditure Data" (SSA), Pub. No. 76-11927 (Social Security Administration, Jan. 1976), U.S. Dept. of Health, Education and Welfare, p. 4.

Note: Outlays are deflated using GNP deflator.

will increase the range of beneficial interventions. A distressing amount of waste exists—excess administrative costs, for example, but a number of studies show that even totally eliminating the waste would slow the accelerating costs of medical care only briefly.

A second characteristic that distinguishes health care from most other services is that insurance, provided as a fringe benefit of employment, pays for most of the medical costs for today's workers and their families. Standard economic theory suggests that the cost of such insurance, like that of pensions, results in lower money wages, so that workers pay for this insurance themselves.[8]

But there are two health-care programs that could impose burdens on future workers: Medicare (which serves the aged and disabled) and Medicaid (which serves the *indigent* aged, blind, and disabled). They account for 29 percent of personal health-care spending, and the Health Care Financing Administration projects the share to rise to 33 percent by the end of the century. It will then represent about 4 percent of GNP. If the United States continues the Medicare and Medicaid systems in their present forms, current workers, notably the baby-boom cohorts, will indeed impose burdens on future workers who may have to pay Medicare and Medicaid costs much larger than those current workers are shouldering today. In contrast to the financing of social security pensions, current payroll taxes are grossly insufficient to pay for promised Medicare benefits. Unlike the social security system, Medicare is not projected to accumulate significant reserves that would add to national saving, the capital stock, and future capacity to produce. Current revenues are supposed to completely support Medicaid, like other government expenditures. In fact, current taxes are not even meeting that goal.

Current projections indicate that the costs of paying Medicare hospital insurance for the elderly and disabled will become so high that by the year 2035, the year the last of the baby-boomers reach age 65, the current age of eligibility for Medicare benefits,[9] workers will face wage reductions of about 2 percent, relative to the burdens imposed in 1986. No published studies exist that show similar projections of the cost of Medicare physician benefits, which will be similar in magnitude, or of Medicaid.

And there is more. Many private employers now promise health benefits to retirees but have not set aside reserves in anticipation of the costs of these obligations. The present value of the future cost of such benefits is estimated at from $169 billion to $275 billion.[10]

Long-Term Care.   Whatever shortcomings may be ascribed to current methods of paying for acute care, existing arrangements reflect a recognition that these services must be paid for. Arrangements for paying for long-term care do not even display this virtue. Public programs, mostly Medicaid, now meet about half of the costs of long-term care. Remaining payments come largely from payments by those who require the services or by their immediate families. Private insurance covers barely 1 percent of total outlays.

Current estimates project that the rate of increase in the costs of nursing home care will match that of acute care. Demography plays little part in the rising costs of acute care, since young and old may need to rely on it. But elders and the disabled are the major beneficiaries of long-term care. Its costs are projected by the Health Care Financing Administration to rise by more than one-third over the next two decades, purely because of the rising numbers of the very old and the disabled. Increases in service costs will add about as much to outlays.

The United States has deployed few instruments to meet these rising costs. The Medicaid program requires that people must establish that their income is sufficiently low and their assets sufficiently few to qualify for assistance. This requirement means that the elderly and the disabled, other than those who are already poor, cannot receive assistance unless they spend their estates or otherwise divest their assets. Private insurers are working hard but with little success to design insurance that will provide significant protection at a price that workers or their employers will find attractive. While these efforts may eventually succeed, the Health Care Financing Administration, which oversees Medicaid, projects that private insurance will cover no more than 5 percent of total nursing home costs by the year 2000.

The United States must find a way to pay for long-term care, principally home care for those who require medical and social assistance to remain outside institutions and nursing home care for those who cannot remain independent. That the society will offer this care, which will represent a sizable call on resources at the time they must be provided, is beyond dispute. That nothing is being done now to increase productive capacity to anticipate these costs is equally evident.

The major distinction between social security or private pensions, on the one hand, and the costs of health care, on the other, is not that the latter are projected to rise more than the former—although they are. The distinction, rather, is that Congress finances social security and private employers finance private pensions in ways that add to national saving and raise productive capacity by amounts commensurate with the additional costs that private and public pensions will impose. Future workers, therefore, will be no better or worse off than they would be if the number of retirees did not increase. The added current saving and future output just about offset the extra goods and services the increased numbers of the elderly will consume.

In contrast, health care paid through taxes and private benefits for retirees are financed in ways that do not add to national saving. Unless policy is changed, the predictable additions to future costs for these benefits will have to be met by an economy that has not increased its productive capacity. Accordingly, they will cut into future production, reducing consumption for purposes other than health care or investment. Based on current projections, the reduction in consumption will be on the order of 4 percent by 2035.

This reduction could be largely offset if the taxes or premiums for health benefits were set at levels sufficient to pay for the cost of benefits projected over the next several decades. Cutting public health benefits would not reduce the burden unless such a policy led to denying some services, as the diversion of current production to pay for a given amount of health services is roughly similar whether the diversion is accomplished through taxes and government spending or through premiums and private insurance.

The Federal Deficit. The Congressional Budget Office projects that the deficit on the activities of government, outside the social security and Medicare trust funds, in 1991 are running at more than $300 billion per year. This massive deficit represents the most serious burden that the baby-boom generation and others active today are imposing on future workers. By cutting national saving and capital formation through their refusal to shoulder the burden of the cost of current government services, this generation is bequeathing to tomorrow's workers less wealth than would result if currently active cohorts were paying their way by contributing enough in taxes to balance the federal budget.

The solution requires only that the population today pay for the goods and services the government provides, not—as in the case of pension and health benefits—that it amass assets in anticipation of future costs. The annual costs of failing for one more year to close the deficit are small, but the cumulative costs become large if the government deficit continues.[11] A solution must entail an end to the fiction that additions to social security reserves can be used to pay for government consumption elsewhere in the budget and simultaneously add to the nation's capacity to meet future pension and health costs.

Compared to What?

Between now and the time when the baby-boom generation retires, the economy and per-capita consumption are likely to grow. Exactly how much hinges on the growth of productivity and the increase in the capital stock per worker? If annual growth of productivity remains at the post-World War II average of 1 percent per year[12] and gross saving remains at its post-World War II average of 16.5 percent of the GNP, net wages will rise 22 percent by the year 2000, 65 percent by 2020, and 93 percent by 2040. Even if national saving does not increase in anticipation of the added cost that increased numbers of retirees will impose, future workers will enjoy rises in net wages several times larger than the added costs they will be called upon to bear for retirement benefits.

Of course, growth may proceed less rapidly. If productivity expands no more rapidly than it has since 1973, net wages will rise only 9 percent by the year 2000, 27 percent by 2020, and 44 percent by 2040. Even at such depressed rates, the increases in wages are larger than the anticipated increases in the costs of health care for retirees. If the growth of productivity remains low, however, the political resistance to paying the higher taxes necessary to support such benefits is likely to intensify.

RETIREMENT POLICY

The critical questions for retirement policy do not concern the affordability of benefits promised under current law. Current workers are paying for promised pensions, public and private, through taxes or premiums, which lead to reduced current money wages. But they are not paying enough for promised health benefits to cover all the costs they will impose on future workers, and they are reducing future productive capacity by their failure to pay enough in taxes to cover the costs of current government consumption. While these burdens will be supportable as long as the growth of productivity proceeds at even minimal rates, the failure of the current generation to save enough to support its own retirement would raise questions of intergenerational equity.

The central questions of retirement policy revolve around two issues. First, what steps, if any, should be taken now to relieve future workers of burdens that currently promised benefits will impose? Relief could come in the form of promising fewer benefits to future retirees than current law provides. For example, should the elderly be denied certain health services that are available to younger people? Because current workers are in the process of paying fully for the retirement pensions they will receive, no curtailment can be justi-

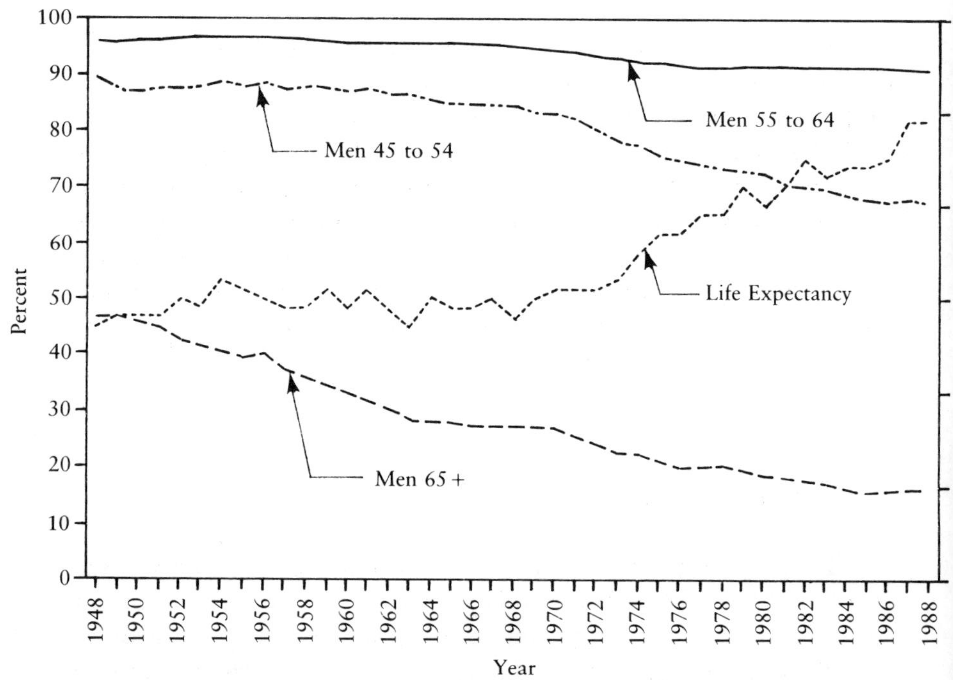

Figure 5-7.   Male labor-force participation: rates and life expectancy at age 65 (in years)

Sources: For male life expectancy at age 65, see "Social Security Area Population Projections, 1988," Actuarial Study #105 (SSA), Pub. No. 11-11552 (Social Security Administration, June 1989), U.S. Dept. of Health and Human Services. For labor-force participation, see "Labor Force Statistics Derived from the Current Population Survey, 1948–87," Bulletin 2307, U.S. Dept. of Labor, Bureau of Labor Statistics, August 1988, pp. 34, 37, 39; and "Employment and Earnings" U.S. Dept. of Labor, Bureau of Labor Statistics, Jan. 1988, pp. 15–16.

fied on the grounds that they will burden future workers; justification would have to rest on other grounds.

The second set of issues concerns the role that the elderly are expected to play in the economy and society at large. In particular, should steps be taken to reverse the trend toward retirement at a progressively younger age? While reversing the trend could rest on a belief that benefits are too costly, it could also reflect a judgment that increasingly early retirement is bad for people despite its apparent appeal.

The Retirement Age

Life expectancy and retirement rates have risen steadily throughout the twentieth century (Figures 5-7 and 5-8 show trends after World War II). This trend predates the advent of social security and the subsequent proliferation of private pensions and has continued since. People, it seems, prefer to use part of their rising incomes to

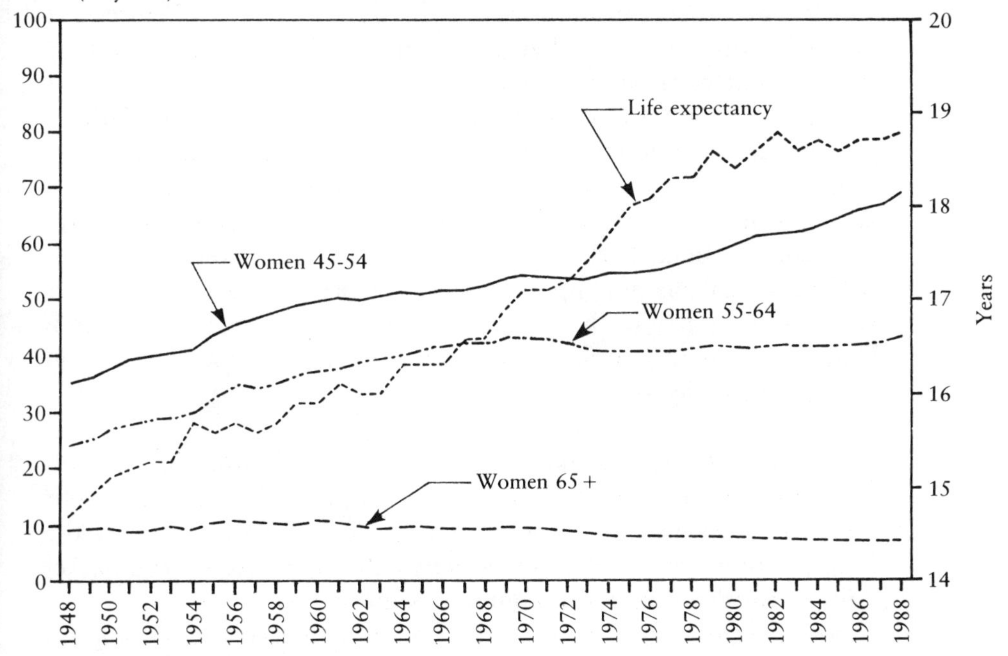

Figure 5-8. Female labor-force participation: rates and life expectancy at age 65 (in years)

Sources: See Figure 5-7 sources.

augment the proportion of their lives spent at leisure rather than at work. This trend manifests itself also in the lower incidence of child labor, the shortening of the work week, and the availability of vacations, often with pay. In the jargon of economics, leisure is a "normal" good, defined as one for which demand rises with income.[13] Economists routinely assume that income is used to purchase goods and services that provide utility or satisfaction and that work, which generates the income to buy these goods and services, must be a burden at the margin; otherwise, people would work more than they do, thereby earning additional income to support added consumption.

This line of argument is indisputably correct; it in no way conflicts with the observation that for many work is a source of satisfaction, social status, and sense of self-worth. These benefits come from the work experience as a whole. Work and the satisfactions associated with it are so gratifying to some that they do little else. For others, work is nothing more than a nasty means to the desirable end of income to pay for essential and not-so-essential consumption. The prohibition of mandatory retirement rules, starting in the mid 1970s, had no significant effect on the trends shown in Figures 5-7 and 5-8, which suggests that people are retiring early because they want to, not because they have to.

The practical question is whether the incentives embodied in various policies should change to encourage people to remain at work longer than they do.[14] The economic case for such a change would rest on one of these grounds: that people think rationally about retirement, but make bad decisions because bad incentives distort their decisions; that people impose costs on or provide benefits to others who are not party to their retirement decision; or that people think irrationally about retirement, and carefully designed incentives could improve their decisions.

Nonneutralities.   Current policies clearly encourage retirement. The most common variety of private pension, the defined-benefit plan, provides lifetime benefits whose present value declines the longer retirement is delayed.[15] Whether the Age Discrimination Act will permit these results to continue is unclear.

Social security now also encourages retirement at age 65 but will not do so by 2004. Currently, benefits for those who delay retirement do not rise enough to compensate for the shortened period of expected benefits. The government is gradually increasing the bonus for delayed retirement, however, so that the present expected value of benefits for people who become eligible starting in 2004 will be independent of their retirement age.

Although the elderly are not now being required to pay enough in taxes to cover the costs of the health-care benefits they will receive, this fact raises a question of intergenerational equity but does not indicate that the current system encourages retirement. Medicare benefits are available at age 65 regardless of work status, although Medicare coverage is now secondary to employment-based benefits. Medicaid is available on the basis of a means test that precludes work, but the test is the same regardless of age.

On balance, the trend toward early retirement reflects not the response of the elderly to nonneutral incentives but rather their preferences to use enhanced wealth in part to leave the work force.

Externalities.   A policy that encourages workers to remain in the labor force until later ages than they now do will result in a larger labor force and add to national output. If workers are paid what they add to output—the assumption of standard economic theory— their decision to work or to retire generates no costs or benefits for others through their earnings. But if retirees delay their retirement past age 65 and do not retire until up to age 70, current law reduces the expected value of social security benefits.[16]

In addition, the decision to continue working or to retire affects other workers indirectly by influencing promotion opportunities. Because promotion is based partly on seniority, retirement opens promotion opportunities for younger workers. In effect, policies to encourage older workers to delay retirement are equivalent to policies that reduce or defer promotion opportunities for younger workers.

Promotion opportunities depend not only on the retirement of older workers, of course, but also on the growth rate of the labor force. When the population is growing, the number of younger cohorts is always greater than older ones. When the population is stable, the number of younger cohorts is about the same as older ones. If managers and others in positions of authority come predominantly from the ranks of older workers, the growth in the number of such positions and the proportion of older cohorts who will find themselves in such positions will be larger if the population is growing than if it is stable.[17] As shown in Figure 5-5, growth of the U.S.

labor force is now slowing and will stop entirely early in the next century. Thus, demographic events will confront workers who are now or soon will be entering the labor force with poorer promotion opportunities than older workers have had.

To increase the retirement age would further reduce promotion opportunities by slowing the exit from senior positions of older workers who would otherwise have vacated them.[18] Those in the labor force during the transition will find opportunities for promotion sharply deferred at best, reduced or eliminated at worst.

Policies to encourage workers to continue working until later ages are unlikely to be effective until near the end of this century or the beginning of the next one. The effective date of any curtailments of benefits is likely to be set in the future because workers near retirement cannot change saving and consumption decisions made in anticipation of a particular retirement date. Furthermore, some time would be allowed for businesses to modify private retirement systems that are integrated with social security. In 1983, for example, Congress enacted a gradual increase in the age at which unreduced social security benefits can be claimed but deferred the effective date until early in the next century.

Thus, any advance in actual retirement ages is likely to occur just when growth of the labor force ends, thereby magnifying the effects of slow growth in the labor force on promotion opportunities of younger workers. Raising the retirement age may well be a good idea, but the basis for such an increase must be found in its effect on workers themselves, not in supposed beneficial effects for society at large.

Why Interfere with Individual Retirement Decisions?

If the trend toward early retirement largely reflects individual preferences, what basis is there for trying to change the trend? I have no good answer to this question, but I do not think that it is the right question to ask. The implicit presumption of the question is that any individual decision that is not distorted by nonneutral incentives and that does not impose cost on or generate benefits for others should be allowed to stand, because people are in the best position to decide what is in their own best interest. This principle places the burden of proof on those who would interfere with market decisions made by individual consumers or businesses.

But the principle of letting everyone decide according to his or her own best interest is not applicable to retirement policy. My decision to retire is influenced by the decisions of my contemporaries. When others retire will influence my decision on the age at which I think it is in my best interest to retire. It may even affect when it is, in fact, best for me to retire. One of these dependent choices will be better for me than are others, and one collective set of these choices by all workers will be better for most workers than are others. There is no reason in theory to expect that I and all my colleagues, acting independently, will establish an environment that produces the best collective outcome.[19] To put the matter directly, retirement is not only a private decision but also a social act that others influence and that affects others.

Furthermore, the principle that external incentives should not taint individual decisions on retirement is fatally compromised, because we have decided that some people behave adversely to their own interests or because private institutions cannot handle certain problems that collective institutions can solve.[20] We mandate through government programs that people save for retirement pensions and health-care benefits because we realize that many people are too myopic to plan for distant contingencies, and we are unwilling to let the elderly face the consequences of such myopia. Private employers establish pension plans in part for similar reasons.[21]

In short, current policy assures workers at least a basic income and for many a good deal more *when they reach 62* (the age at which social security retirement benefits first become available) or some other age. Policy forces workers to accumulate enough income to retire, presumably on the ground that they might not do so without compulsion. While policies do not force or even much encourage them to retire, the policies give them the means to do so, and most take the opportunity.

What Should Be Done?

The case for changing the system of benefits for retirees does not rest on the cost of the current system. Future workers will be able to afford what current programs promise if today's workers pay in taxes, premiums, and contributions enough to prepay the costs of the benefits they will eventually receive and if current workers pay in taxes enough to cover the cost of other government services. Even if they do not, current programs will be affordable if growth of productivity does not fall below today's already depressed levels.

Nor should a change in retirement policies rest on romantic notions regarding the satisfactions that workers derive from their jobs. This line of argument, usually advanced by incumbents of well-paid, sedentary professions, has little relevance for the many workers whose jobs are physically demanding and mentally unrewarding. That prohibition of mandatory retirement led to no upsurge in labor-force participation by the elderly suggests that harsh restrictions are preventing few from remaining in jobs they love.

Any case for a change in incentives should be put in terms of the role and function of the elderly in future economic and social life. Congress already took one important step. In 1983, it decided that the age at which retirees can claim unreduced social security benefits should gradually increase from 65 to 67 over a twenty-five-year period starting in 2002. Retirees can continue to claim benefits as early as age 62, but the pension amount would be reduced more than now. This change will amount to a cut in social security benefits of 12 to 14 percent when fully effective. Congress also decided that workers should receive sufficiently higher benefits for deferring retirement so that the expected value of lifetime benefits would be independent of the age at which they were initially claimed. Furthermore, Congress stipulated that taxable income should include up to half of social security benefits, provided that the beneficiary's income exceed certain limits ($32,000 for couples and $25,000 for single people). Since Congress did not index these thresholds, this change means that eventually nearly half of benefits will be included in taxable income.

These changes reflected the congressional judgment that people who are living longer should work somewhat longer, that social security should not penalize workers who remain active beyond the normal retirement ages, and that reductions in benefits should not affect workers about to retire.

Should Congress decide to make a concerted attack on the deficit, two additional changes in social security deserve serious consideration. First, the income tax treatment of social security remains more favorable than that of private pensions. To establish parity, personal income should include far more than half of benefits without any threshold. Only the return of the employee's own payroll taxes, which are subject to income tax when earned, should be excluded from income tax. A good case based on principles of income taxation can be made also for including in the personal income tax base the subsidy value of Medicare insurance coverage. While I would support such an imputation, it would create the new principle that the government should tax in-kind benefits, as well as cash. Congress has consistently rejected this principle as it applies to employer-financed fringe benefits, including health insurance, group life insurance, and other noncash benefits.

A second change concerns the age at which full benefits can be claimed. The increase from 65 to 67 could be completed in less than twenty-five years without imposing undue hardship. While many argue for further increases in the age of full benefits, such amendments would intensify pressures for liberalized disability benefits and, in any event, should lie in the distant future. Furthermore, the age at which unreduced social security pays benefits should align with the age of entitlement for Medicare.

The most important issues concerning government-managed benefits for retirees concern the financing of acute care medical services and the possible liberalization of long-term care benefits. Medicare taxes are just over half of the long-term projected costs. Few regard the current menu of benefits as unduly generous. Accordingly, the deficit is likely to be made up either by raising taxes or slowing the seemingly inexorable growth of health costs.

Long-term care, an individually variable combination of medical and social services provided both in people's own residences and in nursing homes, has so far defied serious efforts of private insurers to develop and price policies that large numbers of people would want to buy. It is improbable that any long-term care insurance plan will appeal to more than a modest fraction of the population. For that reason, more federal support for the costs of both home health and nursing home care is both desirable and likely as the number of very elderly persons rises (see Figure 5-2).

This menu of actions may strike many as rather anemic. I see no basis for large cuts based on either cost or excessive generosity of current programs. Marginal cuts, through added taxation of benefits or through setting a higher age at which benefits become available, may be necessary for budgetary reasons. Rather, larger increases in benefits for long-term care and possibly in revenues to pay for already legislated acute care benefits will be required.

But the striking characteristic of current public and private programs for the elderly is that they are working rather well. The elderly have achieved rough economic parity with the rest of the population. Surveys document that although most nonelderly persons think the elderly are beset with problems, and the elderly, too, seem to think that other elderly persons are sorely afflicted, the elderly complain no more or less than the nonelderly do about most of the problems of daily living—income, housing, food, attention from relatives, and friendships. Confronted with this evidence, we should not assume we are missing something but recognize that in this area government and private institutions both work reasonably well.

The same cannot be said for policies that affect children and young adults, especially blacks and Hispanics. Functional illiteracy, low educational achievement, teenage pregnancy, and high unemployment all testify to poorly functioning families and failing private and public institutions. It would be a mistake if we used our growing awareness of these problems to justify cuts in private and public programs that for the first time in American history have brought the elderly economic equality.

Notes

1.   All projections in this paper assume that birth rates come to an average 1.9 live births per woman, which is below the rate of 2.1 necessary to sustain the population; that net immigration averages 600,000 per year; and that mortality rates continue their progressive decline.

2.   The statement is based on the Social Security Administration's intermediate demographic assumptions, which project annual net immigration of 600,000 people, consisting of 400,000 legal immigrants and 200,000 illegal immigrants.

3.   This table reveals that all developed countries will end up with slightly more than 20 percent of their populations aged 65 or older, a situation that can be inferred directly from a mental exercise. If the countries eliminated premature mortality, everyone lived 80 years, and birth rates just sustained the population, exactly one-fifth of the population would eventually be 65 or older. While these conditions are not satisfied exactly, they closely approximate actual trends, except for birth rates, which are projected to remain below those necessary to sustain populations and which account for a projected rise of slightly over 20 percent in the fraction of those 65 or older in most countries.

4.   Economists will recognize that this process is simply an expression of the life-cycle theory of consumption behavior. If all cohorts behave in this fashion, the capital stock will grow at a rate equal to the sum of the rates of growth

of income per worker and of population. Whether the resulting capital stock is too high or too low to enable successive cohorts to consume as much as possible over their lifetimes depends on whether the rate of return to saving is greater or less than this sum of growth rates. If the interest rate is higher, then welfare would be increased by a rise in saving. If the interest rate is lower, then welfare would be decreased by a rise in saving. In this model, no individual leaves any unconsumed income at death to add to saving. Nevertheless, each cohort adds to the capital stock because part of its income is unconsumed throughout its life; and the sum of these unconsumed quantities grows as the population rises and output per worker increases.

5.   The rate of return through social security to people reaching retirement age in 1977 was about 8.5 percent in 1986 and is falling steadily. The government, however, raised taxes and cut benefits since those estimates were made. See Aaron (1983).

6.   The statement is based on Myers and Schobel (1983:553–561). The actual rate of return is likely to be somewhat lower, as Myers and Schobel base their calculations on current tax rates. Congress, however, will have to raise payroll-tax rates if it retains the current benefit formula and if it maintains long-term actuarial balance in social security, as it has done in the past. See Aaron, Bosworth, and Burtless (1988). If Congress raises payroll taxes, the actual rate of return will be lower still, reinforcing the statement.

7.   This statement takes other fiscal policy as given. Under this assumption, additions to social security reserves increase the federal budget surplus (or reduce the deficit). The Gramm-Rudman-Hollings deficit-reduction targets short-circuit this result, however, by measuring the budget deficit *inclusive* of social security surpluses, thereby stipulating that each additional dollar of social security surplus can be offset by an added dollar of deficit elsewhere in the budget.

8.   Health insurance, like pension accruals but unlike cash wages, is excluded from the personal income tax base. This tax concession should also be regarded as one of the costs of private health insurance, as it requires that some other tax be increased or some other public expenditure be reduced to offset the revenue loss. In either case, this element of the cost of health insurance is paid by current taxpayers. Only if the tax concession can be charged with increasing the national debt, raising government borrowing, and reducing national saving would this part of the burden of health insurance be shifted to the future.

9.   Covered workers and their dependents who become disabled or suffer from end-stage renal disease are eligible for Medicare benefits before age 65.

10.   The Employee Benefit Research Institute (EBRI) prepared the lower estimate; the Government Accounting Office prepared the higher. I reduced the GAO estimate by roughly 32 percent, ERBI's estimate of the reduction in costs attributable to the 1988 catastrophic health-care cost amendments to the Medicare system. Each estimate includes benefits for current retirees, accrued benefits of active workers, and future accruals of active workers. The difference is traceable to estimates of the numbers of workers who will retire with entitlements to such benefits and to differences in the assumed rates of growth of health-care costs.

11.   The government deficit is about 3 percent of GNP. If one assumes that

the real rate of return to added saving averages 6 percent, the annual loss of future output from such a deficit for one year is 0.18 percent of GNP.

12.   The 1-percent rate refers to total factor productivity, an estimate of the annual growth of output in addition to the growth of a weighted average of the growth rates of the labor force and the capital stock. Output per worker rose faster than this rate because the amount of capital per worker also rose.

13.   The opposite of a normal good is not an "abnormal" good but an "inferior" good, defined as one for which demand falls when income rises.

14.   Posed in this way, the question of retirement policy should be addressed as part of a broader set of decisions regarding age of entry into the labor force, length of work weeks and vacations, and preretirement withdrawals from the labor force for fixed periods. Such issues clearly lie outside the range of this paper, however relevant they may be to public policy.

15.   Note that retirement refers to retirement from a particular job, not to withdrawal from the labor force. "Retirees" could continue to work at other jobs. Few do so.

16.   Current law calls for a gradual increase in the delayed retirement credit, a bonus paid to workers eligible to claim social security benefits but who forbear from doing so. The credit will rise until the bonus fully compensates workers for the delay, so that the expected value of lifetime benefits will be unaffected by the age at which the worker claims them. When this change is complete, the expected cost of social security pensions will be invariant to the date at which the worker claims them.

17.   A simple example illustrates this point. Make three assumptions: that there are two age cohorts, a younger cohort A and an older cohort B; that one-third of the labor force is in managerial positions; and that selection for such positions is entirely on the basis of seniority. If each cohort is twice as large as the next older one, every person in cohort B will occupy a managerial position. If the population is stable, two-thirds of cohort B will occupy such jobs, but one-third will find no openings.

18.   An extension of the example in the preceding footnote illustrates the problem. Suppose that in addition to cohorts A and B there is a third, retired cohort C. With cohort C retired, this example yields the same estimates as the preceding one of the numbers of workers who rise to managerial positions. If each cohort is twice the size of the one that went before, a shift so that none of cohort C retires would mean that only two-thirds of cohort B would rise to managerial positions; the rest would have to wait until they are older to do so. If population is stable, all managers would be drawn from the older cohort C, and no one from cohort B would occupy a managerial position. In short, a rise in the retirement age defers promotion. If promotion and retirement are probabilistic at each age, workers at each age would find the chances of promotion reduced, and workers during the period when the retirement age is increasing but who do not extend their working lives would experience reduced, not merely deferred, chances of promotion.

19.   This problem, to which I only allude, arises in other settings, racial integration, for example. Thomas Schelling (1971) showed that even if the overwhelming majority prefers to live in racially integrated housing, individual deci-

sions may cause an initially integrated housing pattern gradually to unwind into almost total segregation. In this case, each person acts in his or her own best interest *given the initial situation*, but each person's actions alter the initial situation for others, leading to an outcome that all regard as inferior.

20.   Inflation is one such problem. Private insurers are unable to offer indexed pensions because they cannot invest in indexed assets. The government can offer benefits adjusted for inflation because of the power to tax.

21.   Employers face other important motivations to provide pensions, including the exclusion from personal income tax of employer contributions to qualified pension plans. Furthermore, pension entitlements act like "golden handcuffs," bonding employees to the firm because departure before certain ages reduces the value of already-accumulated pension rights.

REFERENCES

Aaron, Henry J. 1983. *Economic Effects of Social Security*. Washington, D.C.: Brookings Institution.

Aaron, Henry J., Barry P. Bosworth, and Gary Burtless. 1988. *Can America Afford to Grow Old?* Washington, D.C.: Brookings Institution.

Boskin, Michael. 1986. *Too Many Promises: The Uncertain Future of Social Security*. Homewood, Ill: Dow Jones-Irwin.

Longman, Philip. 1987. *Born To Pay: The New Politics of Aging in America*. Boston: Houghton Mifflin.

Myers, Robert J., and Bruce D. Schobel. 1983. "A Money's-Worth Analysis of Social Security Retirement Benefits." *Transactions*, vol. 53, pp. 533–561. (Society of Actuaries).

Schelling, Thomas. 1971. "Dynamic Models of Segregation." *Journal of Mathematical Sociology*, vol. 1, pp. 143–186.

6 Foreign Aid to the Less Developed Countries

HENRY J. BRUTON

One of the genuinely important facts about the world is that there exists a large number of people whose income is so low that they can barely survive or so low that they have little occasion to share in the opportunities and the excitement that the world offers. These low-income people live in a world with other people whose incomes are much higher and who can avail themselves of the goods, services, and opportunities that make possible a comfortable and rewarding life, a life in which they can realize most or all their potentialities for personal growth and increased understanding.

In many countries a vast majority of the population is very poor, and in other countries the poor are a smaller proportion of the population. It is customary to speak of poor or less developed countries as those countries characterized by massive and continuing poverty, a situation most easily measured by low income per capita—low relative both to the achievement and maintenance of physical health standards and to per-capita income in other countries. I shall use *less developed country* in this sense. Such language is convenient, but it can be misleading. There are poor people in all countries, and there are rich people in all countries. Indeed, some of the world's richest people reside in countries where most of the population is exceedingly poor.

These are "genuinely important facts" because they impinge on so many aspects of the lives of us all. Large inequalities in income are a major source of international tension and ill will. They invite dependency and make real political and economic independence difficult to maintain. Certainly, not all the tensions and unrest in the world are due to the existence of widespread poverty in the midst of riches, but equally certainly, such inequalities contribute to the tension that we see all around us. Since widespread and continuing turmoil anywhere creates uncertainty and instability everywhere, the elimination of massive poverty and reduction in inequalities in the availability of goods, services, and opportunities among the world's population have benefits for almost everyone.

It is, however, crucial to make explicit that poverty and enormous inequalities are unjust, and the pursuit of justice is a fundamental objective of any worthy society. What constitutes justice with respect to international economic issues is, of course, a question that has no final answer, and I can only announce my general position.[1]

While we should be willing to share our output of consumer goods with the poor (especially in cases of famine or other catastrophe), our primary obligation is to help people find a way to eliminate their poverty, that is, to help them increase their productivity. So the usual arguments about distributive justice do not concern us. Our obligation, to use slightly different language, is to help eliminate the source of the poverty, not simply compensate for the existence of poverty by supplying goods and services.

The first section of my essay presents some data to establish the broad outlines of the extent of poverty and international inequality and, where possible, their changes over time. Several general hypotheses arise about the process and consequences of the growth of gross domestic product (GDP), about the purposes of economic development, and about the role of rich countries in the development of poor countries. A brief review of the "theory of development" follows this discussion. The purpose of this section is to establish a point of departure to help us think about development of less developed countries in the 1990s and the role of the United States in that development. Are we doing enough? The presently most talked about issue of developing countries—the debt crises—is not discussed due to lack of space.

Poverty and International Inequality

Tables 1 through 5 show the growth of GDP in constant prices, exports, and imports for a variety of time periods and a variety of developing countries. The most obvious observation is that the growth rates vary widely among the countries and across time for any given country. Any selection of time periods of similar lengths would show the same variation. Since population growth rates are much less volatile in general, the variation is due almost entirely to variations in the rates of growth of GDP. Some generalizations, however, seem defensible.

GPD per Capita Growth Rates

Growth rates were somewhat higher in the 1960s than in the 1950s. Indeed, the 1960s seem to have been the most impressive of the post-fifties period. In our group of less developed countries, Ghana was the only country that did not achieve a positive average annual rate of growth in the 1960–70 years (Table 6-1). The 1970s were almost as good, and about one-half of the countries achieved a higher growth rate in the 1970s than in the previous decade.

In the 1980–85 period, growth rates in many countries declined markedly. Indeed, the decline began in general around the mid-1970s. Only India, Pakistan, Sri Lanka, and China grew more rapidly than in the 1970s. The strong showing of China and (somewhat less so) India in the years 1980–85 stands out. Botswana also did remarkably well, and a few other countries (e.g., Turkey, Egypt, Korea, Malaysia) achieved acceptable growth rates in the 1980s, albeit somewhat lower than over the previous decade or decade and a half.

The widespread negative growth rates from 1980 to 1985 are concentrated among sub-Sahara African and Latin American countries, generally, the poorest and the richest, respectively, (in per-capita GDP) of the developing countries. India and Sri Lanka, two countries with weak records in the 1960s and 1970s, picked up in the 1980s, and China's growth rate more than doubled in this period. Only Korea, in our list, seemed to grow in a more or less constant way.

Comparison of Rich and Poor Countries

The last two columns of Table 6-1 are ratios of per-capita GDP in the identified country to that in the United States. These ratios are based on purchasing power parity estimates (Summers and Heston 1984), which always show smaller differences between rich and poor than do estimates based on exchange rates. As of 1980, these ratios show some relative "catching up," that is, most of the less

Table 6-1. Average annual rate of growth of GDP per capita (selected less developed countries)

	1950–60	1960–70	1970–80	1980–85	1950–75	1965–85	Country GDP per capita as a % of U.S. GDP per capita	
							1955	1980
Botswana	.8	3.3	10.2	8.6	3.1	8.3	7[a]	21
Egypt	.9	2.1	5.3	2.4	1.4	3.1	10	15
Ghana	1.9	−.3	−3.1	−4.0	.7	2.2	19	9
Ivory Coast	0	4.3	1.7	−5.5	2.0	.9	14[a]	18
Kenya	1.0	2.8	3.1	−1.0	1.8	1.9	9	6
Nigeria	2.1	.6	4.0	−6.7	2.6	2.2	13	20
Tanzania	3.7	3.3	1.5	−2.6	2.6	0	5[a]	6
Bangladesh	N.A.	1.3	1.3	1.0	N.A.	.4	7[a]	5
India	2.3	1.1	1.5	3.0	1.5	1.7	7	6
Pakistan	N.A.	3.9	1.6	2.9	N.A.	2.6	7	8
Sri Lanka	1.3	2.2	2.5	3.7	1.6	2.9	18	10
Taiwan	4.8	5.9	8.1	3.9	5.3	7.1	12	31
Indonesia	1.6	1.9	5.3	1.4	2.0	4.8	7[a]	10
Korea	2.6	6.1	7.8	6.4	5.1	6.6	12	25
Malaysia	.8	3.7	5.4	3.0	2.6	4.4	17	29
Philippines	3.2	2.1	3.6	−3.0	2.8	2.3	12	13
Thailand	2.6	5.4	4.7	3.0	3.6	4.0	8	15
Iran	3.0	8.4	−.6	N.A.	5.1	N.A.	14	24
Argentina	2.1	2.8	.6	−3.0	1.9	.2	39	40
Brazil	3.1	2.5	6.2	−1.0	3.7	4.3	15	27
Chile	1.2	2.4	.7	−2.8	.7	−.2	30	30
Colombia	1.3	2.1	4.0	0	2.0	2.9	22	24

Table 6-1 (Continued)

	1950–60	1960–70	1970–80	1980–85	1950–75	1965–85	Country GDP per capita as a % of U.S. GDP per capita	
							1955	1980
Ecuador	1.9	N.A.	5.8	− 1.4	2.5	3.5	14	20
Mexico	2.4	3.9	2.1	− 1.8	2.7	2.7	24	32
Costa Rica	2.6	3.1	3.3	− 2.2	2.6	1.4	23	28
China	N.A.	3.3	4.0	8.6	N.A.	4.8	9	14
Turkey	3.5	3.5	3.5	2.0	3.7	2.6	18	26

Sources: Estimates for 1950–60 and 1950–75 are from Morawetz 1977, Table A-1. These rates refer to GNP per capita in 1974 U.S. dollars. They are not, therefore, exactly comparable to the estimates for the other periods. The growth rate for Taiwan in the 1965–85 column refers to 1965–81 and is from Scitovsky (1985). Growth rates for Taiwan for 1970–80 and 1980–85 are from *Statistical Yearbook of the Republic of China,* various years.

Estimates for the other periods are from *World Development Reports,* various issues. Estimates for 1960–70, 1970–80, 1980–85, and 1965–85 were computed by subtracting the rate of growth of population from the rate of growth of GDP in constant prices. Intervals may not be exactly those indicated in the headings for all countries. The ratios of the developing country GDP per capita to that of the United States (columns 7 and 8) are from Summers and Heston (1984).

The estimates in column 7 marked *a* refer to 1960.

Table 6-2. Absolute differences between the GDP per capita in less developed countries and the United States: estimates over time

	1 1950	2 1975	3 1955	4 1980	5 1976	6 1985
Botswana	2,238	4,938	4,834[b]	6,395	7,780	8,589
Egypt	2,176	4,952	4,631	6,912	7,610	8,819
Ghana	2,025	4,811	4,173	7,350	7,310	9,049
Ivory Coast	2,096	4,778	4,361[b]	6,679	7,280	8,769
Kenya	2,250	5,038	4,713	7,629	7,650	9,139
Nigeria	2,229	4,951	4,437	6,613	7,510	8,629
Tanzania	2,294	5,078	4,838[b]	7,597	7,710	9,139
Bangladesh	3,117[a]	5,135	4,840[b]	7,657	7,780	9,279
India	2,284	5,099	4,746	7,591	7,740	9,159
Pakistan	3,135[a]	5,107	4,754	7,426	7,720	9,049
Sri Lanka	2,288	5,104	4,364	7,251	7,690	9,049
Taiwan	2,154	4,421	4,465	5,567	6,820	N.A.
Indonesia	2,275	5,069	4,825	7,355	7,650	8,899
Korea	2,232	4,734	4,597	6,082	7,220	7,279
Malaysia	2,028	4,573	4,339	5,885	7,030	7,429
Philippines	2,210	4,898	4,550	7,067	7,480	8,849
Thailand	2,246	4,919	4,736	6,908	7,510	8,629
Iran	1,995	3,917	4,108	6,293	5,960	7,781
Argentina	1,471	3,774	3,138	4,880	6,340	6,662
Brazil	2,006	4,311	4,370	5,937	6,750	7,789
Chile	1,783	4,538	3,623	5,717	6,840	7,999
Colombia	2,070	4,728	4,010	6,207	7,260	8,109
Ecuador	2,103	4,735	4,411	6,533	7,250	8,239
Mexico	1,816	4,146	3,897	5,542	6,800	7,349
Costa Rica	1,933	4,404	4,038	5,919	6,850	8,129
China	N.A.	N.A.	4,678	6,954	7,480	9,119
Turkey	2,063	4,445	4,188[b]	6,020	6,900	8,349

Sources: Columns 1 and 2 Morawetz (1977) Table A-8. Data are in 1974 U.S. dollars. Estimates in column 1 marked with an *a* are for 1960.

Columns 3 and 4, Summers and Heston (1984). Estimates for column 3 marked with a *b* are for 1960.

Columns 5 and 6 computed from GDP per-capita data in *World Development Reports*, 1978 and 1987. The 1985 estimate (in the 1987 *World Development Report*) has been deflated by the increase in the U.S. GDP deflation between 1976 and 1985. Evidently the three groups of data are not exactly comparable.

developed countries grew at a somewhat faster percentage rate than did the United States. Some countries gained by a considerable margin, some by a more modest margin, and some few fell further behind. Were these ratios available for 1985, there would doubtless be more countries that fell further behind.

Table 6-2, however, shows that the absolute differences between the per-capita GDP of the United States and those of the developing countries increased across the board for all intervals. The data in columns 1 and 2 show that between 1950 and 1975 absolute differences more than doubled in almost all instances. The differences continued to rise in the decade after 1975. Only Korea was just about able to hold its own in this period. These countries, therefore, were not catching up in an absolute sense. This is due, of course, to the large absolute differences in GDP per capita at the outset of the period. For the absolute differences to fall over time requires that the inverse of the ratio of the growth rates exceed the ratio of the initial per-capita GDP. Thus, if the per-capita GDP of a developing country is one-third that of the United States, its growth rate must be more than three times greater to reduce the absolute gap. This is unlikely, and it is even more unlikely that the poorer countries can, in this sense, "catch up."[2]

Growth Rates in Developed Countries

Table 6-3 shows per-capita growth rates for ten European countries, the United States, Canada, and Japan. The evidence in this table is similar to that of Table 6-1. The 1960–70 interval shows generally the highest growth rates, up somewhat over the previous decade. The 1970s begin to show a modest decline, except here and there, and an almost across-the-board sharp fall in the first half off the 1980s.[3] It is useful to note that in the 1980s there are no negative rates of growth shown in Table 6-3, unlike those shown in Table 6-2.

Growth rates in the 1870–1913 period were also well below those for the 1950–75 period. The United States and Canada are the only countries in the table that show a (slightly) lower growth rate during 1950–60 than during 1870–1913. During the latter period, international trade was fairly unrestricted and unimpeded, and the British pound was a solid international currency. So it was a good period for economic activity, and yet growth rates of GDP per capita were well below those for the 1950–75 period. Estimates of GDP in Mitchell (1975) for the United Kingdom and Germany go back to 1850, and for the fifty-year period 1850–1900, annual rates of growth of per-capita GDP averaged about 1.5 percent for both countries, similar to the post-1980 figures.

Table 6-3. Average annual rates of growth of GDP per capita (Western Europe, Northern North America, and Japan)

	1870–1913	1950–60	1960–70	1970–80	1980–85	1950–75	1965–85
Belgium	1.7	2.4	4.2	2.8	.6	3.4	2.8
Denmark	2.1	2.5	4.4	2.1	2.3	2.9	1.8
France	1.4	3.5	4.5	3.0	.5	3.8	2.8
Germany	1.8[a]	6.8	3.5	2.6	1.5	4.5	2.7
Italy	.7	5.4	4.7	2.4	.5	4.3	2.6
Netherlands	.8[b]	3.2	3.9	2.1	.3	3.3	2.0
Norway	1.4[a]	2.6	3.6	4.3	3.0	3.3	3.3
Sweden	2.3	2.8	3.7	1.4	1.9	3.0	1.8
Switzerland	1.3[c]	3.0	2.7	.1	1.0	2.6	1.4
United Kingdom	1.3	2.4	2.4	1.8	1.9	2.2	2.4
Canada	2.0	1.2	3.8	2.8	1.3	2.4	2.4
United States	2.2[a]	1.5	3.0	2.0	1.5	2.0	1.7
Japan	1.5	7.3	9.9	3.9	3.8	7.6	4.7

Sources: Estimates for 1870–1913 are from Maddison (1964:30). Estimates marked *a* are for 1871–1913; *b* for 1900–1913; and *c* for 1890–1913. The estimate for Japan for 1870–1913 is from Maddison (1987).

Estimates for 1950–60 and 1950–75 are from Morawetz (1977).

Estimates for other intervals are from various issues of *World Development Report.* Germany, after 1950, is the Federal Republic of Germany, so boundaries after 1950 are not the same as those for the 1870–1913 period.

Are Developing Countries Catching Up?

Table 6-3 adds a piece of evidence to the catching-up story. Japan did more or less catch up. Estimates from Maddison (1987: Table A-4) show that Japan's per-capita GDP was about 29 percent of that of the United States in 1870. In 1950, it was about 18 percent, and by 1985 Japan's GDP per capita ($11,300) was just slightly less than the average of industrial market economies ($11,810) and was some 68 percent of that of the United States.[4] The absolute difference between per-capita GDP in Japan and the United States increased from $1,402 in 1870 to $6,775 in 1950 and declined steadily thereafter to $3,594 in 1984 (Maddison 1987: Table A-4). So the big catching up took place in the twenty years after 1950, when Japan's average annual growth rate was 8.2 percent, compared to 2.2 for the United States. Korea, whose GDP per-capita growth rate after 1960 was almost as high as that of Japan, did not narrow the absolute gap at all over this period. The reason is simply that as late as 1960, GDP per capita in Korea was 6 percent of that of the average of the Organization for Economic Cooperation and Development (OECD) countries (Morawetz 1977:Table A-7). To make a dent in the absolute difference, Korea's growth rate would have had to be about 16 times that of the West. Such a difference obviously was not possible. Of course, if Korea continues its spectacular growth rates, it will at some point begin to close the absolute gap. Korea's growth rate in the 1980–85 period remained impressive, but it too was substantially lower than in the 1970s. The same general point applies to Taiwan, another exceptionally fast growing economy (Li 1988).

Thus, income inequality among nations will be with us for the indefinite future. Since, catching up is not an achievable target, it is necessary to identify explicitly what the target or objective should be in the years immediately ahead. I will argue later that the effort to catch up has, in fact, led to policies and strategies that have penalized societies in a variety of ways. Iran is the most obvious example of a country that tried to catch up and thereby caused great problems for its people. It is not by any means, the only, example. Increasingly, objectives framed in terms of reducing poverty and establishing a more flexible, responsive economy—an economy with substantial transformation capacity—are especially relevant (Bruton 1989).

Foreign Trade

It is generally recognized that unusually high rates of growth of foreign trade characterize the 1950–75 period. Numerous observers have argued that an important—according to many the most important—explanation of Korea's and Taiwan's rapid growth was their exploitation of this strong foreign trade market. Similarly, countries whose policies have impeded foreign trade in a variety of ways have often been criticized by economists for not exploiting foreign trade markets and their (frequent) slow growth explained in terms of these impediments. The success of an "outward oriented" development strategy depends heavily on whether or not world trade is expanding strongly. It is therefore helpful to have some appreciation of the extent to which growth of world trade in the 1950–80 period was in fact exceptionally high. *Exceptionally high* means that policymakers

Table 6-4. Growth rates in real terms of GDP, exports and imports: selected intervals for the West

	1870–1913		1960–70			1970–80			1980–85		
	GDP	X	GDP	X	M	GDP	X	M	GDP	X	M
Belgium	2.6	3.5	4.7	10.9	10.3	3.0	4.9	5.5	.7	3.4	1.1
Denmark	3.2	N.A.	5.4	7.1	8.2	2.5	4.7	3.1	2.4	6.0	3.8
France	1.7	2.8	5.5	8.2	11.0	3.5	6.8	6.9	1.1	2.2	1.1
Germany	2.8	5.1	4.4	10.1	10.0	2.6	5.8	5.9	1.3	4.6	2.6
Italy	1.4	N.A.	5.3	13.6	9.7	3.0	6.7	3.7	.8	4.7	3.2
Netherlands	2.1	4.6	5.2	9.9	9.5	2.9	5.3	4.0	.7	3.4	2.6
Norway	2.2[a]	N.A.	4.4	9.1	9.7	4.8	7.3	4.5	3.3	5.8	4.2
Sweden	3.0[b]	3.8[d]	4.4	7.7	7.2	1.7	2.4	2.3	2.0	6.4	3.8
Switzerland	2.0[c]	N.A.	4.3	8.5	9.0	.4	4.1	4.4	1.2	3.5	3.6
United Kingdom	1.9	2.1	2.9	4.8	5.0	1.9	7.5	4.1	2.0	2.6	4.3
Canada	3.8	6.5	5.6	10.0	9.1	3.9	4.4	6.0	2.4	8.8	5.4
United States	4.2	3.8	4.3	6.0	9.8	3.0	6.9	4.8	2.5	6.6	8.4
Japan	2.5	N.A.	10.9	17.2	13.7	5.0	8.9	4.4	3.8	7.3	2.4

Sources: Maddison (1964:166) and *World Development Report*, 1982 and 1987.
[a]1871–1913.
[b]1900–1913.
[c]1890–1913.
[d]1893–1913.
X refers to exports.
M refers to imports (figures not available, 1870–1913).

do not expect such a rate to continue, and they should act on the presumption that the growth rate of world trade will tend to decline to usual levels.

The ratio of both exports and imports to GNP seems to have risen over time for most OECD countries. For those eight countries for which data are available for the 1870–1913 period (see Table 6-4), exports in real terms grew more rapidly for all save the United States. In the post-1960 years, both export- and import-growth rates for the countries shown in Table 6-4 exceed that of GDP in all cases except imports of Japan after 1970. In 1950, the ratios of exports and of imports to GDP were generally lower than in 1913 (Maddison 1964). This surely reflects the consequences of the two world wars and the depression of the 1930s. After 1950, trade grew rapidly as nations removed the numerous impediments to international transactions. By 1973, the ratios of trade to GDP were, with notable exceptions (especially Switzerland and the Netherlands), similar to those of 1913. The ratios were up again in 1985, but this seems largely a consequence of slow GDP growth rather than of a significant change in the volume of foreign trade in the various economies. Even so, rates of growth of exports especially, and imports to a slightly lesser extent, were lower in the 1980–85 years than in the two previous decades.

Over extended periods, one expects foreign trade to increase relative to GDP because of falling costs of transportation. A steady decline in transport costs will not only increase the flow of existing merchandise trade but will also result in new products becoming tradable. The effect of falling costs of transportation is perhaps paramount in the trends for the 1870–1913 period shown in Table 6-4. Import rates are not available but export-growth rates in this period are generally well below those for the 1960–70 and 1970–80 decades. The postwar adjustments in trade policies, combined with the rapid entry into world trade of a number of developing countries, affect the latter growth rates. Neither factor can continue indefinitely.

The hypothesis then for the West is this: Both exports and imports grew more rapidly in the 1950–80 years than the countries can expect over the near future. Growth of foreign trade will continue absolutely, and relatively to GDP, because transportation costs will fall. The splurge in the growth rate due to the peculiar circumstances of the 1950–80 years will fade away. Changing foreign trade poli-

Table 6-5. Growth rates of GDP, exports, and imports for less developed countries

	1960–70			1970–80			1980–85		
	GDP	Exports	Imports	GDP	Exports	Imports	GDP	Exports	Imports
Egypt	4.3	3.2	–1.1	7.4	– .7	8.8	5.2	3.9	8.0
Ghana	2.1	.2	–1.5	–.1	–8.4	–3.3	– .7	– 7.9	– 8.6
Ivory Coast	8.0	8.8	9.7	6.7	4.6	8.1	– 1.7	1.8	– 10.7
Kenya	6.0	7.2	6.6	6.5	–1.0	–1.0	3.1	– 3.9	– 9.0
Nigeria	3.1	6.6	1.6	6.5	2.6	20.0	– 3.4	– 9.9	– 11.5
Tanzania	6.0	3.4	6.0	4.9	–7.3	– .3	.8	– 11.1	– 3.9
Bangladesh	3.7	6.5	7.0	3.9	–1.9	3.5	3.6	7.1	3.1
India	3.4	3.0	– .9	3.6	3.7	2.8	5.2	4.6	2.2
Pakistan	6.7	8.2	5.3	4.7	1.2	4.3	6.0	2.4	3.9
Sri Lanka	4.6	4.7	– .2	4.1	–2.4	1.1	5.1	7.3	1.5
Indonesia	3.9	4.0	2.0	7.6	8.7	11.9	3.5	1.1	4.9
Korea	8.6	34.1	20.5	9.5	23.0	11.8	7.9	13.0	9.8
Malaysia	6.5	5.8	2.3	7.8	7.4	7.0	5.5	10.7	6.4
Philippines	5.1	2.2	7.1	6.3	7.0	3.4	– .5	– 2.1	– 5.9
Thailand	8.4	5.2	11.2	7.2	11.8	5.4	5.1	8.4	2.8
Iran	11.3	12.6	11.4	2.5	–9.7	12.3	N.A.	N.A.	N.A.
Argentina	4.2	3.4	.3	2.2	9.3	2.1	– 1.4	3.2	– 17.2
Brazil	8.4	5.1	4.9	8.4	7.5	4.2	1.3	6.6	– 9.1
Chile	4.5	.6	4.7	2.4	10.9	2.8	– 1.1	2.3	– 12.5
Colombia	5.1	2.2	2.5	5.9	1.9	5.7	1.9	1.6	– 1.4
Ecuador	N.A.	2.9	11.5	8.8	7.5	9.9	1.5	6.3	– 4.3
Mexico	7.2	2.8	6.4	5.2	13.4	7.0	.8	10.1	– 11.3
Costa Rica	6.5	9.6	9.9	5.8	3.5	3.8	.5	.4	– 4.4
China	5.2	N.A.	N.A.	5.8	N.A.	N.A.	9.8	8.8	17.6
Turkey	6.0	N.A.	N.A.	5.9	1.7	3.3	4.5	25.3	10.1

Sources: World Development Report, 1982 and 1987.

cies will have some effects, but the effects are likely to be modest during the next decade or so. Indeed if policies have a major effect, it may well be to reduce trade/GDP ratios.

Export-import data for the less developed countries show diversity (Table 6-5), and no historical series exist to serve as a basis of comparison. There are many factors at work. On the import side, foreign aid can affect trade growth rates for some of the countries to a marked degree, as can sharp changes in certain commodity prices. The precariousness of the foreign trade sector in these countries is evident from a glance at the 1980–85 columns. Negative growth rates (in real terms) mean that the rate of increase in the availability of foreign goods is declining below previous levels, and countries must adjust in one way or another. The estimates in Table 6-5 suggest that most of the countries shown adjusted by a reduced growth of GDP.

The most obvious observation, however, is that the growth of foreign trade does not generally exceed that of GDP for the developing countries, as it did for the OECD countries. Only for Korea does the growth of both exports and imports exceed that of GDP in the decades 1960–70 and 1970–80 and the 1980–85 interval. The generally haphazard relationship between the growth of GDP and that of foreign trade in developing countries, compared to the more stable relationship in developed countries, is doubtless due in part to different trade policies in the developing countries over the period. Many of the developing countries actively pursued policies that dampened both import and export growth, but the mixture of countries and the change over the three periods strongly suggest that policies as such are not the only relevant explanation, and in some, perhaps most, instances not the most important. More generally, one may argue that for many countries (including many not included in the tables), such features as their structure, technology and labor skills, and infrastructure, caused foreign trade to be lower relative to the growth of GDP than in the developed countries. This is true even if the trade GDP ratio is high. This latter statement applies most directly to the traditional sector and less so to "modern" sectors imposed on the society. The growth of GDP seems to have its origins much more in the basic characteristics of the domestic economy, in its traditions, organizations, structure, and culture, than in the extent of its exporting and importing.

Theories of Economic Development

To try to get a handle on a way of approaching the development issues, a brief survey of development theory is helpful.[5]

The Harrod Model

In the late 1940s and early 1950s, when concern with development became a live practical issue in all parts of the world, economics did not offer a "development theory" that could serve as the basis for the design of policies. The most readily available argument at the time was the dynamization of the Keynesian income-determination model, first worked out by R. F. Harrod (1939, 1948). Harrod noted that investment, a key variable in the determination of the level of aggregate demand in Keynes's short run, would result in a larger capital stock over multiple short runs. Investment that helped resolve today's aggregate demand problem became capital tomorrow and thereby increased the productive capacity of the economy. Full utilization of capacity therefore required that aggregate demand grow along with this capacity. Harrod's formulation led to the result that capacity would grow at a rate determined by the ratio of the saving rate to the productivity of capital. The latter is measured by the relationship between capital stock and the flow of output. The higher the saving rate and the lower the capital-output ratio (i.e., the higher the productivity of capital), the greater the growth rate of capacity. Attention in the West at this time was given mainly to the problem of insuring that demand would grow at this rate. That this was the direction of attention is due, of course, to the widespread belief that the basic problem of the economies of the West was that of oversaving.

The Harrod argument was widely used in analyses of development. The most obvious difference between countries with high percapita GDP and those with low was that the capital stock per unit of labor in the former was much higher than in the latter. More physical capital therefore was the key to raising GDP in developing countries, and to do this required an increase in saving or more foreign assistance. The Harrod formulation indeed made development, that is, growth of GDP, look easy: All that was necessary was to increase the rate of saving and investment. The argument also led to a simple role for foreign assistance: If the domestic saving rate was too low to achieve the targeted rate of growth, aid could provide the additional savings that were necessary.[6]

The Dual Economy Model

The Harrod formulation was also more or less the basis of the most widely employed development model, that of the dual economy, worked out initially by W. A. Lewis (1954) and enriched by Fei and Ranis (1964), among others. The less developed economy is initially characterized by a small modern sector and a large traditional sector. The modern sector is a replica of the economies in the West, and development means increasing the size of this sector.

Therefore, all investment is to be in this sector and labor is to be drawn from the traditional sector until the entire economy is made over in the image of the West. When that time arrives, the country has overcome underdevelopment. The policy implication of this model is clear: Achieve a high rate of capital formation in the modern sector until it absorbs all the labor from the traditional sector.

There are four aspects to emphasize about this way of thinking about development: (1) Capital formation is the mainspring of development; (2) relative prices of capital and labor have no role to play; (3) development means, is defined as, becoming like the West, and therefore the capacity to import is an especially strategic consideration; development then is essentially the "displacement" of existing economic organizations of the low-income country by those of the West; (4) foreign assistance was conceived as supplying additional savings, plus modern technical and administrative knowledge.

The irrelevance of factor prices arose from one or more of three possible assumptions: The technology of the West was so much more productive than that prevailing in the low-income countries, that any factor-combination issue was easily resolved in favor of Western technology. It became expedient then to assume that the advanced technology fixed the production coefficients. Second, the assumption could be made that with a horizontal supply curve of labor (i.e., widespread unemployment), the ratio of factor prices would remain unchanged until all labor was fully employed in the modern sector. With this assumption, there may well be a variety of production techniques available, but the same one would be chosen by producers until the economy was fully modernized. Third, some observers argued (or assumed) that tradition so dominated economic agents in the developing countries that they would respond slowly, if at all, to price signals, and hence considerations other than factor prices determined factor combinations. This last assumption, plus a variety of others about the inappropriateness of the market, led to a great emphasis on physical planning as the main policy instrument in the 1950s and 1960s.

The New Orthodoxy: A Market Approach

The approach (combined, of course, with many details and special adjustments) began to change by the early 1960s. Perhaps the first fundamental change was in response to the evidence that an inappropriate exchange rate and distorted factor prices almost inevitably led to misallocation and hence to less output from available resources than was technically possible. More fundamentally, such distortions forced the economy to slow growth or to stop it completely to correct the distortions. Allocation, and hence relative prices, did matter, and to ignore them was to court disaster. Empirical evidence of the responsiveness of farmers to price signals was especially convincing and widespread, but so were the responses of other sectors of the economy. Getting prices right became the key—as important, if not more so, as high rates of capital formation.

The second, equally far-reaching change was the gradual decline in the emphasis on the role of investment, and a corresponding rise in the role of productivity growth as the mainspring of development. This shift occurred in large part as a consequence of the empirical evidence that showed that the contribution to the growth of GDP and to that of individual sectors of the economy of new capital was decidedly modest. Rich countries had become rich because the productivity of all their factors had grown slowly, but regularly, year after year after year. The question then became how to create an economic environment in the developing countries that built productivity growth into all sectors. Economists thought that the major sources of productivity growth were technical research and development (R and D) and "human capital formation," the improvement in the quality of labor. Despite the considerable empirical evidence to support this position, policies that would increase productivity were much more difficult to work out and to design than were policies to increase the rate of investment. Large expenditures on R and D and on education and other forms of training often had considerable effect on productivity growth, but often there was disappointment with the results, especially as employment opportunities rarely kept pace with the supply of educated labor. There is still no general theory of productivity growth.[7]

A significant number of economists emphasize the importance of "correct" allocation. It is not clear, however, if their emphasis rests on the arguments of getting the most from given resources or whether they believe (for unexplored reasons) that correct allocation itself contributes to productivity growth. At any rate, the argument has resulted in downplaying physical, comprehensive planning and in pushing hard for greater reliance on the market. The view includes as well a rather uncompromising condemnation of the government as a prisoner of special interests and hence a major source of the problem, rather than of a solution. (See, e.g., Lal 1985.)

The third major modification that emerged over the 1960s and early 1970s refers specifically to international trade. Many economists attributed the apparent success of Korea and Taiwan in their overall development efforts to their even greater success in exporting. The import-substitution strategy of the 1950s and early 60s, followed by many developing countries, aimed at protecting the developing economy from foreign competition and reducing reliance on foreign trade. The new arguments reversed this strategy: Exporting was crucial to successful development, and an outward-oriented policy was the key to success. As already shown, world trade boomed in the 1960s and early 1970s and thereby created considerable opportunities for exporting.

There were two specifically identified advantages of exporting: First, it contributed to productivity growth, although the exact way it did this is not completely clear. Second, the rapid growth of exports helped to prevent a balance of payment bottleneck from emerging and thereby helped to prevent a stop/go sequence that, as already noted, defeats productivity growth.

Attention was also given to other possible sources of distortion, such as tax and subsidy systems and various institutions (e.g., labor unions and extended families). Part of the policy task includes modifying these arrangements so that there are fewer and fewer distortions. Development economics and microeconomics then become essentially the same. Inequality in the distribution of income, it is further argued by this point of view, will be resolved automatically if these policies are implemented. The same observation holds for unemployment. Both unemployment and inequality were common problems in the capital-accumulation models.

In their summary of this approach, Bruton and Clark (1987) argued that a country will most effectively facilitate its development if the following conditions prevail:

1. Appropriate budget and monetary policies achieve overall macro-stability.
2. Factor and product prices accurately reflect relative scarcities. Of special importance are exchange rates, wage and interest rates, and prices of agricultural commodities. There should, therefore, be few if any direct controls or subsidies.
3. The economy is reasonably open. Tariffs should be low and uni-

form, exchange and import controls should be essentially nonexistent, and foreign investment allowed, even encouraged.
4. A nondistorting and well-administered tax system should be in place.
5. Publicly owned (or partly owned) enterprises should be run exactly as if they were privately owned, profit-seeking firms.

In an environment characterized by these conditions, the domestic saving rate (plus foreign aid, loans, and investment) would permit a rate of investment that would produce an acceptable rate of growth. Macro-stability and "correct" prices facilitate the process of identifying and selecting those investment opportunities that have the highest social rate of return, including investment in improved labor quality and in R and D. Great weight is placed on the reliability of the results obtained from formal project evaluation. The "correct" prices of domestic factors of production and of foreign exchange will help to insure that exports increase in such a fashion that no foreign exchange (or other) bottlenecks appear. The investments in physical and human capital, the accumulation of new technical knowledge, and the absence of bottlenecks generate growth of output of goods and services.

While this approach is not a pure laissez-faire approach, the general implication of this new orthodoxy is that the role of the government in the economy should be modest indeed. Proponents of this new orthodoxy are willing to explain the failure of a country to grow by "wrong policies," that is, policies not consistent with those just listed. Proponents frequently cite Korea and Taiwan as successes because they, proponents claim, generally followed these policies, and India's and other countries' slow growth is accounted for by their failure to do so.

Problems with the New Orthodoxy

The new orthodoxy has gained considerable academic support, but its strongest exponents are the World Bank and the International Monetary Fund. It is difficult to evaluate the extent to which policymakers in governments around the developing world accept these arguments. It seems clear that had the Bank and Fund not pushed this approach, and often made its acceptance a condition for assistance, policymakers in developing countries would not look so favorably upon the policies. One can argue that even Korea and Taiwan have not followed such policies very closely and that their success is due largely to policies (and other characteristics) the new orthodoxy does not contemplate. These countries have achieved high rates of growth of exports. This perhaps is the only undisputed aspect of their postwar experience.

A number of objections to the new orthodoxy have been expressed with varying degrees of support.

1. This new orthodoxy, like the capital-accumulation approach, rests on the notion that development is essentially a matter of the displacement of the indigenous with the imported.
2. The new orthodoxy defines development as growth of GDP per capita. It gives little attention, however, to the role of institutions, values, culture, religion, and other intangible factors, as important sources of welfare. Critics sometimes argue, moreover, that in its concern to extend the influence of markets, the new orthodoxy is willing to sacrifice them willy-nilly for more goods and services.
3. The approach places blame for such problems as slow growth, inequality, inflation, balance of payments problems, and the misuse of aid primarily on "wrong policies" of the developing countries. Critics argue that it gives little attention either to the policies of the West that affect the developing country's capacity to grow or to the more basic difficulties that characterize the developing countries—incomplete markets, inexperienced governments, colonial heritage, and institutions that have evolved to help relieve some of the costs of poverty and are ill suited to facilitate growth.
4. The new orthodoxy treats the role of the government superficially. The nature and extent of the division of labor between the public and private sectors is heavily dependent on a variety of factors specific to the country under consideration—history and culture are especially important. Critics of the new orthodoxy, however, frequently note the difference between the role of government in Korea and in Taiwan, and indeed the role of government varies markedly among countries generally looked upon as successful.
5. Most of the empirical evidence in support of the new orthodoxy applies to the post-1950 years, which, as already emphasized, appear to be unusual years for growth of both GDP and for world trade. Data and other evidence for the pre-1940 period are less supportive of the approach.

The Search for a New New Orthodoxy

The objections have attracted a sizable following, but it is generally agreed that no *new new* orthodoxy has yet emerged to the market approach. In addition to the lacunae just listed, some more positive arguments are available that do point the direction in which a new new approach may, at some time, be found.

The most obvious point is that we need to understand development, in contrast to displacement. Any approach should seek to explain why and how economies change, not simply how they may duplicate the already-rich West, and thereby cast off their indigenous characteristics. This means that the country must use *its* resources, in contrast to trying to create—or import—resources equivalent to those in countries with high per-capita GDP. Developing countries must place their primary focus on the sources of productivity growth, not simply on the allocation of resources of given productivity. The main role for the price system is to ensure that no bottlenecks appear that force the economy to stop for their correction. This condition alone is sufficient to deny the equivalence of microeconomics and development economics. Poor people are poor because their productivity is low, and the basic development question is how to raise this low productivity.

Numerous observers accept that some protection is necessary early in the development effort. (The new orthodoxy is occasionally ambiguous on whether trade should be free or limited in some way or other.) Protection is necessary to create opportunities for searching for and learning new technologies and new management procedures. The protection must not distort the economy to any significant degree and should not penalize exports. For reasons elaborated below, a significantly undervalued exchange rate is an effective means of providing such nondistorting protection.[8] As productivity rises, so too will transformation capacity, and a substantial transformation capacity among its resources makes it possible for a country to live comfortably in the world community.[9] The objective on the production side is to create, behind this protection, a more flexible, responsive economy, in which productivity growth is occurring regularly.

Specific attention must also be given to "institutions." The relevant notion of institution in the present context is that of conventions of economic and social behavior that supplement explicit laws or contracts or that limit the way the market works. Institutions are a "set of rights and obligations in force . . . defining (1) what markets exist, taking markets in the broadest sense, to include all voluntary exchanges, and (2) how economic relations are regulated in areas where markets do not exist" (Matthews 1986:905). Such institutions vary widely from country to country, and affect what is doable at a given time. Some institutions have direct links with basic values and therefore are themselves important sources of welfare. They are a determinant of what kind of economic change will in fact increase social welfare. The destruction of these institutions in the name of development imposes major costs on the community. Institutions then limit what a society can do at a given time, so may affect how something is done. This point leads to the last issue that must be included in any approach to development.

Development and other economics has not had much to say about the composition of consumption, especially of increased consumption. This is, in part, a consequence of the common practice of equating development with displacement, so, the assumption is simply that people in the developing world would want the same things that those in the rich countries want. It is also due, in part, to the common assumption of economics textbooks that economic actors have complete and unambiguous information about their preferences and about their substitutability rates among goods and services in response to changes in relative prices. Evidence suggests that these assumptions interfere with, rather than illuminate, our understanding of a significant component of welfare.

The obvious point is that people in developing countries must learn what kind of consumption does in fact enhance welfare, just as they must learn how to increase capacity consumers in newly independent nations who are experiencing new consumption opportunities cannot know a priori what consumption composition will yield the greatest welfare. In particular, they must learn that the preferences of people in the currently richer countries are not necessarily theirs, and that, in fact, they must find their own. Thus, any theory of development must include some hypothesis about preference formation and about how new preferences that result in greater welfare come into being. Evidently, where incomes are very low, simply more food, better shelter, improved health are understandably much in demand as income rises. It is, however, also evident that choice problems appear at relatively low incomes. Many choices go deep indeed, including those concerning work and leisure, kind and place of work, and family-sharing arrangements. Something more than text book indifference curves are needed to illuminate these choices.

Albert Hirschman (1982) emphasized that people often think they want one thing, and when it is acquired they find that they do not really want it. It is becoming evident, for example, that the increasing availability of goods and services in developing countries (and industrialized countries as well) has resulted in considerable disappointment; such goods and services have not produced the satisfaction anticipated, and, even worse, have frequently been acquired at the sacrifice of other things that yielded greater welfare. Tibor Scitovsky (1986) emphasized the importance of "creative consumption" as a means to a more rewarding life. Michael McPherson (1983) argued that want formation does have analyzable structures, that wants are really means to deeper ends, and that we must move beyond simple observation of overt behavior to understand the sources of personal development. Poverty is demoralizing, then, not only because it may deprive people of their physical needs but also because it deprives them of the opportunities to achieve wants of a deeper significance. Permanent poverty may discourage articulation, even awareness, of wants. This preference-finding process also requires some protection.

The Development Process in Summary

To put all these pieces together into a neat, well-specified model is hardly possible. It is useful, however, to try to summarize the main ideas. Each country has at some initial period a labor force with a set of characteristics—including skills, experience, and commitment—and a capital stock that embodies technical knowledge and other qualities and is of a particular age distribution. In each country, there is a body of knowledge that is not embodied in existing capital, that is distributed among the economic agents in some way, and that helps to determine the productivity of the capital and labor. These productive resources are set in an institutional and social environment that directly affects their productivity. In this environment are also sources of meaning and, hence, of welfare and equity. Such institutions and social arrangements impose constraints on what individual economic agents and the government deem appropriate and acceptable, and indeed on their capacities to perceive, to understand, arguments and ideas about alternative modes of economic endeavor and economic policy.

Growth of measured GDP occurs as resources increase in quantity and in productivity. Continued growth of factor productivity is necessary for continued growth of output. Productivity growth, in turn, depends in some small part on investment but primarily on the functioning of other aspects of the system, especially searching and learning. The growing economy is one where there are strong and evident inducements to search and to learn and where there are relatively few obstacles to searching and learning, as well as to producing.

Growth takes place in a social and institutional environment and is limited and directed by this environment. Equity and justice require—among other things—that this environment be respected; search takes place within the constraints created by the environment, and it is in this sense that it is respected. The kind of inducements that are appropriate and possible depend as well on the extent to which these social institutions, practices, and perceptions produce entrepreneurial activity and generate a genuine interest in "more" and "other" among the population. Investment that does not conform, does not mesh with the society, will be less equitable—and therefore less productive of increased welfare and indeed probably of physical output—than is investment compatible with these basic and deep-seated characteristics of the society. In particular, a society may avoid bottlenecks in the form of social unrest and tensions; as noted, bottlenecks can defeat productivity growth.

Policymaking enters in several ways into this approach. How economic actors perceive reality is relevant to their action. So it is for government officials as well, and history and experience also affect their perceptions. They, too, are subject to bounded rationality, to lack of information, to pressures from many sides, and to internal disagreements. Great difficulty in designing and implementing specific policies therefore exists. To get a coherent, effective policy in place in these circumstances is all but impossible. Governments, too, must therefore search and learn. Both are difficult.

If, then, the objective of development is not simply to catch up with the West in terms of GDP per capita, what is it? The objective may be set in terms of creating a genuinely independent economy

and society in which search, discovery, and informed choice are inherent characteristics; these phenomena must take place in an indigenous setting that controls and directs them. The indigenous setting
is crucial. It reflects that institutions and traditions, cultural and political values bear on the concept and hence on the choice of policies
and specific objectives. An indigenously based development is less
likely to produce the tensions and upheavals, the disappointment
and disaffection that imported change tends to produce. One can
also expect that an approach to development built around these notions will contribute directly to the reduction of poverty and to the
emergence of an increasingly flexible economy with greater transformation capacity.

THE ROLE OF FOREIGN AID IN DEVELOPMENT

Given this broad picture, the final question is, what should the
role of the United States and other donors be? I begin with some
brief comments about foreign aid in general, and then turn directly
to the United States's role in the 1990s.

Purposes of Foreign Aid

The basic idea of foreign aid has, from the beginning, been the
following: Donors presume that the developing country is pressing
against a particular constraint, and they then make aid available to
release that constraint. Usually, the donors further assume that the
recipient country is pursuing economic and other policies that legiti-
mize the constraint, that is, the constraint is one that the country,
without aid, cannot be expected to overcome.[10] The clearest example
has already been mentioned: aid to increase the rate of capital formation.

This way of approaching foreign aid rests on three especially important assumptions: (1) the United States (the West in general) can
supply what the country needs for development, that is, physical
capital; (2) the principal bottlenecks in the less developed countries
are saving capacity and the absence of a domestic capital-goods sector; (3) the developing country is willing and able to implement
those policies that are most conducive to achieving development. All
these assumptions became suspect as we accumulated understanding

and experience with development and aid. The role that foreign aid could play then became increasingly unclear.[11]

In addition, it became evident early on that there were numerous, extremely complex practical questions about aid. How should donors distribute aid among the less developed countries? Should aid have strings, and if so, what kind? Should aid be for specific projects or for general support? Should the developing countries use aid enhancing the role of women to try to accomplish objectives that are important in the donor country, but less so, or not at all, in the receiving country? Should aid go to the poorest countries or to those countries that could use it most productively? How much aid should go to each country? To what extent does aid, any aid, violate the sovereignty of the recipient? These questions have no final answers, of course, and are usually solved in large part by default and by ad hoc decisions in a given situation. They do, however, add great complexity to the design of an aid policy or to the construction of a general theory of aid and development, as well as to exacerbating the political issues.[12]

Relationships between donor and recipient are invariably awkward, and the creation of a genuine atmosphere of cooperation, common purpose, and learning between donor and recipient has proved difficult to establish.[13] Stanley Please (1984), a longtime officer of the World Bank, noted that the Bank has often been arrogant and uninterested in the recipient country's views and aspirations. The World Bank in particular, but other donor agencies as well, has come to have very firm views of development policy.[14] Its capacity to listen, to take into account specific circumstances and histories, to learn, and to adjust has been found increasingly wanting. The consequence is less effective aid and limited learning on the part of both donors and recipients. One might well argue that this situation is an inevitable consequence of giving and receiving aid. It is difficult, indeed, for an individual or group of individuals, who have within their power the decision to provide or withhold enormous sums of money to a recipient, not to feel and betray a sense of knowing what is best for the recipient.

Success and Failure in Foreign Aid

Although any evaluation of aid is filled with pitfalls, the available evidence does entitle us to say that there are many instances of successful aid efforts. Success here means that a specific aid project had the effect intended and no unwanted side effects. Poats (1985:255), in his review of twenty-five years of aid, finds evidence that about one-third of aid-financed individual capital projects achieved or surpassed their stated objective. Another one-third were satisfactory in that they came reasonably close to achieving their original objectives, and another one-third were disappointments. Only about 10 percent, he concludes, were complete losses. The study of aid commissioned by the World Bank and the International Monetary Fund (Cassen et al. 1986) concludes that "the majority of aid is successful in terms of its own objectives," but that a "significant proportion [of aid] does not succeed. . . . [C]onsidering the difficult circumstances in which aid operates, one might conclude that the record compared well with the average for complex human endeavor" (Cassen et al. 1986:294,295). Cassen laments in particular that we seem to have learned little about aid from past mistakes, while Poats (1985) emphasizes that we have.

Evidence is clearest on aid for specific physical projects that foreign contractors can frequently carry out. They, for example, can build roads, improve harbors and ports, and construct schools and other buildings. Such projects have a clear-cut identity, a beginning and an end. Tracing through the long-term consequences of these kinds of projects is more difficult, and there is evidence that some of these kinds of projects, though completed and available for use, have not broken a real bottleneck in the development process.

The consensus seems to be that technical assistance is less effective than project aid, although it is important to appreciate the numerous major successes (Poats 1985; Cassen et al. 1986; Mosley, 1987). Technical assistance is less common now than in the 1960s and 1970s. In part, this is because newly trained nationals of the developing countries are now available who can perform tasks previously done by expatriates but also because many developing countries have major doubts about its effectiveness. The evidence of the capacity of aid donors to effect policy change in the receiving country is equally mixed, as, of course, is the capacity of donors to know what the right policy is.

Perhaps the most important failure has been the general inability of aid to have much direct effect on poverty, either to relieve it or to compensate for its existence. Food aid has, in certain instances, helped the very poor, but frequently at the expense of the long-run development of a more productive agricultural sector. The failure of aid to affect poverty is partly a matter of the development policies the country follows, but also a matter of the design and implementation of aid policies.

Aid Policies for the 1990s

Two general approaches for foreign aid policies for the 1990s may be identified. The first is to keep the present general approach and to try to make it work better. Countless books and special studies follow this approach. The second is to devise a substantially new approach. I try to do a little of both.

Improving Present Programs.   There is little doubt that developed and developing countries could improve the effectiveness of the present aid industry without modifying its basic structure. The evidence that aid has worked well in numerous instances suggests that these arrangements are not without merit. Donors and recipients could make specific changes that would help to make arrangements more effective. Some of these may be briefly identified here, although in general they are well known.

There should be much more cooperation among aid agencies, the World Bank, the IMF, regional development banks, and other parties. Similarly, a country receiving aid very much needs a central aid-management office to try to coordinate aid proposals and availabilities. Government officials of recipients not only spend unnecessary time with the numerous aid people, but there is duplication and competition among donors, project proposals emerging from incomplete information about other projects that dampen the effectiveness of individual projects and indeed the whole aid package.

Donors and recipients may find ways to bring about more genuine cooperation between them. The word "genuine" is important, because there is now the appearance of cooperation. One would think that having a single organization (e.g., the World Bank or another single multilateral agency) manage all aid would enhance cooperation, but there are problems. An agency that manages all the aid available has a great deal of leverage, and leverage is rarely conductive to genuine cooperation between giver and receiver. But competition among aid agencies does not seem to result in improved aid administration. Also, large bureaucracies are seldom sources of imaginative and innovative ideas. Thus, Mason and Asher write that it "cannot be said that the [World] Bank has been an outstanding leader in applying new techniques of project appraisal or analysis of development processes. . . . The bank has perhaps been less venturesome than some other project lenders, at least until recently, in exploring new avenues of investment" (Mason and Asher 1973:257–298) They go on to say that World Bank's view of development process has been narrower and more limited than that of a number of organizations.

It does seem that there should be a style, a technique, a manner that could evolve to bring about such cooperation. The evidence, one must acknowledge, does not support such a position. (See, e.g., Morss and Morss 1986:96) Since a single agency will not emerge, one can only exhort all aid-providing groups to recognize that recipients have knowledge, insight, and understanding that is highly relevant to establishing an effective aid program. Less developed countries should cultivate the important capacity of saying no firmly and finally to aid offers they do not like. Aid donors, and international development banks, should learn that moving money is not what development is about and that ignorance is common among all members of the human race.

Aid donors, in particular, should try to learn the objectives of the government and of the society receiving aid. Aid programs that aim at objectives of little interest to the aid-receiving society or to which the latter is explicitly opposed are surely misguided. Sovereignty deserves respect. On the other hand, it is legitimate for donor and recipient to discuss the objectives of aid as equal partners in the search for ways to enhance the welfare of recipients.

We need to find ways to learn more about how aid is working. Repeating programs, projects, arrangements, or techniques that have failed frequently is obviously absurd. We must find some way to accumulate evidence on what works and what does not in such a way that we can widely communicate and use it.

Eliminate the distinction (for aid purposes) between foreign exchange and domestic currency costs. Also eliminate aid tying. Neither of these common practices has any acceptable justification, and both are a major source of irritation and conflict. Aid funding should always include some recognition of the recurring costs that the project may create when it is operative.

Some headway in all these obstacles to move effective aid has been made over recent decades, but there is still much to do. These proposals would leave the basic aid arrangements and methods largely unchanged from their present form. Even so, it would take an enormous effort to effect these changes to any significant extent. These changes do not address such practical problems as which countries get aid, how much, and in what form.

Indigenous Development. I would like now to discuss very briefly alternative ideas that seem to follow directly from the ideas and concepts discussed above as the adjustment and deepening of the new orthodoxy of development theory. In particular, we want an approach to aid that enables aid to contribute to real development in contrast to an approach that facilitates displacement.

Indigenous development is essentially a process of learning, so the idea is to create an environment in which searching and learning takes place as a matter of routine. The economic agents must themselves initiate the search, and they necessarily have to begin from where they are. Learning requires that something new becomes available that has some overlap or link with the old. Big leaps from one technique or activity to another that is completely different—that is, that does not overlap with the existing and known—usually defeats learning and discourages search. (For further elaboration on this point, see Hirschman 1968, 1987, and Bruton 1985a and 1985b, 1989.) Modest steps are much more likely to be both firm and consistent with genuine intentions.

This argument rests on the notion that there is underutilized technical knowledge in the community, that is, if economic agents set out to search for knowledge, they can find it. That this is the case seems reasonably well established (Chambers 1983; Bruton 1985b). The capacity to find seems especially evident when the searcher seeks the answer to a specific question arising out of the efforts to increase output. The argument also assumes that private entrepreneurship and organizational capacity are present in appropriate amounts. This assumption is defensible when the new activities are consistent with the experience and knowledge of the community. Entrepreneurship becomes a problem if the new activities are large scale and alien to the society.

So, the initial step is the appearance, in the developing country, of a strong inducement to search on the part of economic agents. The most effective way to do this is to push the economy hard, but to make the availability of additional capital and imports expensive and forbid most direct private foreign investment. When an economy is pressed hard, however, the most likely problem is that the balance of payments will deteriorate. To prevent this, the developing country should effect a major undervaluation of the local currency. The undervaluation of domestic currency creates widespread opportunities for import replacement and new exports without completely eliminating foreign competition. The new opportunities will also be "near" existing techniques and therefore conducive to learning as well as to increasing employment and output.

Protection in this manner does not distort to any significant degree, nor would it result in the creation of large-scale white elephants. The creation of widespread opportunities by this means is important as it results in the economy gaining experience in a large number of new activities, that is, it helps to create transformation capacity, the capacity of an economy to move resources from one activity to another with only modest loss of productivity. High transformation capacity is one necessary condition for the emergence of the kind of economy defined earlier as the objective of development. Specialization is the high-risk policy if transformation capacity is low, and the developing country must learn transformation; generally, it learns by doing.[15]

How Can Foreign Aid Help?   The United States and other countries can help the development process along in a number of ways.

1. The donor must be willing to import any and everything that the developing country can export at competitive prices, given its exchange rate. Where such imports harm activities in the United States, aid funds may be used to facilitate the development (in the United States) of new activities. The exact way that this can be done is not completely clear, but the general point is to use foreign aid funds to remove obstacles to importing into the United States. This is different from giving imports from less developed countries preferences. There would be no such preferences. The only advantage the developing country would have would be the undervalued domestic currency that would make exporting unusually profitable.

2. The added incentive to export provided by the undervalued exchange rate should create inducements in the developing country to search for ways to enter export markets. The economic agents in the developing country have an incentive to seek out information, data,

plans of present and potential importers. The agents may use aid to cover costs that an importer may have in working with an exporter from the developing country. The initiative however—and this is crucial—must come from the exporter.

3. The strong undervaluation will create new investment opportunities. Investment in new activities, even more than in familiar ones, is an uncertain activity. The developing country may use aid to provide some form of insurance against failure. The donor must not provide insurance free, but could provide it at a subsidized price. There would be an educational and publicizing task, but this should be left to the agency providing the insurance.

4. As argued above, there is underutilized knowledge available in the less developed country, that is, knowledge that could be found by economic agents on their own who engaged in search. This will at some point lead to a blank wall where some more formal, organized help is necessary. Aid may be a means to remove or circumvent these walls. This does not mean large-scale support for elaborate research institutions, most—but not all, by any means—of which have not proved effective. What is wanted are organizations that can respond to specific questions identified by economic agents seeking to produce more with given resources. This, for the most part, calls for small operations staffed by people with great practical experience in the activities of the economy, and knowledge of the society, its organizations, institutions, and history.

An illustration may help to make this point clearer. In several places in Africa one finds extensive junkyards, usually divided into numerous stalls. In an individual stall will be a collection of parts, pieces, and things that constitute the "capital" of the junk dealers. The dealers sell physical products, but more important they sell knowledge and technology. They sell ideas, and then supply an item that can implement that idea. The dealers are often extraordinarily clever in turning useless things into useful things in response to a specific request from a client. Clients are generally small-scale domestic enterprises and households. Evidently, it makes no sense for dealers to try to invent independently of the problems that their clients specify. The face-to-face meetings between the searcher and the potential rescuer is about as precise and continuous as it can be.

These African junkyards are an example of a type of investment in knowledge accumulation that apparently has yielded high returns. Increasingly, researchers are documenting similar examples, although no inventory seems available. The examples attest to an inventiveness on the part of certain members of the society and to both the idea of search and the availability of a supply of new knowledge. The knowledge thus created is invariably "appropriate," emerging from within the society rather than being imposed on it from without.[16]

Jon Sigurdson (1986:71–72) makes a similar point with respect to Japan. He writes that "the production plants in Japan do not rely on a specific technology but a system under which production is gradually improved in response to requests by users and in co-operation with machinery makers." Aid used to support these indigenous research activities could make significant contributions to the growth of productivity. Aid that helps resolve a problem that people have recognized and are willing to confront is always more acceptable than is aid aimed at more general, more distant targets.

5. Aid in the form of technical assistance has, as noted, a mixed history. Its dubious record tempts one to rule it out completely but that seems a bit extreme. Rather, it seems better to provide foreign technical assistance when it is a genuine request from a developing country and when the latter shares significantly in the costs. The donor should forthwith end the aid when it becomes evident that the country is either not committed to its use or not able to use it.

6. Infrastructure projects offer opportunities and pitfalls. Among the opportunities are the project's specific identity and the ability of the donors and recipients generally to carry it through. It is also abundantly clear that many developing countries "need" roads, dams and irrigation systems, and transportation facilities. At the same time, there are numerous expensive projects that have little or no effect on the productivity of the economy, and some that have been downright harmful to that productivity. Large-scale projects are difficult to manage and to maintain once completed and always seem to have consequences far beyond those contemplated in the usual benefit-cost analyses. On the other hand, some analysts say that small-scale projects are not really enough, a view I wish to dispute below.

Clearly, there is a role for foreign aid here. In recent years the United States has financed very few infrastructure projects because of lack of funds. Even with available funds, the aid program might do more on supporting the maintenance and management of existing infrastructure facilities. A priority objective may well be, however, to find ways to ensure that the infrastructure constructed is more productive than in the past and to resist the appeal of supporting giant infrastructure projects just because they can often be done fairly expeditiously.

Aid may be exceptionally helpful on small-scale, very labor-intensive infrastructure projects. In rural areas, in particular, there are opportunities to organize labor-underemployed generally or seasonably idle—to construct roads, bridges, water-control devices, and the like. Aid funds simply can pay wages to the workers on such projects. This is essentially a means of providing the liquidity to a government to finance the activities. Such use of aid has the further advantage of providing income to some of the very poorest groups in the country. These projects will be small, but they could be numerous. If they get too big, the organizational problems become unmanageably severe.

7. Aid to facilitate policies aimed directly at creating employment and productivity growth among low-income people may pay off handsomely. Three examples will help illustrate this point.

In some countries, the Ministry of Agriculture has detailed data on most farms. The government also sets the price for a number of farm products. A policy that rewards increased yields with higher prices would surely induce the search for ways to get yields up year after year. The government may need to do very little else to bring about a more dynamic agriculture.

Governments may design a similar kind of policy for employment in manufacturing. Tax-rate adjustment or a direct subsidy might reward a firm that increased the labor intensity of its operations from year to year. For example, a rise in labor's share of value added at unchanged wage rates could measure increased labor intensity. A rise in productivity with no change in wage rates means that the firm reduces its unit labor costs, and this provides an incentive to hire more labor.

In many developing countries, it is advantageous to keep food prices low in urban areas. Governments, however, frequently keep food prices low in a way that penalizes agriculture, either by taxes or price controls on agricultural products. But a policy of "buy high, sell low," made possible by aid, will permit strong incentives for agricultural development by giving farmers high prices for their output and still keep urban prices low by subsidizing food prices there.

There are other examples, but these three make the general point clear. Aid that rewards increased yields as well as increased productivity and employment not only helps the low-income groups directly but also contributes to the creation of a tradition of search and learning, trial and error in the community.

8. Where a country runs into an unexpected difficulty for which it cannot be held responsible while pursuing a range of policies that conform to those discussed above, the donor can immediately make a lump-sum loan (possibly a grant), with no limitations on its use and without exhortation or arm twisting.

Evidently, there are many more issues to confront if the approach suggested above were to be taken seriously. The general point is simple: The developing countries must themselves create a demand for aid, and the donor countries must stand prepared to meet that demand. This general approach not only serves real development objectives effectively but also resolves some of the practical problems (e.g., aid tying) referred to above: Donors provide aid to those who demand it.

Two general points follow from these examples. The first is that the approach not only pays little heed to catching-up but also plays down the notion of international competitiveness. Undervaluation will encourage exports, especially new exports. But more fundamentally, it provides the protection and the incentives that lead to searching, learning, and more effective transformation capacity, the capacity to seize and to create opportunities. It therefore decreases dependence on foreign trade, or, more accurately perhaps, it recognizes that foreign trade is extremely risky until transformation capacity is extensive. It is a means of creating independence, self-reliance, increased productivity, and a base, a foundation from which change may proceed in a reasonably untraumatic fashion.

The second point refers to the possibility that implicitly in this approach we are asking the developing countries to "reinvent the wheel." To some extent this is correct, simply because it is the way to learn. Albert Hirschman writes that

Humans have to reinvent a great many things—from learning how to walk to the proper use of language and this intensive practice in reinvention and re-creation is surely a necessary, although not sufficient, condition for the subsequent generation of genuine creativity. The problem in industrial research and development is not how to minimize reinvention but how to achieve the best possible balance between reinvention and taking advantage of the existing stock of knowledge for the purpose of accelerating both industrialization and creativity. (Hirschman 1987:24)

This statement and many of the preceding arguments remind us that development is necessarily a slow process. Get-rich-quick schemes do not work. The emphasis on searching and learning, on productivity growth, on endogeny and institutions also helps make clear that genuine social and economic change that produces a continuing expansion of social welfare is a slow, long-term process. Therefore, aid is a long-term matter, and it is essential to establish it on a solid institutional basis.

Is the United States Doing Enough?

Foreign aid has very few devoted advocates in any part of the government. The demands on the federal budget of the many domestic activities reviewed in other chapters of this book are all of much greater direct concern to the Congress and to the president than are matters of foreign aid. This is neither surprising nor necessarily evidence of selfishness or of an uncaring attitude.

To emphasize the point again, much of the tension in the world is due to the vast inequalities that prevail among nations, and this continued tension creates many problems for all of us. Similarly, reliable polls indicate that many Americans appreciate how unjust the enormous inequalities are. A foreign aid program aimed largely at removing this source of injustice will, I suggest, be more appealing than a defense of foreign aid built around the argument that it serves our political and economic interests—although of course it does. Perhaps the most difficult task is that of creating a genuine realization in Congress and in the executive branch that foreign aid is something most Americans are willing to support.

If these two branches of the U.S. government came to this realization—and I do not mean to understate the difficulty of accomplishing it—then the task of using our aid in more effective ways than in the past would be much easier. The discussion above of how aid can be used much more effectively now than in the past suggests the kind of approach that will in fact make our aid programs much more effective. Indeed these arguments do not call for a large increase in the aid budget. They call rather for an acceptance that aid really should be used simply and directly to help the developing countries create a flexible, responsive economy where productivity is growing as a routine matter over almost all sectors.

If we commit ourselves in this way and find ways to make our aid more effective, then it is more or less certain that over time we can use more money productively—including aid funds to help domestic industries accommodate to increased imports from the developing countries. Anywhere aid can be used productively, there should be aid. The budget consequences of this approach will be relatively modest, especially if the economy continues to grow. The prospects are not exactly bright, but neither are they hopeless, and there is no doubt at all that our obligations and opportunities are great indeed.

NOTES

I am grateful to Brian Levy, Michael McPherson, Joseph Pechman, and Hans Singer for comments on a previous draft of this paper. A more complete version of the paper is available as Research Memorandum 111, Center for Development Economics, Williams College, Williamstown, Massachusetts. The paper was completed summer 1988.

1.   The literature on this (as on all topics) is unlimited. I found Beitz (1979), Hoffmann (1981), Rawls (1971), and Little (1982, chapter 16) especially helpful.

2.   According to data reported in Helmers (1979:260), the 25 percent of the world's population with the lowest income earned 12.5 percent of the world's income in 1860, against 3.2 percent in 1960.

3.   Maddison (1987) has a particularly illuminating set of data that show that a big decline in such variables as growth rates of GDP and productivity for six countries (France, Germany, Japan, Netherlands, United Kingdom, and the United States) began around 1973.

4.   Summers and Heston (1984) show Japan's per-capita GDP to be 72 percent of that of the United States in 1980.

5.   An excellent short survey of development theory may be found in chapter 2 of Killick (1978). Little (1982) is a fine book-length study of development economics. Little is, however, convinced that there is no such thing as development economics. A good review of the early theorizing on development may be found in chapter 2 of Mikesell (1968).

6.   Another reason for the attraction of the capital-accumulation formulation was the general success of the Marshall Plan. The United States provided investable funds to Europe after the war, and the European countries used these funds in such a manner that they restored productive capacity in a relatively short time. The same, it seemed, should have been possible for the countries of Asia, Africa, and Latin America.

7.   There is, of course, an enormous literature on productivity growth. Denison, Jorgenson, Nelson, Griliches, Mansfield, and many others have studied

productivity growth with care and insight. The point in the text means that we cannot define the conditions under which productivity growth will take place.

8.   The undervalued exchange rate does discriminate in favor of tradeables relative to nontradeables. This distortion should be modest in most instances and will not have adverse effects on exports or the balance of payments.

9.   Charles P. Kindleberger made popular the very useful term *transformation capacity* in various writings, e.g., Kindleberger 1977.

10.   A complementary point has to do with the role of foreign exchange in development. Under specific assumptions, a country may have a sufficiently high saving rate but be unable to convert the savings into exports (or into domestically produced capital goods) and hence to earn the foreign exchange to import the capital goods necessary for growth. Researchers now seem generally to recognize that this situation is largely a consequence of misguided trade and investment policies (Chenery 1987). The basic paper on the foreign exchange constraint is Chenery and Strout (1966).

11.   Inconclusive and doubtful statistical investigations of the relationship between aid and development further cloud the picture. Perhaps the most satisfactory empirical studies are those of Mosley, Hudson, and Horrell (1987) and Mosley (1987). The evidence they offer suggests that the link between aid and development is extremely precarious. See, however, the articles by Papanek cited by Mosley. Papanek's findings do show some evidence of a positive relationship.

12.   The large revenues from oil exports that a number of countries receive are similar to financial aid with no strings attached. It is difficult to find an oil-exporting country that has been able to use such funds to establish, or begin to establish, a flexible, responsive economy with widespread productivity growth. Oil revenues are extreme, of course, but help us to understand the point. The main result of large revenues from oil exports was to make huge amounts of imports possible. Bruton in Ranis, Morris, and Leiserson (1984) examines the problems created by "unlimited" amounts of foreign exchange.

13.   It is also relevant to note that an "Aid Industry" exists (Morss and Morss 1986). This industry has its own objectives, not the least of which is to remain in existence. This industry not only constitutes a lobby for aid but is also active in helping governments of developing countries work up aid requests and applications. Indeed, in numerous instances the donor originates the aid request. This practice is not necessarily harmful, but it reminds us that the "demand" for aid does not result entirely from the recipient country's own conceptions and objectives. Aid agencies are obliged to "move funds," and their officials are very much aware that to do this often requires helping the recipient ask for aid.

14.   This view is essentially that of the "new orthodoxy" described above but *not* the qualifications and addenda described above as the beginnings of a *new new* orthodoxy.

15.   Foreign exchange, by the definition of undervaluation, will accumulate. This, of course, is directly contrary to the foreign exchange-gap notion. The point here is that undervaluation (and hence foreign exchange accumulation) is the most effective means of inducing search, learning, and productivity growth. Undervaluation results in a wide range of new investment opportunities and

facilitates new exports that induce immediately applicable technical knowledge (Bruton 1989).

16.   I owe this example to my former colleague Robert Schneider. For other examples and a further development of this point see Freeman (1973).

BIBLIOGRAPHY

Beitz, C. R. 1979. *Political Theory and International Relations.* Princeton: Princeton University Press.

Bruton, H. J. 1985a. "The Search for a Development Economics." *World Development* 13:1099–1124.

——. 1985b. "On the Production of a National Technology." In Jeffrey James and Susumu Watanabe, eds., *Technology, Institutions and Government Policies*, pp. 81–115. London: Macmillan.

——. 1989. "Import Substitution as a Development Strategy." In H. B. Chenery and T. N. Srinivason, eds., *Handbook in Development Economics*, pp. 1601–1644. Amsterdam: North-Holland.

Bruton, H. J., and P. G. Clark. 1987. "An Approach to Development Policy Analysis." In Paul G. Clark, ed., *Development Policies and Economics Training.* Williamstown, Mass.: Center for Development Economics, Williams College, pp. 77–112.

Cassen, Robert, and Associates. 1986. *Does Aid Work?* Oxford: Clarendon Press.

Chambers, R. 1983. *Rural Development.* London: Longman.

Chenery, H. B. 1987. "Foreign Aid." In *The New Palgrove, A Dictionary of Economics.* London: Macmillan.

Chenery, H. B., and A. Strout. 1966. "Foreign Assistance and Economic Development." *American Economic Review* 56:679–733.

Fei, J. C., and G. Ranis. 1964. *Development of the Labor Surplus Economy.* Homewood, Ill.: Richard Irwin.

Freeman, C. 1973. "A Study of Success and Failure in Industrial Innovation." In B. R. Williams, ed., *Science and Technology in Economic Growth*, pp. 227–245. London: Macmillan.

Harrod, R. F. 1939. "An Essay in Dynamic Theory." *Economic Journal* 69:14–33.

——. 1948. *Towards a Dynamic Economics.* London: Macmillan.

Helmers, F.L.C.H. 1979. *Project Planning and Income Distribution.* The Hague: Martinus Nijhoff.

Hirschman, A. O. 1968. "The Political Economy of Import Substituting Industrialization in Latin America." *Quarterly Journal of Economics* 82:1–32.

——. 1982. *Shifting Involvements*, Princeton: Princeton University Press.

——. 1987. "The Political Economy of Latin American Development." *Latin American Research Review* 22:7–36.

Hoffman, S. 1981. *Duties Beyond Borders.* Syracuse, N.Y.: Syracuse University Press.

Killick, T. 1978. *Development Economics in Action.* New York: St. Martin's Press.

Kindleberger, C. P. 1977. *Economic Development.* New York, McGraw-Hill.

Lal, D. 1985. *The Poverty of Development Economics.* Cambridge: Harvard University Press.

Lewis, W. A. 1954. "Economic Development with Unlimited Supplies of Labor." *The Manchester School* 22:139–91.

Li, K. T. 1988. *The Evolution of Policy Behind Taiwan's Development Success.* New Haven: Yale University Press.

Little, I.M.D. 1982. *Economic Development: Theory, Policy, and International Relations.* New York: Barie Books.

Maddison, A. 1964. *Economic Growth in the West.* New York: Twentieth Century Fund.

——. 1987. "Growth and Slowdown in Advanced Capitalist Economics." *Journal of Economic Literature* 25:649–698.

Mason, E. S., and R. E. Asher. 1973. *The World Bank Since Bretton Woods.* Washington, D.C.: Brookings Institution.

Matthews, R.C.O. 1986. "The Economics of Institutions and the Sources of Growth," *Economic Journal* 96:903–918.

McPherson, M. S. 1983. "Want Formation, Morality, and Some Interpretive Aspects of Economic Inquiry." In N. Hann, R. N. Bellah, P. Rabinow, W. M. Sullivan, eds., *Social Science as Moral Inquiry,* pp. 96–124. New York: Columbia University Press.

Mikesell, R. F. 1968. *The Economics of Foreign Aid.* Chicago: Aldine.

Mitchell, B. R. 1975. *European Historical Statistics, 1750–1970.* New York: Columbia University Press.

Morawetz, D. 1977. *Twenty-five Years of Economic Development.* Baltimore: Johns Hopkins University Press.

Morss, E. R., and V. A. Morss. 1986. *The Future of Western Development Assistance.* Boulder, Colo.: Westview Press.

——. 1987. *Foreign Aid: Its Defense and Reforms.* Lexington: University Press of Kentucky.

Mosley, P., J. Hudson, and S. Horrell. 1987. "Aid, the Public Sector and the Market in Less Developed Countries." *The Economic Journal* 97:616–641.

Please, S. 1984. *The Hobbled Giant: Essays on the World Bank.* Boulder, Colo.: Westview Press.

Poats, R. M. 1985. *Twenty-five Years of Development Cooperation.* Paris: Organization for Economic Cooperation and Development.

Ranis, G., C. T. Morris, and M. Leiserson, eds. 1984. *Comparative Development Perspectives—Essays in Honor of Lloyd Reynolds.* Boulder, Colo.: Westview Press.

Rawls, J. 1971. *A Theory of Justice.* Cambridge: Harvard University Press.

Scitovsky, T. 1985. "Economic Development in Taiwan and South Korea: 1965–81." *Food Research Institute Studies* 19:215–264.

——. 1986. *Human Desire and Economic Satisfaction.* New York: New York University Press.

Sigurdson, J. 1986. "High Technology in Japan and Sweden." In Erik Baark

and Andrew Jamison, eds., *Technological Development in China, India, and Japan*, pp. 57–85. New York: St. Martin's Press.
Summers, R., and A. Heston. 1984. "Improved International Comparisons of Real Product and Its Composition, 1950–1980." *The Review of Income and Wealth*, ser. 30 (June):207–262.

7 Social Needs and Tight Budgets: Why Not Try Economic Efficiency?

Edward M. Gramlich

Economists seem to be of two minds regarding economic efficiencies. On the one hand, they proclaim that there is no free lunch, that having more of x means having less of y. On the other hand, they teach that distortions in the system lead to inefficient outcomes, the resolution of which permits more consumption of x and y.

This same conflict is played out in the budget arena. On the one hand, there are a series of important social problems needing attention. The share of income received by low-income groups has decreased and measured poverty has risen, sharply so for children. The numbers of underclass neighborhoods have increased, as has homelessness. Health and nursing home expenses of the aged have accelerated, and the share of people without health insurance remains high. Measures of educational attainment remain low, particularly for children of low socioeconomic status. Various measures show that levels of air and water pollution either remain high or have increased. Living standards in many parts of the world are low and getting lower. There are, of course, offsetting signs of progress in some areas, but the list of social problems that are normally thought of as requiring public sector intervention is long enough to cause concern.

At the same time, the capacity of the federal government to intervene productively in these areas seems distinctly limited. Many of the limits are organizational or structural, referring to the design of programs, the implicit incentives, and so forth—problems that might in principle be corrected without a great deal of new money. But many problems require new money as well, and there the cupboard seems bare. The obvious manifestation of this bare cupboard is the continuing string of massive federal budget deficits. Moreover, the favorite measure of most economists, net national saving rates, remains near postwar low levels.

The obvious solution to the twin problems of large spending needs coexisting with large budget deficits is for large tax increases. But there politics seem to block the road. All recent national presidential elections have been won by the candidate who took the harder line against raising taxes. Many states have recently adopted tax-limit amendments to their constitutions, and the anti-tax lobby rises with great ferocity any time a lonely politician as much as suggests higher gas taxes, higher sin taxes, taxes to finance deposit insurance, taxes to finance health care for the aged, or anything else. More general tax increases, such as a rise in income tax rates or a value-added tax, are never even suggested by anybody trying to win political elections.

How can the United States resolve this impasse between social need and the unwillingness to raise taxes? Why not try economic efficiency? If there are distortions in the system, it is at least in principle possible to find ways to spend more on social problems, reduce deficits, and improve economic efficiency simultaneously. In this paper I list some of the more obvious distortions and how they can be remedied. These remedies do not change the underlying tension between social needs and budget exigencies, and they will certainly be costly to some parties—in that sense there is still no free lunch. But by partially resolving the budgetary impasse, they can make for potentially significant improvements. After describing the long and growing list of problems that might require more spending, and recalling why the budget problem is serious and cannot be ignored, I advertise my list of potential remedies.

SOCIAL PROBLEMS AND SPENDING

Other papers in this volume cover the main problems in different areas. Here I only recapitulate that material to make the case that the list of items on the nation's social agenda is long and growing. The other papers make the important point that lasting solutions to most of these problems require more than money; throwing money alone at problems will not do. But it is still hard to imagine lasting solutions that do not entail at least some new public funds; throwing structural change alone at problems will not do either.

The discussion below focuses on three of the most important problems on the nation's agenda: poverty, health care, and education. Solutions to these three seem to be the most costly. After briefly reviewing the situation in each area, I summarize trends in public spending in these areas and for nondefense spending in general.

Poverty

In the first decade following President Lyndon B. Johnson's declaration of war on poverty, the country made noticeable progress. The share of the population living below the official poverty line, called the poverty rate, fell from 20 percent in 1963 to 11 percent in 1973. Since then, progress has been halted. By 1987, even after a sustained business-cycle expansion, the poverty rate was still 13.5 percent.

There are several reasons why these gross numbers may not be as disturbing as they seem. The official poverty counts are based on Census Bureau numbers, and there are several problems with the way the Census counts income. It ignores in-kind benefits, such as health insurance and food stamps, and by using pre-tax income, it ignores the gains from tax cuts that take the poor off the tax roles. Moreover, Jencks (1984) pointed out that consumption-based measures of low-income status generally show more improvement than income-based measures, such as those from the Census.

At the same time, there are several more ominous trends. Because of the rise in numbers of single-parent families, the poverty rate for children has risen more than the overall poverty rate. A growing share of poor people live in underclass areas with high crime and bad schools (Ellwood 1988). A growing share of poor people cannot afford decent housing, and another growing share of poor people cannot afford any housing at all.

Nobody would claim that money alone could solve all these problems. Welfare programs have well-known work-disincentive effects, and a debate continues over whether present welfare programs encourage family-splitting (Murray 1984 gives the case that they do, and Ellwood 1988 gives the case that they do not). Efforts to revitalize low-income neighborhoods have not been very successful, and public housing programs have been plagued with inefficiency and corruption. At the same time, it is hard to imagine a successful attack on these problems that does not entail at least some new money. One cause of the trend that shows a rise in poverty is the minimal rise since 1973 in real output per capita; another is a sharp drop since 1973 in real benefit payments for public assistance and food stamps. One cause of increased homelessness over the period is the greater expense for housing of all types; another is the sharp cut in low-income housing subsidies.

Health Care

Whereas problems in the welfare area may be partially attributed to declines in public spending, problems in the health care area convey a different image of a sink that can absorb endless amounts of money, and yet the problems persist. Two decades ago, the two largest health insurance programs—Medicare for the aged and Medicaid for the poor—were just coming into existence. In the late 1980s, expenditures on these programs exceeded 2 percent of gross national product (GNP). They will probably rise to nearly 3 percent of GNP by the mid-1990s, and they are growing more rapidly than any other type of federal spending, even including national defense and interest payments. Important in this picture is that the relative price of medical care has risen at a rate 1.35 times the rate of increase of consumer prices in general.

The main reason that both health care spending and prices rise so much more rapidly than do other public and private goods is that the structure of present health-insurance programs gives inadequate incentive to control costs or economize on expensive treatments. How to introduce such incentives is a deep question I will not get into. But even with these large spending increases, two very basic health-care needs remain:

- Many people—a full 15 percent of the population—still lack any sort of health insurance whatever. Given the high and rising expense of health care, it becomes increasingly difficult to imagine how people can survive without health insurance in today's society.

- Most people lack any insurance for long-term nursing home expenses. With the aging of America and advancing technology, the nursing-home-eligible population—those over 85 years of age—is expected to increase at the astounding rate of 4 percent a year for the next two decades, making this gap in available coverage massive.

Whether policymakers will improve the structural incentives or not, these pressures for spending increases will continue.

Education

Poverty is a national problem partly because of a lack of spending, and health care is a national problem in spite of large spending. Education, on the other hand, is a problem that is by and large a state and local responsibility. There are some federal grants for disadvantaged schools, but federal spending has always been less than 10 percent of total spending on education.

One difficulty in appraising the seriousness of educational problems is that no direct measure of educational status exists. Incomes and the prevalence of health insurance can be accurately measured; how well people are educated cannot be accurately measured. What can be measured is how well students do on standardized tests, and those measures seem largely reassuring. After a long period of decline, most test score measures are now on the upswing (Congressional Budget Office 1986). Minority students and others in disadvantaged schools rank below nonminorities, but these scores are improving as well, and even closing the gap some. Beyond the test scores, however, there is still plenty of casual evidence of terrible conditions in certain disadvantaged schools—high dropout rates, crime in the schools, and teenage pregnancy.

The story for input measures—money spent on public schools—is just as ambiguous. Total spending at all levels rose steadily from 3 percent of GNP in the mid-1950s to over 5 percent in 1989. Roughly half of this rise was due to relative price increases for public education; half was due to real increases in spending. But again, cross-sectional evidence that real spending levels are significantly lower in disadvantaged schools tempers this favorable evidence of improvements over time. While important structural changes in schools and their governance should certainly be considered, it is again impossible to see how to pull up education levels of disadvantaged children without new sources of finance for disadvantaged schools.

Trends in Public Spending

I will now briefly show how these salient trends in public spending look in the overall distribution of national output between pri-

Figure 7-1. Nondefense spending by function, 1955–86, as percent of GNP

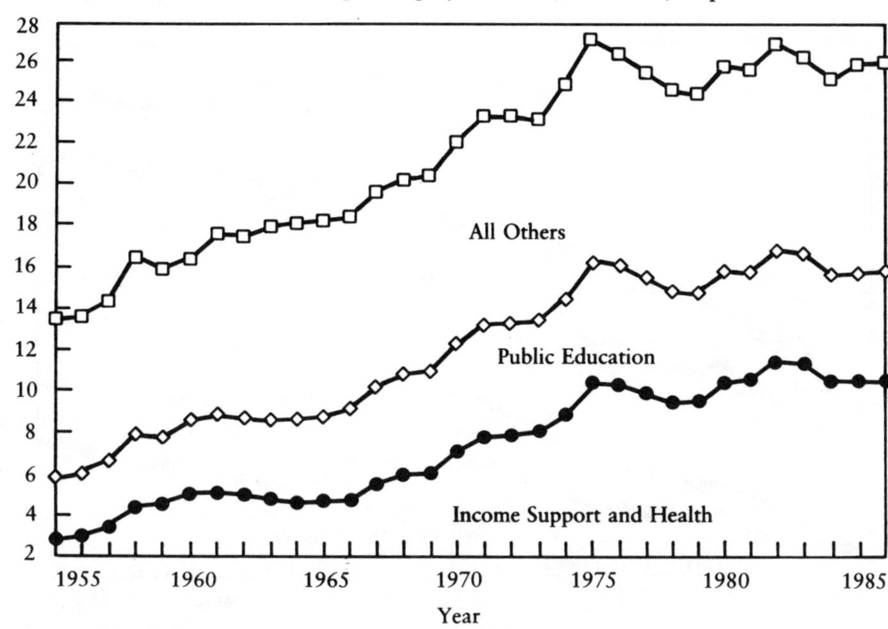

Source: U.S. Department of Commerce, Bureau of Economic Analysis, *Survey of Current Business*, various years (Washington, D.C.: Government Printing Office).

vate uses and nondefense-program spending. In the latter is all direct public spending, less defense spending less interest payments. The data subtract grants from the federal government to state and local governments to avoid double counting.

Figure 7-1 shows nondefense program spending by function as a share of GNP. Over the 1955-1986 period, spending for income support and health programs grew from 3 percent of GNP to close to 11 percent, with part of the growth in the health programs and the remainder largely in social security. Programs for low-income support—public assistance, food stamps, and public housing—also were one component responsible for growth up to the mid-1970s, but since that time they declined relative to GNP.

As mentioned, spending for public education also grew as a share of GNP, from 3 to 5 percent over the period. The remainder (Figure 7-1's "all others"), spending in all other nondefense areas—transportation, public safety, environmental protection, agriculture, labor training—remained relatively stable, rising from 8 to 10 percent of GNP over the three decades. The total peaked at 27 percent of GNP

Figure 7-2.   Nondefense spending by government, 1955–88, as percent of GNP

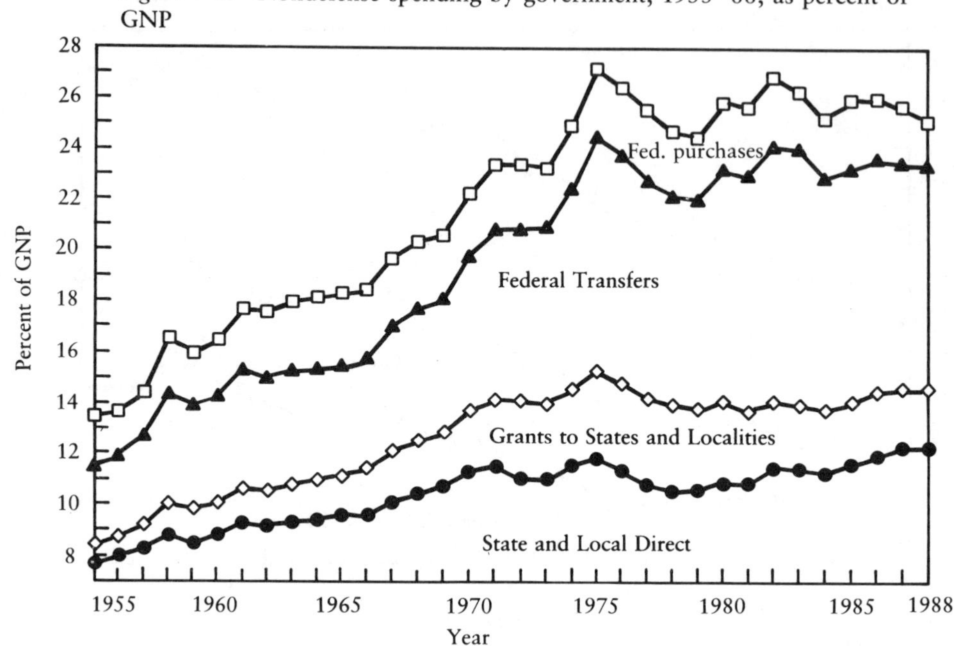

Source: U.S. Department of Commerce, Bureau of Economic Analysis, *Survey of Current Business,* various years (Washington, D.C.: Government Printing Office).

Note: The second line refers to the total spending of state and local governments. Deducting federal grants from that total gives the first line. Hence the difference between the two lines is just federal grants to states and localities. If one is interested in what state and local spending would be *in the absence* of grants, the answer is somewhere between these two lines. If all of grants raise spending, state and local spending in the absence of grants would be the first line. If all of grants lower state and local taxes and have no impact on spending, state and local spending in the absence of grants would be the second line, just what total state and local spending is in actuality.

back in 1975 and in 1989 was 25 percent of GNP. But unemployment insurance, one of the components of income support, is very cyclical, and when adjusted for cyclical variation, the share of nondefense spending in GNP was in 1989 approximately what it was in the mid-1970s. The cyclically adjusted spending share rose from 15 percent of GNP in 1955 to 25 percent of GNP in 1974, and has since held steady at that level.

Figure 7-2 shows these trends by level of government spending. The total is obviously the same total as in Figure 7-1. Total spending by states and localities (the second line) rose from 8 percent in 1955 to 14 percent in 1988, again with all the growth occurring before 1975. Grants from the federal government to states and localities grew some over the period.

In any event, the largest growth in spending over the period was for federal transfers for income support—mainly social security—and health programs, the same growth that we saw in Figure 7-1. Federal purchases of goods and services for nondefense programs are relatively small and stable by comparison, consisting of not much more than the wages of nondefense civil servants.

CAN BUDGET DEFICITS BE IGNORED?

Given the rise in indicators of national need and the unwillingness to raise taxes, it is tempting to conclude that budget deficits should simply be ignored. Public spending needs are immediate and visible; the costs of deficits are long term and subtle. Moreover, economists on both the right and the left have given voice to this skepticism about the effect of budget deficits by arguing that deficits are not harmful, or at any rate are less harmful than altering fiscal policy to correct the deficits (on the left, see Eisner 1989; on the right, see Kotlikoff 1986 and Barro 1989). Since it is so critical to the topic here, I want to argue that deficits are harmful and should be corrected. Failure to correct them will make the social problems worse, not better, in the long run.

The Impact of Deficits on Living Standards

Budget deficits play a different role in the short and long run. In the short run, they can arise from cyclical declines in tax revenues, operate to stabilize the economy, and prevent GNP from falling. In the long run, the flexibility of wages and prices naturally stabilize such business cycles, and deficits absorb private saving that would otherwise be funneled back into private investment. Hence, while deficits can boost output in the short run, by reducing the rate of private capital formation, they lower output in the long run.

Making the case that deficits cause long-term harm requires several logical steps. The first is the answer to the question of whether increases in the budget deficit lower national saving rates. Since federal saving or dissaving is one component of national saving, na-

Figure 7-3. National and federal saving, 1955–88, as percent of GNP

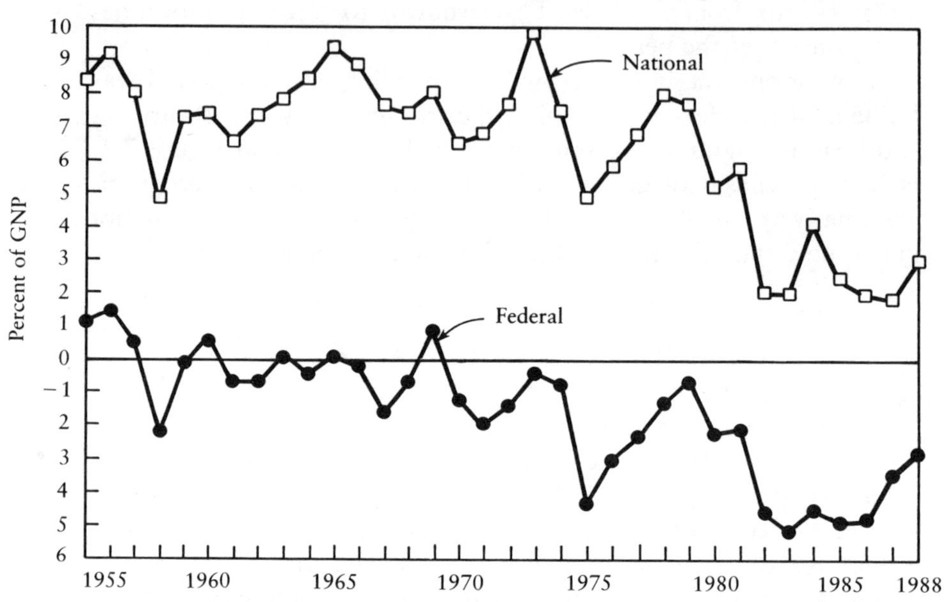

Source: U.S. Department of Commerce, Bureau of Economic Analysis, *Survey of Current Business,* various years (Washington, D.C.: Government Printing Office).

Note: The test of whether the federal budget surplus (FS) influences overall national saving (NS) is conducted either in level or first difference form by statistical regressions of the following form.

Level regression:

$$\frac{NS}{Y} = 8.37 + 1.081 \; \frac{FS}{Y} - .052 \; U, \quad R^2 = .793, \quad SE = 1.10$$
$$\phantom{\frac{NS}{Y} = 8.37 + } (6.1) \phantom{\frac{FS}{Y}} (-0.2)$$

Difference regression:

$$\Delta\!\left(\frac{NS}{Y}\right) = \; .553 \; \Delta\!\left(\frac{FS}{Y}\right) - .623 \; \Delta U, \quad R^2 = .743, \quad SE = .79$$
$$\phantom{\Delta\!\left(\frac{NS}{Y}\right) = } (2.9) \phantom{\Delta\!\left(\frac{FS}{Y}\right)} (-2.6)$$

NS = Net national saving (gross saving less depreciation)
FS = Federal budget surplus (negative if a deficit)
Y = GNP
U = Unemployment rate (to correct for cycle)
Standard errors are in parentheses.

tional savings rates will be automatically reduced unless deficits are offset by contrary movements in private saving, as Barro would argue, or unless some cyclical phenomena break the correlation, as Eisner would argue. Without getting into the many technicalities raised by either argument (discussed in Bernheim 1989 and Gramlich 1989), the basic facts seem rather clearly to argue that increases in budget deficits do lead to lower national saving rates.

The time series are in Figure 7-3, and it seems plain that the rise in the federal deficit has led to a corresponding drop in net national saving (gross saving less depreciation). It also seems clear that net national saving rates are at extremely low levels these days, lower than at any time since World War II. The regressions at the bottom of Figure 3 are meant to take this argument beyond the eyeball stage—the federal surplus variable is seen to be strongly significant with the proper sign whether in levels or first differences. It raises national saving dollar for dollar in the level regression, and by half of this amount in the first difference regression.

Given that the deficit reduces the net national saving rates, what next? In a closed economy, where international capital flows do not exist, reduced saving implies reduced investment, and this leads to reduced growth of the capital stock and lower levels of GNP per capita in the long run (see Gramlich 1984, Tobin 1986, and Romer 1988 for successively more complex treatments). In an open economy, where international capital flows are important, reduced saving implies higher foreign borrowing, and this higher foreign borrowing also leads to reduced levels of GNP in the long run, as resources are devoted to repaying dividends and interest to foreigners (see Ribe and Beeman 1986). Either way, there is a shift of consumption resources from the future to the present, or a drop in the rate of improvement of living standards.

This drop in the rate of improvement of living standards is all too evident from the data. As Figure 7-4 shows, there was a sharp drop in the rate of the GNP per worker—that is, productivity improvement—between 1975 and 1988. From the cyclical peak of 1955 to the cyclical peak of 1973, U.S. GNP per worker rose at an annual rate of 1.7 percent; from the cyclical peak of 1973 to the cyclical peak of 1988 the annual improvement in GNP per worker was down to 0.1 percent. Had GNP per worker continued growing at its earlier rate in the post-1973 period, it would have been 23 percent higher by 1988.

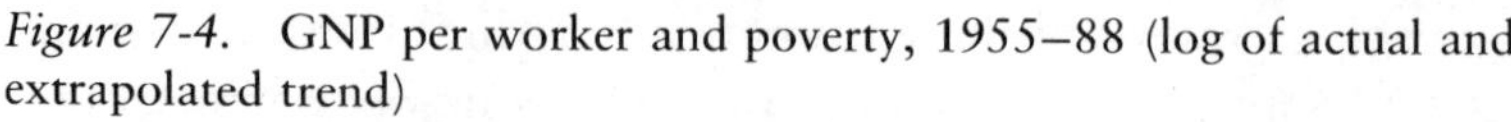

Figure 7-4.   GNP per worker and poverty, 1955–88 (log of actual and extrapolated trend)

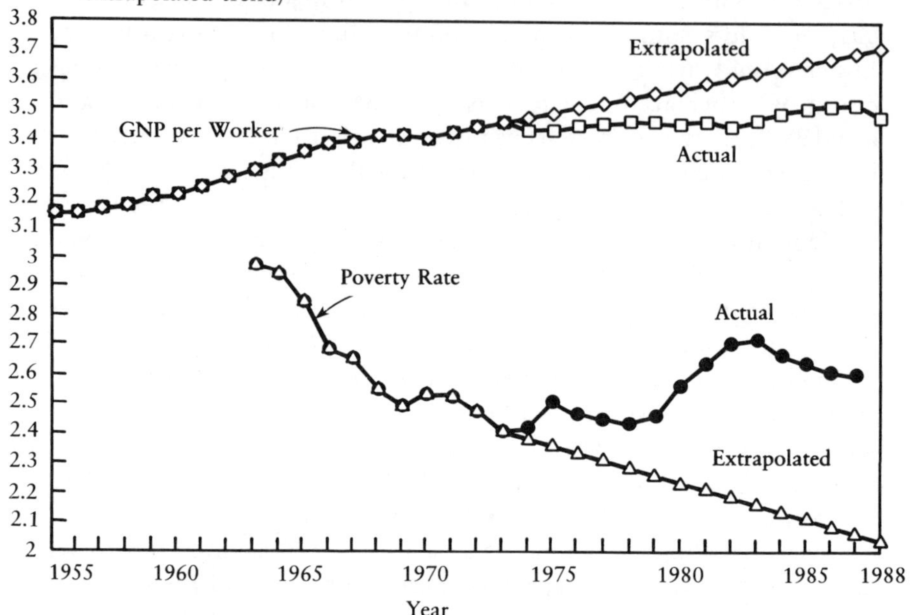

Source: U.S. Department of Commerce, Bureau of Economic Analysis, *Survey of Current Business*, various years (Washington, D.C.: Government Printing Office).

Note: GNP per worker is extrapolated from the average growth rate between 1955 and 1973, and the poverty rate is extrapolated by inserting this GNP per worker into the first difference regression.

Level regression:

$$\ln P = 9.51 - 2.115 \ \ln \frac{Y}{L} + .196 \ln U, \quad R^2 = .420, \ SE = .122$$
$$\quad\quad\quad (-4.0) \quad\quad\quad (2.0)$$

Difference regression:

$$\Delta\ln P = \quad\quad -1.457 \ \Delta\ln\frac{Y}{L} + .197 \ \Delta\ln U, \quad R^2 = .603, \ SE = .041$$
$$(-2.6) \quad\quad\quad (3.2)$$

P = Percent of population living in poverty
Y = Real GNP
L = Employed labor force
U = Unemployment rate
Difference equation used to extrapolate poverty

Since the drop in productivity occurred before most of the short-fall in national saving and capital stock, there must certainly have been other causes. But while not enough time has elapsed to assess the results of the recent experiment with low national saving rates and capital formation, the low national saving rates of the 1980s must also play some role in prolonging the present productivity slowdown.

The Impact of Living Standards on Social Problems

No reason necessarily exists to explain why social problem indicators should depend on the level of living standards. At least among the developed countries of the world, societies can be slightly poorer or slightly richer, and raise a high or a low share of their population out of poverty, depending on their wage distribution, their degree of altruism, and other factors.

While almost any relationship can hold in principle, for the United States it seems clear that the right model is President John F. Kennedy's saying that "a rising tide lifts all boats." Historically, a striking relationship exists between the level and growth of overall income and the reduction in poverty and other measures of social problems. This relationship can be seen in Figure 7-4. Up until 1973, when aggregate income was growing at a healthy rate (1.7 percent per year), the poverty rate was declining at a healthy rate (5.6 percent per year). Since that time, the growth of aggregate income has dropped sharply and the poverty rate has actually increased.

The regressions at the bottom of Figure 7-4 again try to formalize the relationship. These regressions are in log form, to represent that poverty should decline asymptotically as aggregate income rises. Whether in levels or first differences, the negative impact of aggregate income is strong and significant, as is the positive impact of unemployment. The level equation has a standard error of 12 percent of the poverty rate, the first difference standard error is only 4 percent. When this first difference equation is used to predict the poverty rate if aggregate income had kept on growing at its earlier rate, the predicted poverty rate in 1988 was only 7.7 percent, as is shown in the bottom line, less than three-fifths of the actual poverty rate.

There are other ways to measure the impact of economic growth on social indicators. Similar regressions can be fit to the nondefense program spending levels shown in Figures 7-1 and 7-2. These regressions show that nondefense program spending would be on the order of 25 percent higher had income growth continued at its former rate. While one would not want to take any such calculations too literally, it seems clear that productivity slowdown has a major downward impact both on the living standards of the poor and on the level of social spending.

This is the reason why the United States cannot ignore budget deficits. They are important in determining the level of living standards in the long run, and living standards in turn feed back onto social problems, such as poverty, homelessness, and inadequate health care. In the United States, a minimum requirement for an attack on the nation's social problems seems to be that overall living standards should be rising at healthy rates; and living standards are unlikely to rise at healthy rates again until government reduces its budget deficits.

ECONOMIC EFFICIENCY, TAX-FINANCED PUBLIC SPENDING

The political impasse is about finding ways to attend to social problems without raising deficits or taxes. The economic puzzle is deeper: Should decision makers agree on levels of government spending and then finance this spending by taxes, or agree on tax levels and adjust spending to meet taxes? In this country, the usual approach of economists is to decide on spending levels first and assume that taxes can adjust. In a country like Sweden, where marginal tax rates are close to their practical maximum, the usual approach is to consider taxes as given and try to work spending down to this predetermined level. In this section, I dust off an old argument that gives a general approach for dealing with this question.

Economists base their aversion to taxation on their belief that taxes distort economic activity. An income tax penalizes work and rewards leisure, for reasons unrelated to the intrinsic values of work and leisure. By taxing saving when an individual first saves and again when that person earns interest, an income tax also penalizes saving and rewards consumption, for reasons unrelated to the intrinsic values of saving and consumption. A payroll tax raises the cost of labor, an excise tax does the same to the cost of the taxed commodity, and a property tax does the same for property and improvements.

However, these penalties do not cause economic distortions if behavior is insensitive to tax rates. If the demand or supply of an activity or a good is inelastic, the government can tax the activity or the good without distorting the pattern of resource allocation that would otherwise hold. This is why the distortion implicit in any tax is proportional to some measure of the sensitivity of demand and supply to the tax. It can also be shown that the distortionary cost of any tax is proportional to the square of the tax rate.

As Pigou (1947) first recognized, this reasoning suggests that the general answer to the question of whether one should make decisions about spending and trust the tax system to finance this spending, or go at it the other way around, depends on the distortionary cost of the tax to be used to finance this spending. If tax rates are already high and the sensitivity of activity to this tax is high, the true social cost of added spending includes the added distortion and is also high. If the distortionary cost is low, or better yet, if raising some tax rates would reduce economic inefficiency, the true cost of the spending is much lower (see also Atkinson and Stiglitz 1980).

This is all shown in Figure 7-5. The downward-sloping line is the demand for some public service, say a public transportation system, which shows at each level of spending how much additional benefit society would derive from a small increment in the level of service. (Economists refer to this as the "marginal social benefit" curve.) The horizontal line shows the cost of providing each marginal increment of spending if a perfectly nondistortionary tax, say a user fee, financed the spending. That is, if no distortions were introduced by raising the funds to pay for the marginal increment of the service (one more bus route, say), each dollar of added service would cost society one dollar. However, when financed by a distortionary tax, such as a local income tax, each incremental dollar of spending will cost society more than a dollar, and the added cost of another dollar's worth of service rises with the level of the service provided, since the impact of the distortion becomes more severe.

The higher of the two upward-sloping supply curves captures the distortion, which combines the resource cost of adding to the level of service with the cost of the distortion. Notice that as the quantity of public services increases, the distortionary cost increases disproportionately, because the tax rate is rising to finance the higher level

Figure 7-5. Tax-financed public spending

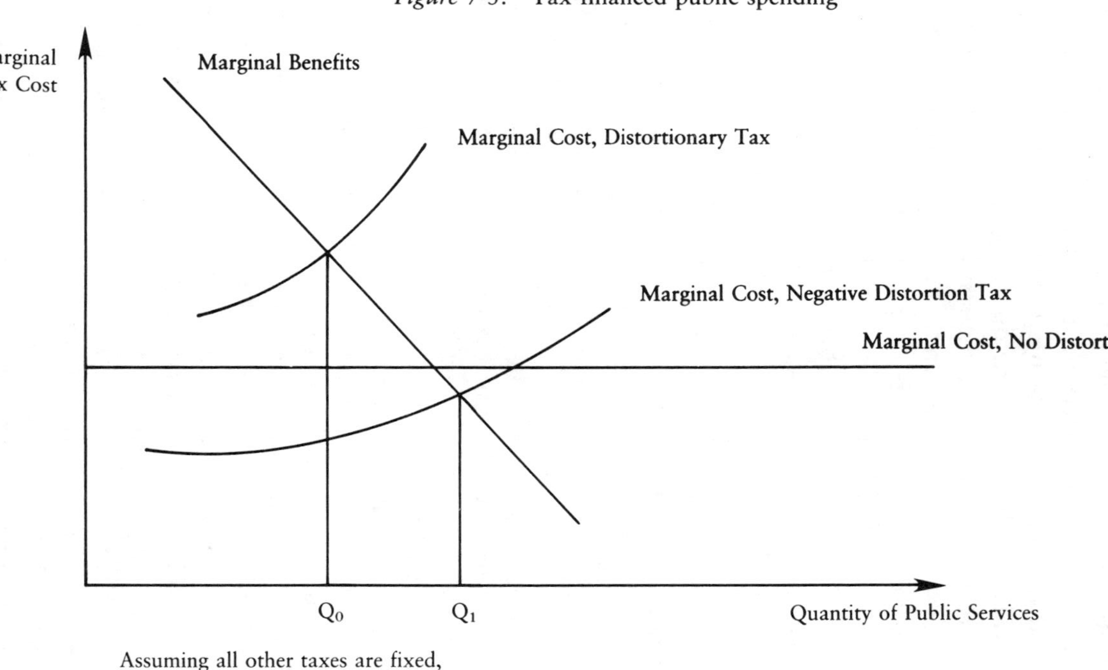

Assuming all other taxes are fixed,
   Q_0 is quantity if financed by a distortionary tax
   Q_1 is quantity if financed by a negative distortion tax

If other taxes are not fixed, negative distortion taxes should be used until they become equally distortionary with existing taxes, and the overall optimum is where MB equals the new MC.

of service. The lower of the two upward-sloping curves shows that the picture is different if the distortionary tax is targeted toward an activity that is socially beneficial to discourage—for example, if the government imposes excise taxes on goods with negative external effects (e.g., through a cigarette tax) or if closing loopholes in the tax system raises the needed revenues. The overall marginal cost of such a "negative distortion tax" is still upward sloping, but it is lower throughout than that of a distortionary tax, which lacks this favorable side effect of discouraging activities that are not socially beneficial.[1]

The optimum quantity of the public service is that at which the cost of adding to the level of service just equals the social benefit of that increment. Graphically, this is the point at which the marginal benefit line intersects the marginal cost curve. On the figure, the marginal benefit intersects the three marginal cost lines at points specific to those lines. This illustrates that choosing the relevant marginal cost curve depends on which taxes finance the expenditure on the service. If a distortionary tax finances the service, the optimal quantity of services that the tax will finance is Q_0. If a negative distortion tax finances the service, the optimal quantity is the larger amount Q_1. This simple argument shows why Swedes and Americans can have different ways of thinking about optimal social output and even different optimal quantities of precisely the same public service. For our purposes, it shows the important role of eliminating economic inefficiencies: If negative distortion taxes can be found, optimal social spending is much greater.

This diagram assumes first that all other taxes are fixed, and the government is just designating one tax to serve as the marginal source of finance. If decision makers were to confront the broader problem of deciding all taxes and spending simultaneously, the general way to proceed would be to use all taxes until their marginal costs were the same and then have the marginal benefits of spending equal this common marginal cost. The diagram also assumes that the jurisdiction is in budgetary equilibrium, where spending equals taxes, and the only question is the one of how to finance any added spending. If, as suggested above, there is a need to reduce deficits, some low-priority types of spending should be cut, and some of the good negative distortion taxes should be used up in rectifying the budget imbalance. Again, there would not be full budgetary adjustment until the marginal costs of all taxes were the same, until the marginal benefits of spending equalled this common marginal cost, and until budget deficits and national saving rates were at their desired levels.

It is impossible to conduct such a simultaneous budgetary analysis here. Instead, I will focus on incremental policy changes that seem to move toward this overall optimum point by reducing budget deficits, making use of negative distortion taxes, or some combination. On the tax side, I mention only three specific measures: closing tax loopholes, levying energy taxes, and levying externality taxes. A fourth measure, child-support enforcement, is discussed in this section because it raises issues common to those of other taxes.

Closing Tax Loopholes

Measures that close tax loopholes qualify as negative distortion taxes because uneven tax rates distort the pattern of economic activity. But it is not straightforward to identify a tax loophole or a distortion, because one's definition hinges on whether one views income or expenditures as the desired tax base—a very controversial topic among economists (Pechman 1980). For this discussion I sidestep that debate by considering loopholes to be only those changes that would be moves toward both a comprehensive income and expenditure tax.

To take perhaps the most obvious case, consider the deduction of mortgage interest on the personal income tax. This mortgage-interest deduction is a tax loophole under either an income or an expenditure tax because the interest cost of borrowing is deductible but the return, the return from owning a home, the rent one does not have to pay, is not taxable. Distortions of this sort can cause, first, what is known as an arbitrage problem, where homeowners switch their borrowing to deductible form without making any change in their saving or investment behavior. In this case, the deduction causes a straight transfer to these borrowers, with no impact on the pattern of spending at all. There is no distortion in the pattern of spending, but there is an unwarranted tax giveaway. Gordon and Slemrod (1988) find the astonishing result that because of tax arbitrage, the U.S. government actually loses revenue in trying to tax capital income. The same exists for many European countries.

But the interest deduction can distort as well. It can increase investment in housing as compared to other forms of capital, such as plant and equipment investment, and thus shift the country away from the optimal allocation of investment funds. It can also encourage borrowing at the expense of self-financing of homes. For the business sector, the deductibility of interest but not of dividends encourages firms to use debt finance excessively and increases the risk of bankruptcy. It is also one of the factors behind the recent surge in leveraged buyouts, which are ultimately attempts to switch from equity to debt finance.

There are other such loopholes. The federal income tax deduction for state and local taxes might seem to stimulate valuable state and local spending, but a careful analysis leads to skepticism. Most voters in state and local elections do not itemize deductions, so it is quite unlikely that the tax deduction will raise public spending at the margin in most communities. In these communities, the deduction is a simple giveaway to high-income taxpayers. But the deduction should raise public spending in high-income communities with lots of itemizers, and these communities would not seem to need the subsidy (Gramlich 1985).

Another important loophole involves fringe benefits. Firms can deduct these fringe benefits, the most important of which is employer-paid health insurance, but they are not taxable to individual workers. This loophole encourages firms to pay employees more in tax-free form and less in taxable form than the underlying demands would merit.

The CBO (1988) estimated that if Congress completely eliminated by 1993 fourteen such loopholes, government revenues would rise by the whopping total of $137 billion, 2.1 percent of GNP, and more than the baseline deficit in that year. Such a change would also represent a social revolution in America, and a sober analyst might bet against its full occurrence. But that is not the point. The point is that full or partial loophole-closing measures could raise up to this amount of revenue. And there are many such partial approaches that could generate substantial revenue gains while they make large reductions in tax distortions:

- Deductions could be capped or allowed only in excess of a certain share of taxpayer income.
- Deductions could be made partial—only a fraction of some expense could be made deductible.
- Deductions could only be allowed at the lower bracket marginal tax rate, 15 percent.

- Deductibility rules could be tightened, say by not allowing mortgage deductions on second homes or for certain types of state and local taxes.
- The distortionary impact of deductions could be lessened by raising the standard deduction and adjusting other parameters of the tax system to raise revenue.

With so many possibilities, it makes little sense to suggest a specific plan. There are many that could reduce significantly the impasse between social needs and budget deficits. It is not particularly noteworthy that up to 2 percent of GNP, the nation can have as much revenue as it is willing to raise. It is noteworthy that revenues on this scale can be raised while at the same time raising the efficiency of the tax system.

Energy Taxes

The second type of negative distortion tax involves energy. Since the oil crisis of the mid-1970s, it has been generally recognized that the U.S. economy is vulnerable to price or supply shocks and that there is a long-run interest in conserving energy, more so than if a free market existed. Moreover, since the United States consumes a significant share of the world's energy, U.S. energy taxes will reduce U.S. demand, world demand, and the world price. In that sense, they will be shifted partly onto foreign suppliers of energy. When to these factors is added the artificial encouragement that the income tax still gives to energy exploration, there is a good case for raising the price of energy through an energy tax.

There are several ways to do it. The most neutral is a tax on all forms of energy use, called a British thermal unit (BTU) tax. Such a tax would have neutral effects on domestic supplies of energy and imports and on different fuel sources—oil, natural gas, coal, and other sources of power. It would raise the most revenue at the lowest tax rates for any set tax rate. The tax could favor domestic supplies at the expense of imports by adding an oil-import fee. On the one hand, that would increase incentives to invest in domestic supplies; on the other, there would be an incentive to drain America's supplies of oil first. Or, by adding a gasoline tax, the tax could be levied against unnecessary driving more than necessary heating oil.

As with closing loopholes, there are many options, all of which could raise significant amounts of revenue. A broad-based tax on all forms of energy could raise up to $40 billion, an oil-import fee of $5 a barrel could raise more than $20 billion, as could a gasoline tax of $.20 a gallon. There is also no reason not to combine these taxes, with a low-rate, broad-based tax supplemented by additional levies on gasoline and on oil imports. In each case, the distortion is likely to be small or negative because present energy prices may well be too low in the sense that they do not cover the social cost, and because the tax will be partly shifted abroad in the form of lower world prices for energy.

Externality Taxes

Negative externalities occur when certain private activities impose costs on others, costs that do not reflect the prices paid by those private parties engaging in the activity. The remedy is to impose a tax on these negative externality activities to make the prices better conform to true social costs. Many examples of such negative externality taxes are now assessed, such as the fairly low rates on cigarettes, wine, beer, spirits, and emissions of hazardous materials. But in each case, analysts figure these tax rates well below the levels necessary to bring about the efficient outcome where the price structure reflects all external costs. The CBO (1988) worked out a conservative option for taxing smoking, drinking, and emissions, raising federal revenue $20 billion in the process. Again we have the situation where the government could raise revenue while it makes consumption choices better reflect true social costs (including the higher expected medical expenses).

Child-Support Enforcement

The Aid to Families with Dependent Children (AFDC) program, commonly known as welfare, makes most of its $11 billion in payments to female-headed families with children. For a variety of legal, political, and institutional reasons, taxpayers in general make most of these payments, with absent fathers having to pay very little for the support of their offspring. Only 60 percent of mothers eligible for child support get court awards, and these awards are generally considered to be inadequate. Only half the parents with awards receive the full amount due them, and a quarter receive nothing.

The system has been changing gradually over time. By 1988, each state had a child-support enforcement (CSE) program, an expedited procedure for establishing paternity, obtaining support orders for payment amounts, and providing for automatic withholding of child-support payments when absent parents fall behind in their payments. The Welfare Reform Act of 1988 introduced financial penalties for states that did not establish paternity in at least half of the cases and provided for immediate withholding of support payments even before absent parents fell behind in their payments. But it did not nationalize the program—meaning that absent parents can generally escape the automatic withholding by moving out of state. The changes up to 1988 brought in about $3 billion in child-support payments from absent fathers, lowering public welfare costs a like amount, and the 1988 changes brought in some more. But even with the recent changes, only 10 percent of AFDC households now receive any financial support from absent parents (Garfinkel and Wong 1987), and as long as the program is run by states, there is a real limit on how much can ever be brought in.

CSE payments to mothers and the federal government could be increased by:

- Nationalizing the withholding system to collect automatically from absent parents, no matter which state they live in.
- Replacing the present court orders for payment amounts with a flat-rate increase in the payroll tax, a certain amount per child. Such a change would enable both the mother and the government to keep pace with inflation over time and share in any real income gains of the absent parent.
- Requiring that states establish paternity in all cases.

These changes would directly raise income-support levels for low-income families with children and reduce federal and state welfare costs. The changes would improve fairness in the welfare system, in the sense that those responsible for a budget problem would have to pay for it. And there could be efficiency improvements as well. An effective CSE program would place an added low-rate tax on absent fathers to pay the support costs of the mother and children. Since payments would go to the mother as a matter of right, the government would not tax away, in the form of lower welfare benefits, rises in her earnings, eliminating this high-rate tax on the mother's earnings. Hence, a low tax rate on the absent father's earnings would replace a high tax rate on the mother's earnings. This may not seem worth writing home about, but given that the distortion cost is proportional to the square of the tax rate, the change could cut the distortionary cost substantially. Again we have the happy confluence of rises in social spending, cuts in the federal deficit, and increases in economic efficiency.

Economic Efficiency, Grant-Financed Public Spending

Just as negative distortion taxes can help resolve the impasse between social needs and low national saving, so also can improvements in the structure of grants from the federal government to states and localities. These grants now amount to about 2.5 percent of GNP, as we saw back in Figure 7-2. Some are open ended, where states can spend as much as they want, with the federal government matching all this spending at some predetermined rate. Some are close ended, where the federal government matches state spending at a predetermined rate, but only up to a predetermined limit. One irony of the federal grant system is that close-ended grants are used where open-ended grants would make more sense, and open-ended grants are used where close-ended would make more sense. Both sides can gain improved outcomes.

Let us first examine the case where there are positive externalities—that is, spending by one state on, say, pollution control, roads, education, or hospitals, makes citizens in other states better off. In such cases, efficient grants should be open ended, but most actual, real world grants are close-ended. The situation is shown in Figure 7-6. As before, a horizontal line shows the marginal cost (in terms of resources) for the public service in question, say pollution control. But this time there are two demand functions: the lower one gives the marginal benefit of the program to a particular state or community, and the upper one gives the marginal benefit of the program to all states combined. These two demand functions differ because of the positive externalities; some outside the state benefit from the pollution control.

The hatched line shows the cost to the state of providing this service under the typical present close-ended federal grant. Up to the output corresponding to the grant limit, Q_L, the federal government pays a generous share of the cost of the public service, usually 80

Figure 7-6.   Grant-financed public spending where externalities exist

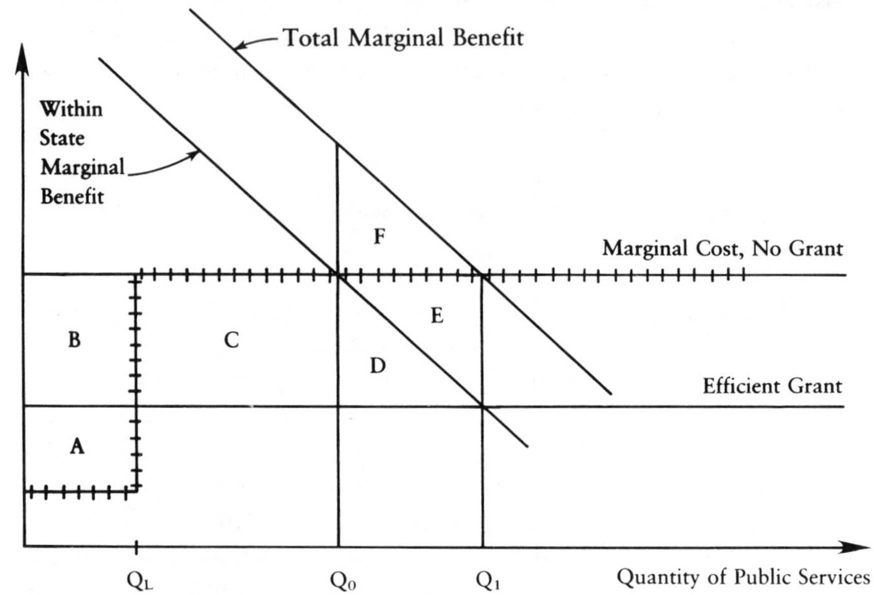

Present close-ended grants
Q_0 is spending level with present grants
Q_1 is spending level with open-ended, low matching grants
Q_L is grant limit for present close-ended grants

Federal tax saving is area $A - C - D - E$
State gain is area $C + D - A$
Out-of-state gain is area $E + F$
Efficiency gain is area F

percent or more, so the cost facing the community is low. After this level, no further federal funds are available, and the marginal cost to the community reverts to the no-grant cost curve. The state, equating the marginal benefits to its citizens to the marginal cost it faces, will select a level of spending of Q_0 in this case, less than the social optimum where the overall marginal benefit equals the overall marginal cost, because there is no price subsidy at the margin. In the pollution-control example, the state would be ignoring the marginal benefits received by those out-of-state when it determined its spending level.

Efficiency could be served by switching to an open-ended grant, where the state would continue to receive a subsidy on each added dollar of spending, though at a less generous matching rate. That rate should be set so that spending equals the optimal level Q_1, where the federal contribution is equal to the amount of benefit going to out-of-state residents. The principle used here is simply that first laid down by Lindahl (see his article in Musgrave and Peacock 1985) in his attempt to determine how different citizens should be taxed for public goods from which all benefit.

Were grants to be made open-ended, the federal government would gain revenue from a reduced matching rate and would lose revenue from a higher level of service selected by the state. The net effect on federal revenues is shown by area A-C-D-E in Figure 7-6. If the current federal matching share is generous and if the state or local spending demand is not price sensitive, as seems to be the case for most matching grants, the net effect on federal revenue will be positive, implying reduced federal spending.

But the change to the open-ended grants will serve the goal of economic efficiency, too. The present close-ended grant does not stimulate state spending at the margin, even though more spending is socially desirable. The open-ended grant would encourage spending up to Q_1 because of the price reduction, and society would gain area F in the diagram. Again we have a way to use economic efficiency simultaneously to reduce deficits, and distortionary costs and raise social spending.

Now consider where grants are given for reasons other than externalities and are open-ended, such as for public assistance to low-income families. This situation is shown in Figure 7-7. The figure is drawn so that the preferences of different states for the relevant public service differ, as given by the high- and low-demand function. The key assumption here is that there is some overriding national interest in standardizing benefits, say because direct beneficiaries of the service will move to a state where benefits are better as long as service differentials exist across states. If so, there is a cost to differences in tastes across states, and there is a social benefit in reducing disparities between benefit levels.

Were open-ended grants used, spending would be Q_L in the low- and Q_H high-benefit state. This disparity in benefit levels could be closed by converting the present open-ended grant to the hatched line, resulting in no change in benefits in the high-benefit state but an increase in the low-benefit state. Converting to close-ended grants would reduce the inefficiencies of large disparities in benefits, though

Figure 7-7.   Grant-financed public spending where taste differences are costly

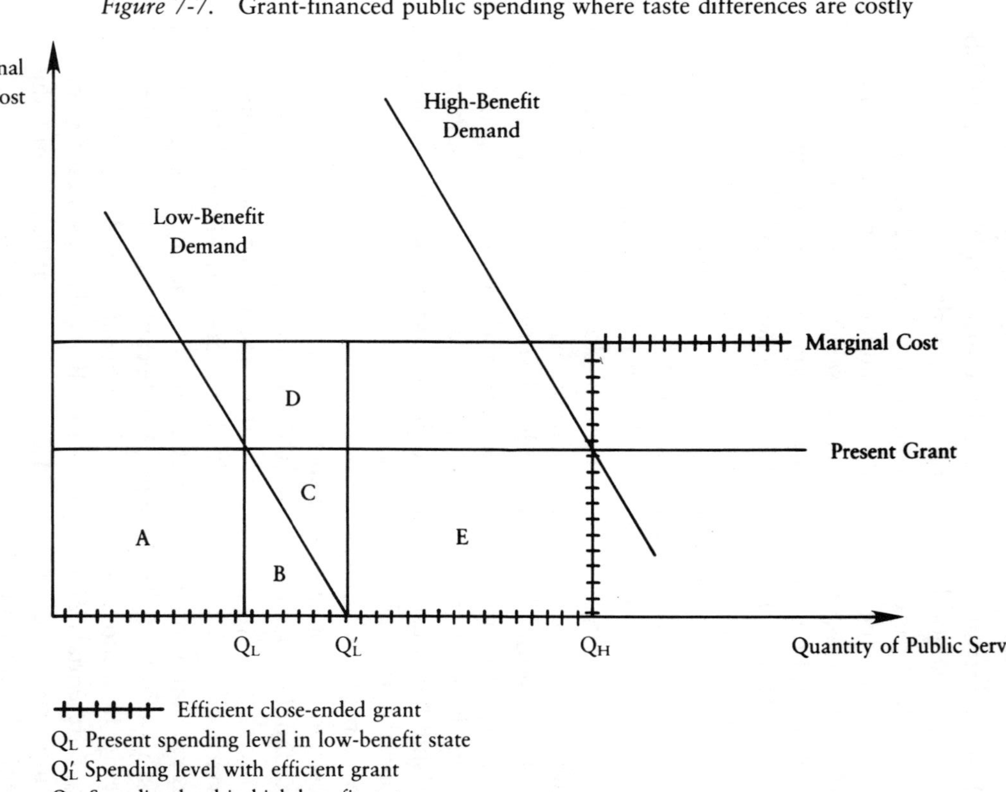

Efficient close-ended grant
Q_L Present spending level in low-benefit state
Q_L' Spending level with efficient grant
Q_H Spending level in high-benefit state

Change in federal outlays on low-benefit state is area $A+B+C+D$
Change in federal outlays in high-benefit state is area $A+B+C+E$

this time there would be an increase in federal budget outlays. This increase is given by area $A + B + C + D$ in the low-benefit state and area $A + B + C + E$ in the high-benefit state. By introducing kinks, or discontinuities, in the grant schedules, this high-benefit state could cut back this latter increase without any change in spending. If, for example, the federal grant paid the full cost up to Q'_L and then switched to the present matching schedule, the federal government would not pay area E to the high-benefit state.

Converting Close-Ended to Open-Ended Grants

There were in 1988 about $30 billion of close-ended grants that could profitably be converted to open-ended grants to deal with externalities. About half are for the interstate highway system; the remainder are for mass transit, airports, sewage treatment, vocational education, and various types of social services. With the interstate highway system it is possible to align grants and state and local spending and to gain an approximate measure of the share of benefits realized by state and by outsiders. There it appears that a conversion to efficient grants would increase total state and local spending by 17 percent but reduce federal outlays by 30 percent (Gramlich 1990). Scaling these numbers up to all grants leads to a federal outlay saving of about $8 billion, a rise in social spending, and of course an improvement in economic efficiency.

Converting Open-Ended to Close-Ended Grants

AFDC is the best example of a program in which grants could be converted to close ended to deal with taste differences. As mentioned above, this program now costs the federal government about $11 billion. The federal government makes open-ended grants to states with federal matching shares that range from 50 percent in high-income states to 80 percent in low-income states. Even with this price differential, state benefit payments differ widely. Combined benefits for AFDC and food stamps for families with no other income are about half the poverty line in low-benefit states and about at the poverty line in high-benefit states. An efficiency cost of these benefits is that they set up costly incentives for families to move to high-benefit states. Others who view income support as a national responsibility and desire nationally standard benefits feel there is an additional problem with horizontal equity: Families of different incomes are treated differently depending on where they live.

Over the years, many proposals have been put forth for standardizing benefits, none of which has made it through the Congress. Another approach would be to forswear outright standardization but to work through the grant formula instead. Rather than making grants open-ended and based on state income, which imperfectly correlates with the benefit levels voted on by states, the matching ratio could be based on benefit levels themselves. Referring to Figure 7-7, an illustrative plan might have the federal government pay all the costs up to 60 percent of the poverty line, 75 percent of the costs up to 80 percent of the poverty line, 50 percent of the costs up to the poverty line, and no costs after that. Such a formula would operate like a close-ended grant, and as the figure shows, it would compress benefits. I previously estimated that it would raise overall AFDC payments to low-income people by about 6 percent, all in low-benefit states. As mentioned above, this change would raise federal costs by about $7 billion at 1988 prices (Gramlich 1987). While raising income-support benefits where they are already so low would seem a high-priority use of marginal funds, and could be defended from an efficiency standpoint given the costs of families moving to high-benefit states, this time a rise in federal spending for AFDC would accompany a rise in social spending.

IMPLICATIONS

The impasse between the desire to raise social spending and the desire to cut deficits and devote more funds to saving and investment seems to set up an irresolvable conflict, a conflict that can be broken only by finding efficiency gains in either the tax system or the grant system. This paper suggests many such gains. On the tax side, closing loopholes simultaneously brings in revenue and reduces budget deficits, improves economic efficiency, and makes possible an increase in social program spending. The same is true for increases in taxes on energy or on activities that generate negative externalities. Increases in child-support enforcement payments directly raise the incomes of low-income families and reduce public welfare outlays, while again lessening transfer-induced distortions. Measures to alter the structure of federal grants also eliminate distortions, raise public spending, and lower federal spending. Since there are no other ways to resolve the impasse, maybe it is time to consider some of these measures.

Notes

1.   Notice that even in the case of a "negative distortion tax," the supply curve still slopes up because as the quantity of public services increases, the tax rate would increase, and eventually the negative distortion would become positive.

References

Atkinson, Anthony B., and Joseph E. Stiglitz. 1980. *Lectures on Public Economics*. New York: McGraw-Hill.

Barro, Robert J. 1989. "The Ricardian Approach to Budget Deficits." *Journal of Economic Perspectives* 3:37–54.

Bernheim, B. Douglas. 1989. "A Neoclassical Perspective on Budget Deficits." *Journal of Economic Perspectives* 3:55–72.

Congressional Budget Office. 1986. *Trends in Educational Achievement*. Washington, D.C.: U.S. Government Printing Office.

——. 1988. *Reducing the Deficit: Spending and Revenue Options*. Washington, D.C.: U.S. Government Printing Office.

——. 1989. *The Economic and Budget Outlook, Fiscal Years 1990–94*, Washington, D.C.: U.S. Government Printing Office.

Eisner, Robert. 1989. "Budget Deficits: Rhetoric and Reality." *Journal of Economic Perspectives* 3:73–93.

Ellwood, David T. 1988. *Poor Support: Poverty in the American Family*. New York: Basic Books.

Garfinkel, Irwin, and Patrick Wong, 1987. "Child Support and Public Policy." Institute for Research on Poverty, Discussion Paper 854-87, Madison, Wis.

Gordon, Roger H., and Joel Slemrod. 1988. "Do We Collect Any Revenue from Taxing Capital Income?" In Lawrence H. Summers, ed., *Tax Policy and the Economy*, vol. 2, pp. 89–130. Cambridge: MIT Press.

Gramlich, Edward M. 1984. "How Bad Are the Large Deficits?" In John L. Palmer and Gregory B. Mills, eds., *Federal Budget Policy in the 1980s*, pp. 43–78. Washington, D.C.: Urban Institute.

——. 1985. "The Deductibility of State and Local Taxes." *National Tax Journal* 38:447–465.

——. 1987. "Cooperation and Competition in Public Welfare Policy." *Journal of Policy Analysis and Management* 6:417–431.

——. 1989. "Budget Deficits and National Saving: Are Politicians Exogenous?" *Journal of Economic Perspectives* 3:23–35.

——. 1990. *A Guide to Benefit-Cost Analysis*. Englewood Cliffs, N.J.: Prentice-Hall.

Jencks, Christopher. 1984. "The Hidden Prosperity of the 1970's." *The Public Interest* 77:37–61.

Kotlikoff, Laurence J. 1986. "Deficit Delusion." *The Public Interest* 84:53–65.

Lindahl, Erik. 1985. "Just Taxation—A Positive Solution." In Richard A. Musgrave and Alan T. Peacock, eds., *Classics in the Theory of Public Finance*, pp. 168–177 London: Macmillan.

Murray, Charles. 1984. *Losing Ground: American Social Policy, 1950-1980*. New York: Basic Books.

Pechman, Joseph A., ed. 1980. *What Should be Taxed: Income or Expenditure?* Washington, D.C.: Brookings Institution.

Pigou, A. C. 1947. *A Study in Public Finance*. London: Macmillan.

Ribe, Frederick C., and William J. Beeman. 1986. "The Monetary-Fiscal Mix and Long-Run Growth in an Open Economy. *American Economic Review* 76:209–212.

Romer, David. 1988. "What Are the Costs of Excessive Deficits?" National Bureau of Economic Research, Discussion Paper #14, Princeton, N.J.

Tobin, James. 1986. "The Monetary-Fiscal Mix: Long-Run Implications." *American Economic Review* 76:213–218.

8 The Politics of Social Policy in the 1990s

Paul E. Peterson

Social policy in the United States has reached a stalemate. As the twentieth century draws to a close, there is a sense of stagnation, of marking time, of an inability to break out of the political and institutional constraints that have gradually encased the policymaking system. As in a nightmare, we seek to escape a threatening, if ill-defined, specter about to engulf us, but our feet are weighed down, our muscles do not respond, and our strength fails us.

The other papers in this volume delineate the social problems facing the United States in the 1990s. They consist of a growing percentage of children living in poverty, a disturbing number of homeless people wandering on the streets of nearly all our major central cities, a seemingly never-ending increase in the cost of public-supported health services, a growing elderly population that a possibly shrinking work force needs to support, and a costly, inefficient system of public education that seems unable to adapt to the needs of the twenty-first century. That these and other social ills persist in a free, democratic, and affluent society is anomalous, even paradoxical. Yet the political energy to resolve, or even address, these issues is curiously dormant.

The Reagan revolution promised otherwise. For better or worse, the seizure of federal power by a conservative political movement bristling with provocative ideas and committed to changing institutional practice raised new prospects and possibilities. The new administration would curtail entitlements, privatize public services, create new choices for consumers through voucher plans and tax credits, shift downward the responsibility for public programs to states and localities through block grants and deregulation of existing programs, and reduce substantially the sheer size of government. The marketplace, the family, private philanthropy, and voluntarism would replace the bureaucrat and the social worker as the main vehicles for American social policy.

Now that the Reagan years have run their course, it is apparent that its promise went largely unfulfilled. Reagan was able to cut taxes, as he had promised. And he was able to block or blunt most new social policy initiatives. He was even partially successful in cutting some domestic expenditures, reducing a few entitlements, and deregulating some social programs. But the general pattern of the 1980s was a political stalemate that left the shape of social policy pretty much as it was the day Ronald Reagan took office. The conditions that gave rise to this stalemate, moreover, are very likely to continue in the decade to come. Social policy rhetoric may no longer ring with conservative presidential slogans. It is less likely that the American Civil Liberties Union will be accused of being the cause of homelessness, or teacher unions of being the source of American miseducation, or excessive welfare benefits of causing poverty, or iron triangles of creating burgeoning budget deficits. The politics of welfare will in this way be kindlier and gentler. But beneath the rhetoric, the political reality may well proceed more or less unchanged.

The primary cause of the current stalemate is not the iron triangle of interests groups, congressional subcommittees, and executive agencies that was once a dominant force in Washington politics. Instead, the primary cause is the division of power between a Republican-controlled executive branch and a Democratic Congress. This division leads to a stalemate not only because each side controls a crucial political institution necessary for promulgating significant change but also because each side holds a political trump card—the Republican one is named "no new taxes," while the Democratic one is labeled "no cuts in social security." With political maneuvering now shaped by these trump cards, the power of special interests and iron triangles, despite presidential rhetoric, has in fact declined significantly, and a continuous political struggle between the two political parties now is defining social policy.

The new visibility of political choice also perpetuates the stalemate. Today the choice is among cuts in domestic expenditures, increases in taxes, and cuts in defense. Acceptance of growing public deficits is made in highly publicized confrontations. Winners and losers are identified and tagged, giving the latter an opportunity to express their delight or chagrin. The system is a rational policy-maker's delight: political leaders who can be held accountable for their decisions self-consciously make clear choices. Unfortunately, such a decision-making system produces no choice at all—except the choice not to change the status quo.

These are the politics of social policy at the national level. At state and local levels, however, politics are less confrontational, less constrained, less visible, and more oriented toward problem solving. The most lasting innovations may thus occur quietly and unobtrusively in a variety of locales, making it difficult to codify and explicate their significance. Yet state and local policymaking, however innovative, has its own bias, its own propensity to focus on economic development rather than the needs of the most disadvantaged. Politicians may well make progress in these quieter spheres of American politics, but the progress cannot compensate entirely for the Washington stalemate.

Major social policy innovation is thus not to be expected in the 1990s. Instead, change is likely to be incremental. Cost containment of health care will remain a lively issue; experimentation with choice in public education will probably increase; programs aimed at the very poor may win political approval, if the government carefully contains their cost; and the price of retirement programs will continue to rise, ever limiting the resources available for other domestic programs. But before spelling out these conclusions in greater detail, let us elaborate the forces that are keeping the contemporary stalemate in place.

THE SEPARATION OF POWER

The separation of power between Congress and the president, virtually unique to the American political system, structures the policy debate system more clearly today than ever before. In the early decades of the American Republic, presidents conceded to Congress most of the policy initiative—at least on domestic issues. After the Civil War, power shifted decidedly toward the executive branch, and congressional and presidential conflicts intensified. But presidents usually brought a partisan majority in Congress with them, which usually mitigated the division between the branches. If presidents sometimes lost the majority in the midterm election, they still had two years to carry out their policy agenda (Sundquist 1987).

The distinctive mark of the contemporary period is the almost perpetual division of power between the two political parties. By 1992, the Republicans will have controlled the White House for twenty of the preceding twenty-four years and twenty-eight of the preceding forty years. During that same time, the Republicans will have controlled both Houses of Congress for only the two years 1953–54, the first half of the first term of Dwight Eisenhower. Republican control of the Senate is somewhat more frequent, but even that has happened for only eight of the twenty-eight years that Republicans controlled the White House.

An Election-Minded Congress

The conditions perpetuating this division of party control are likely to continue into the next century. The numerous advantages incumbents have in reelection contests facilitate Democratic control of Congress. Incumbents gain popularity with their constituents by providing casework services to individuals and taking credit for any federal expenditures targeted to their region. They employ at public expense large staffs—an average of thirty on the House side, fifty on the Senate—that can meet with constituents, mail out newsletters, respond to constituent letters, address holiday greetings, organize television and radio broadcasts back home, raise campaign financing, and discreetly prepare the next campaign. The franking privilege enables members of Congress to perform these services without incurring any postal costs.

The capacity of members of Congress to use their office effectively for reelection has greatly increased in the past few decades (Fiorina 1977). The use of the frank increased from forty-three million pieces in 1954 to over 900 million pieces in 1984 (Ornstein, Mann, and Malbin 1988:174). The size of the average staff of both a senator and a representative grew more than sevenfold in the past fifty years (Ibid.:143). The frequency of congressional visits back home tripled, and the percentage of House staff placed not in Washington but in the congressman's home district rose from 22 percent in 1972 to 41 percent in 1987 (Ibid.:144). For senators, the shift over this same period was from 12 to 34 percent. Campaign expenditures by incumbents also increased dramatically in recent years. Even after controlling for general inflation, campaign expenditures grew more than threefold between 1974 and 1982 (Jacobson 1985:148).

During the 1970s, Congress revised its very organization to better facilitate the reelection prospects of members. As part of the post-Watergate reforms, the House of Representatives weakened the power of committee chairmen by expanding the number of subcommittees within committees and limiting the power of chairmen over the selection of subcommittee chairmen. The number of House committees and subcommittees grew from 130 in 1955 to 193 in 1980, while the Senate committee system expanded from 118 to 205 (Ornstein, Mann, and Malbin 1988:127). With the proliferation of committees, most members of the House could claim that they were either the chairman or ranking minority member of some subcommittee of importance to district residents. At the same time, members of Congress subjected an increasingly number of committee bills to amendment on the floor of Congress, giving individual congressman outside the committee an opportunity to defend constituent interests on a wider range of issues (Smith, 1990; Bach and Smith 1988; Shepsle 1989).

As a consequence, members of Congress are reelected more frequently and by larger margins than ever before. In 1948, only 80 percent of incumbent members of Congress went undefeated. By 1986, the reelection rate of members running for reelection was 98 percent (Ornstein, Mann, and Malbin 1988:56). In addition, the average margin of victory widened. In 1956, the percentage of House incumbents winning by the safe margin of more than 60 percent of the vote was 59 percent; by 1988, the percentage was 88 (Ornstein, Mann, and Malbin 1990: 59).

In this decentralized world of subcommittee politics that persisted into the late seventies, individual members of Congress could play significant policy roles and influence administrative decisions in a host of specific areas. This world provided an environment in which small, narrowly based interest groups could flourish. By supporting particular programs of interest to the group, and building a close alliance with the executive agency that administered the program, as well as the congressional subcommittees with specific responsibility for funding it, the groups worked within the iron triangles that established tight control over program development.

With only limited central congressional controls over subcommittee decision making, each iron triangle could also secure a steady increase in funding for the programmatic activities in which it had an interest (Fiorina 1977). Thus, between 1962 and 1980 the cost of discretionary programs of the domestic budget—the programs most susceptible to the influence of the iron triangles—expanded from 3.6 percent to nearly 5.6 percent of the Gross National Product (GNP) (Peterson, 1990–91:547).

Aid to school districts affected by activities of the federal government illustrates the way in which these discretionary programs could slowly expand during these decades.[1] This "impact aid" program, originally enacted during World War II to assist school districts dramatically impacted by large military concentrations mobilized by the war, continued into the 1980s. Wherever federal personnel live or work, a school district receives money for every child of a federal employee, military or civilian, attending a local school. School districts in Virginia, Maryland, California, Florida, and Texas are among the major recipients of this federal aid, even though it remains to be shown just how they are in more need of federal help than other school districts. Indeed, many are better off because the federal installation in their district generates economic activity that helps sustain the tax base of the local district.

Over the years, presidents have generally sought to reduce the size of the impact-aid program. As President John F. Kennedy observed when he reluctantly signed a law keeping this program alive in 1961:

> undesirable is the continuation for two more years of the current aid-to-impact-areas program, which gives more money to more schools for more years than either logic or economy can justify. This Administration recommended a reduction in the cost of this program, an increase in its eligibility requirements and local participation, its extension for only one year instead of two, and its eventual absorption in a general aid-to-education program. The rejection of all of these requests highlights the air of utter inconsistency which surrounds this program. (*Congressional Quarterly Almanac* 1961:243)

In spite of presidential resistance over the years, the legislation—for which the National Association of Impacted Districts lobbied assiduously—remained popular in Congress. Over 4,000 school districts, located in virtually every congressional district, became beneficiaries of the program as Congress gradually extended program eligibility (U.S. Office of Education 1979:23). In 1956, for example,

Table 8-1. Presidential proposals and congressional appropriations for
educational assistance to districts impacted by the federal government

Fiscal year	Presidential request (millions)	Congressional appropriation (millions)
1970–74	$808.1	$1379.0
1975–78	489.6	1050.5
1981–84	373.3	571.7
1985–87	436.6	611.0

Sources: Congressional Quarterly Almanac (1969:547; 1970:261; 1971:205;
1972:874; 1973:157; 1974:110; 1975:785; 1976:791; 1977:297–98; 1978:106;
1979:237; 1980:225; 1981:501; 1982:252; 1983:505; 1984:422; 1985:335;
1986:200). See also *Budget of the U.S. Government, Fiscal Year 1988* (1987:4–77)
and *Education Week*, January 26, 1988.

children of military personnel on active duty away from home became eligible. In 1958, Congress eased restrictions on monies to
larger school districts, Indian children became eligible, and any child
with a parent in federal employ was counted for purposes of aid
distribution. In 1963, District of Columbia schools became beneficiaries. In 1965, Congress made available construction assistance to
areas suffering a "major disaster." In 1967, it broadened the definition of "minimum school facilities." In 1970, it included children
living in federally subsidized, low-rent housing. In 1974 and again in
1978, Congress attempted to organize these changes into a system-
atic statement on eligibility, which in the end further extended the
benefits and introduced new complexities into eligibility requirements.

All these complex, continuing extensions of eligibility by Congress
help sustain legislative support for the law. As Table 8-1 shows (in
constant dollars), Congress appropriated hundreds of millions of dollars more for impact aid than the president requested in every year
since 1970. From 1975 to 1978, Congress more than doubled the
presidential request.

The Partisan Divide

If it is clear why an election-oriented Congress gave rise to iron-
triangle politics in the 1960s and 1970s, it is less apparent just why
the Democratic party was the partisan beneficiary on the election
machine that had been created. In part, the Democratic advantage is
probably an historical accident. Democrats elected as part of the

New Deal landslide happened to be in office when Congress elaborated these new mechanisms for entrenching the position of incumbents. Two landslide elections that adversely affected Republican incumbents reinforced the Democratic position: the 1958 election, which was during a recession, and the 1974 post-Watergate election, which gave Democrats greatly increased majorities.

But Democratic strength on Capitol Hill is not entirely accidental. The Democrats are a diverse party capable of appealing to an extraordinary range of social, ethnic, and economic interests. Within one coalition they have incorporated blacks, southerners, Hispanics, urban ethnics, environmentalists, Western ranchers, feminists, union members, farmers, developers, defense contractors, and commercial interests in search of government support and protection. Not all these interests support all elements of the Democratic party. But each member of Congress is able to emphasize that portion of the coalition strongest in his or her congressional district without jeopardizing the individuals' relationship to the party leadership.

Republicans are by no means a party of a single mind, but in recent years they have developed a more distinctive political identity. They emphasize the free market, tax reductions, less governmental involvement, lower trade barriers, traditional family values, stronger defense, and fewer ties to special interests. Although individual members of Congress can also tailor the Republican image to suit his or her particular reelection interests, Republicans seem to have less flexibility than do their Democratic counterparts.

Republicans have been more successful in the Senate than in the House of Representatives, probably because trends in presidential elections seem to play a somewhat greater role in statewide elections, which somewhat reduces the incumbency advantage. Twenty-five percent of the incumbent senators were defeated in 1986, a figure not significantly different from the pattern in the 1940s and 1950s (Ornstein, Mann, and Malbin 1988:57). And in the last thirty years, incumbents winning by a safe margin rose from only 39 to 50 percent (ibid.:60). Opponents in Senate contests are usually better known political figures who are better able to run an adequately financed campaign. In 1986, the Senate challengers spent, on average, 53 percent of the amount their incumbent opponent did, as compared with only 37 percent spent by the challengers on the House side.[2] Senate challenges also have less difficulty establishing name recognition, and their critiques of incumbents are more newsworthy.

Republicans were particularly successful in 1980 when economic recession and the Iranian hostage crisis provoked a voter revolt against Democratic incumbents that went well beyond President Jimmy Carter. The Republican sweep of that year gave the Republicans control of the Senate for the next six. But in 1986, the normal pattern reasserted itself, with the Democratic party making differentiated appeals to farmers, southerners, westerners, and minorities, and winning control of the Senate once again in a campaign notable for its lack of a national theme.

The very weaknesses of Republicans in congressional elections, however, give the party strength in presidential contests. Even in the post-Watergate era, Republicans have found it relatively easy to write party rules that emphasize party unity, to settle internal party differences early, to coalesce behind the party nominee, to mobilize the active support of senators and representatives in the presidential campaign, to utilize politically efficacious campaign themes without regard to specific groups within the party, to organize the national party office for fund-raising, voter registration, and other election-related purposes, and, above all, to develop national themes that give coherence to their presidential campaigns (Reichley 1985:175–200). Some analysts believe that in addition Republicans benefit from the electoral college, which gives extra weight to voters from small states, the very states in which Republicans are the strongest (Rosenstone 1983).

Republicans also benefit from their control of the White House at the time when the powers of that office have been used with increasing effectiveness in election campaigns. The White House staff has grown in size and sophistication. It houses a large office of communications with the capacity to use party-funded public opinion polls to monitor weekly, even daily, changes in public opinion on major policy questions. The staff monitors and summarizes carefully news accounts in the press and on television and radio. It carefully organizes for maximum publicity advantage presidential encounters with reporters. With the decline of party organization and the rising importance of television in presidential elections, the capacity of the White House to stage media events both within the United States and overseas has become extraordinarily impressive. The White

House staff designs presidential trips abroad more for their effect on the home audience than for their ostensible diplomatic purpose. In addition, the White House staff includes a large number of special assistants whose main responsibility is to maintain ties with key interest and nationality groups. All this works to the advantage of the party in power, which in recent times has typically been the Republicans.

Democrats, by contrast, find unity in presidential elections extremely problematic. They are regularly subjected to threats of third-party campaigns—whether by George Wallace on the right or Jesse Jackson on the left. Even if they avoid a third-party candidacy, Democrats must make special efforts to unify the party in their platform preparation and vice-presidential selection. Often, many members of Congress will run campaigns that are quite independent of, or sometimes openly hostile to, the national ticket. The party frequently selects Democratic presidential nominees only after a prolonged internal contest that it may not settle until shortly before the party convention. The convention itself becomes more of a unifying effort for the party than a launching pad for the general election. Great differences in ideology and in position on issues make it difficult to enunciate a clear campaign theme. The national party organization has relatively little coherence between elections; it becomes more of a debating forum for internal factions than a well-oiled machine capable of maximizing party support on election day.

All these considerations do not give Republicans a lock on the White House in quite the same way as Democrats seem to have a lock on the House of Representatives. Economic and foreign policy contexts fundamentally affect presidential elections (Hibbs 1987; Kiewiet 1983). Incumbents win if conditions seem relatively good, and challengers win if the economy slips or a foreign policy disaster occurs. Depending on the political context, either party can capture the White House in the decade of the 1990s.

But Republicans still seem to have the edge. A western and southern coalition of support that has remained stable in presidential elections over the past two decades provides a strong base from which to contend for the presidency in the next decade as well. Long-term forces favor the Republicans; Democrats are likely to win only if short-term factors work decidedly in their direction. At the same time, there is little sign that Republicans will be able to surprise the Democrats and capture back even the Senate side of Capitol Hill.

The prospect for the 1990s is a government that is even more divided than was the government of the 1980s.

STRONGER PARTIES, WEAKER GROUPS

Divided government in the 1980s, ironically, strengthened political parties and weakened the power of interest groups. Defying almost all political analyses, and decidedly in contrast to President Reagan's farewell address that criticized the power of iron triangles, the specialized interests were less of a factor in the policymaking process in the past decade than at any point in recent history. Governmental stalemate owes more to the competition for political advantage on the part of Democrats and Republicans than it does to any inside control by narrowly based organizations. And this, curiously enough, is the nub of the problem. Since strongly entrenched partisan interests—not interest groups that an emerging national consensus could override—hold the current stalemate in place, it is all the more likely that the structure of conflict in most of the Reagan era will continue into the next decade.

The intensification of partisanship began with the opening days of the Reagan administration. What happened in 1981 would set the tone for the next two decades. In that crucial year, the administration, led by David Starkman, the head of the Office of Management and Budget, not only secured from Congress a major reduction in tax rates but also assembled into one law, the Omnibus Budget Reconciliation Act (OBRA) of 1981, major cuts in domestic expenditures, elimination of numerous federal programs, and the deregulation and simplification of many others (Peterson and Rom 1988: 213–240). To pass both pieces of legislation, the administration relied first on its control of the Senate by a newly formed Republican majority and then on a unified House Republican minority, coupled with enough conservative Democratic supporters to defeat (in close-roll-call votes) the Democratic leadership in the House of Representatives (Jones 1988).

These legislative successes noticeably altered the decentralized, subcommittee-based decision-making style of Congress in the 1970s. In both the politics of the tax cut and the OBRA legislation, the administration demonstrated the advantages of a more centrally managed decision-making style. It could call upon members of Congress to support a conservative coalition in a highly visible up or down vote on one comprehensive piece of legislation, often called an "omnibus" bill. Constituent interests had to give way to ideological commitment and support for a popular president. Even in a Democratically controlled House of Representatives, the country's most conservative president in fifty years had a 72-percent success rate during his first year (Ornstein, Mann, and Malbin 1988:203–204).

But the consequences of the legislative triumph of 1981 were not exactly what the Reagan administration had anticipated. Within a year, the Democratic leadership used for its own political purposes centralized policy-making, the very tactic that David Stockman had used so successfully. Almost immediately after the passage of OBRA, the Democratic party began to regroup. Aided by the 1982 recession, which adversely affected Reagan's popularity, the Democratic leadership prevented further steep cuts in domestic programs. Then, in the fall elections, held in the depths of the recession, Democrats made enough gains in the House to prevent a conservative coalition of Republicans and southern Democrats from again forming a majority. Presidential victories in the House tumbled from 72 to an average of 47 percent over the next five years. Meanwhile, party-unity scores among Democratic members in Congress climbed to their highest point in thirty years (ibid.:209). Over the next six years, the balance of power in the House remained fairly stable, with the Democratic leadership in increasingly firm control. When the Democrats gained a 55–45 majority of the vote in the Senate in 1986, the division of power in Washington became even more obviously entrenched.

The Democrats not only had the legislative upper hand, but they found that they could turn to their advantage centralized decision making, the new political style inaugurated in 1981. Legislation was no longer being formulated within authorizing and appropriation subcommittees that would rely upon their interest-group allies and supporters within the executive branch to help slip legislation and spending proposals quietly through the legislative maze. The Reagan administration's steadfast opposition to most Democratic proposals, and its threat to veto any legislation outside administrative guidelines, precluded the continuation of this kind of iron-triangle politics, which prevailed in earlier decades.

Instead, the congressional leadership combined most legislation with significant fiscal implications into one large omnibus bill passed at the end of the legislative session, often when the fiscal year was about to expire and a new appropriation was necessary even to maintain the vital functions of government (Schick 1986). By combining a great many policy decisions into one bill, the Democratic leadership made the price of a presidential veto very high. Although the president could still force an accommodation to his wishes on a few issues he regarded as crucial, the maneuver nonetheless forced him to accept many items of legislation with which he did not agree.

In this highly centralized, highly politicized context, a curious policy stalemate evolved. First, the fiscal deficits of the federal government increased rapidly and remained extraordinarily high by postwar standards. Second, President Reagan refused to sign any tax increase large enough to reduce the deficit by a significant amount. He did agree to repeal some of the tax cuts of 1981 that had not yet gone into effect, and he also agreed to minor increases in the tax on gasoline and other user fees. But overall he remained faithful to his pledge not to raise taxes, no matter what the consequence for fiscal deficits or his proposed defense build-up. Third, the Democratic leadership accused the president and the Republican party of wanting to cut social security programs, the social policy that has had the broadest and most intense public support. Finally, with the president and the Democratic leadership each staking a claim to a popular political issue, the fight over the budget was limited to a debate over the appropriate balance in allocating the remaining monies to defense and to other domestic programs.

The pattern of public expenditure reflected this stalemate. After an initial build up in the early 1980s, defense expenditures stabilized at about 6 percent of GNP, only little more than one percent of GNP above the level when Reagan took office (Peterson, 1990–91:549–51). Similarly, expenditures on retirement and Medicare programs for the elderly, after having grown from 3 to 7 percent of GNP during the 1960s and 1970s stabilized at the higher level. Safety-net program expenditures—welfare, food stamps, and Medicaid—also stabilized at about 3 percent of GNP (after having doubled in size during the 1970s) (ibid.). The only component of the national budget to grow substantially was the interest required to finance the public debt.

Expenditures for these programs stabilized because one political party vigorously backed each program, and the other was afraid of the political costs of challenging its opponents' position. The Democratic party was willing to halt the arms build up that had begun during the first years of the Reagan administration, but Democrats were unwilling actually to cut these programs. The Reagan administration won minor adjustments in the social security program as part of a bipartisan compromise in 1983, but it shield away from significantly changing the fundamental policy of letting benefits rise with increases in the cost of living (Light 1985). Also, the Democratic party insisted on protecting from budgetary cuts the entitlement programs aimed at the very poor, and after some initial efforts at achieving savings in this area, the Reagan administration tacitly accepted the Democratic position (Palmer and Sawhill 1984; Weicher 1987).

As a result, Congress made budgetary cuts only in the remaining domestic programs that did not have broad-based partisan support. Expenditures for these remaining programs, ranging from transportation and space exploration to housing, education, and environmental control, increased from 3.6 to 5.6 percent of GNP during the 1970s (Peterson, 1990–91:547). Iron-triangle politics, based upon cooperation among subcommittees, interest groups, and executive agencies, gradually expanded the size of these programs in just the way the impact-aid program had expanded. But during the 1980s, Congress substantially cut these programs, so that by 1989 they constituted once again only 3.7 percent of the nation's GNP (Peterson, 1990–91:551). The impact-aid program, to cite an example discussed above, fell in constant dollars from over a billion-dollar average in the mid-1970s to an average of just over $600 million in the mid-1980s (Table 8-1).

The support of interest groups for these programs was as great in the 1980s as in the 1970s. Their Washington lobbies were as active and energetic in day-to-day legislative maneuvering as ever. But the context in which they operated was now quite different. Because of fiscal deficits, presidential opposition to domestic spending, budget resolutions that pulled together all fiscal decisions into one omnibus piece of legislation, and control over budgetary decisions by party leaders in Congress, policymakers had to make choices between programs of vital interest to the political future of the two major parties and the preferences of previously well entrenched interest groups. In the new age of confrontational politics, the iron triangles lost.

The new, centralized, partisan political system is likely to continue into the 1990s. Budgetary decisions are going to be decided in negotiations between the White House and congressional leaders, informed by analyses supplied by the budget committees. The work of the authorizing and appropriating committees will take place within the general framework set forth by these interparty negotiations in which Republicans play their no-tax-increase and Democrats their no-social-security-cuts trump cards. The forces holding this new policymaking system in place, even after Reagan's militant conservatism has left the scene, are best understood by looking at the way in which the tax legislation of 1981 transformed fiscal policymaking for the indefinite future.

THE FISCAL CONTEXT FOR SOCIAL POLICY

On fiscal matters, the American public seems extraordinarily inconsistent in its policy preferences. As it has for decades, a majority opposes reductions in federal spending in most of the major policy areas, any increase in the federal income tax, and can unbalanced budget. If anything, inconsistency in public opinion has actually become more marked in recent years. Two-thirds to three-fourths of the public regularly support an amendment to the Constitution requiring a balanced budget (*Gallup Report* 1981:12–13). Yet the percentage of the population opposing an increase in the income tax rose from around 55 percent in the 1950s to around 65 percent in the early 1970s to 70 percent in the late 1970s and to as high as 80 percent in 1987 (see Table 8-2).

While tax increases are opposed, support for expenditures remains unabated. Those opposing cuts in health and education expenditures are always overwhelming majorities of the population—seldom does more than 10 percent of the public support cuts in these areas (see Table 8-3). On defense and welfare assistance to the poor, there is more fluctuation over time. In the late 1970s, the percentage favoring cuts in welfare expenditures rose to 60 percent, but by 1987 that percentage fell to 46 percent, about the level it was at in the early 1970s. There is an opposite trend with respect to defense expenditures. Those favoring cuts fell to as low as 23 percent in 1977, but the level has since climbed up to over 40 percent, a level somewhat higher than in the early 1970s when the Vietnam War was coming to an end. Even in the late 1980s there was no majority for cuts in defense expenditures. Only in one policy area—foreign aid—are

Table 8-2. Public opinion on federal income tax

Year	Percentage saying income tax too high
1949	43
1950	56
1951	52
1952	71
1953	59
1957	61
1959	51
1961	46
1962	47
1966	52
1967	58
1969	66
1973	64
1974	69
1975	72
1976	73
1977	69
1978	70
1981	70
1983	77
1984	72
1985	76
1986	73
1987	80
1988	68

Sources: "The Coming Tax Revolt" 1978:30–31; *Gallup Report* 1987:26 and 1988:14. The Gallup pollsters posed the following questions:

1957–67: Do you consider the amount of income tax that you have to pay as too high, too low, or about right?

1969–78: From your personal standpoint, please tell me, for each tax that I read off to you, if you feel it is too high, too low, or about right . . . federal income tax.

1983–88: At present, the federal budget deficit is running at the rate of about 175 billion dollars per year. Basically, there are only a few ways this deficit can be reduced. Please tell me whether you approve or disapprove of each of the following ways to reduce the deficit: raise income taxes?

1988: Would you approve or disapprove of raising personal income taxes to reduce the federal deficit?

Table 8-3.   Public opinion on selected government expenditures

Year	Percentage who say government spends too much on				
	Health	Education	Welfare	Defense	Foreign aid
1973	5	9	51	38	70
1974	5	9	42	31	76
1975	5	11	43	31	73
1976	5	9	60	27	75
1977	7	10	60	23	66
1983	5	*	49	34	78
1987–88	4	7	46	42	72

*Data not available.

Sources: "Assessing the Role of of Government," *Public Opinion* 1987 (November/December):32; *Gallup Report* 1988 (July):4–9. The Gallup pollsters posed the following questions.

1973–87: We are faced with many problems in this country, none of which can be solved easily or inexpensively. I'm going to name some of these problems, and for each one I'd like you to tell me whether you think we're spending too much money on it, too little money, or about the right amount.

1988, education question: Now I am going to ask you a question about government spending. In answering, please bear in mind that sooner or later all government spending has to be taken care of from the money you and other Americans pay in taxes. As I read each program, tell me if the amount of money now spent on that purpose should be increased, kept at the present level, reduced, or ended altogether.

Americans united in supporting cuts in federal expenditure. But foreign aid is such a small part of the federal budget that even if the federal government totally eliminated all foreign aid programs, the size of budget deficits would not be materially reduced.

The public may not be quite as inconsistent as it seems. Very likely, most people believe that there could be more spending in areas they regard as critically important, even with lower taxes, if the government greatly reduced or eliminated expenditures for programs that the public regards as unnecessary. But legislators must make decisions in a context where there is a strong constituency for each and every program, no matter how wasteful any particular voter regards a specific program. Putting together a budget requires compromises that give all participants in the process some of what they regard as vitally important, thereby making it very difficult to shift resources sharply from one policy area to another. If in theory one could increase spending on important policies while at the same time reduce taxes and balance the budget, in practice it is virtually impossible.

Consequently, political leaders find it very difficult to satisfy the public's fiscal demands. On the one side, leaders are under constant pressure to cut taxes—or at the very least not to raise them. In the last three presidential campaigns, the winner was the candidate who either proposed a tax cut or insisted that he would never, never raise taxes. His opponent countered this position by emphasizing that an opposition to a tax increase would necessarily require cuts in popular federal programs, including, most especially, social security. Although this did not prove to be a winning campaign strategy, it did force from the winning candidate promises to keep the social security program intact and to preserve as well most other governmental programs.

In the immediate postwar years, policymakers could manage these inconsistent public demands because they could silently impose tax increases and expenditure cuts whenever the fiscal situation required such unpopular actions. Tax increases occurred silently through the process of bracket creep—the shift of taxpayers to ever higher tax brackets simply as the result of inflation. Inflation pushed worker earnings into higher tax brackets, and taxpayers began paying a higher percentage of their income in taxes, even though their real wages and earnings remained unchanged. Similarly, inflation reduced the value of their social security or other government-assistance paychecks, even though the nominal value of these paychecks remained the same.

From time to time, Congress and the president, working together, could correct this process by noisily enacting tax cuts that reduced the impact of silent bracket creep and by noisily raising social security and other benefits so that they would keep pace with inflation. But, significantly, the unpopular changes—tax increases and benefit cuts—occurred silently, while the popular changes—tax cuts and benefit increases—occurred through the passage of legislation for which both presidents and members of Congress could claim credit. During these halcyon days, taxes and expenditures remained roughly in balance, and fiscal deficits were small.

In recent years, presidents and Congresses have had ever-increasing difficulty in managing these inconsistent public expectations. The institutionalization of a set of policy stabilizers that constrain congressional action gradually eroded much of the flexibility that characterized the policymaking system in the early postwar years. The two most important institutional changes were the indexation of social security in 1972 and the indexation of taxes in 1981. Both have had consequences that were only poorly understood at the time Congress passed the legislation.

At the request of the Nixon administration, Congress passed legislation in 1972 providing for an automatic increase in social security benefits whenever the cost of living rose by more than 3 percent. Benefits had been rising in the 1950s and 1960s at a rate that exceeded changes in the cost of living. By putting social security increases on an automatic basis, Republicans hoped to bring under control the short-term pressures to increase benefits, and so they favored the move, while the AFL-CIO opposed it. However, the new policy did not anticipate that wage increases in the 1970s would fall short of rises in the cost of living, creating a situation where the income of social security recipients would rise more rapidly than that of the average worker.

A second factor compounded the problem. As originally planned, social security indexation, though passed in 1972, was not to go into effect until 1975; policymakers expected that in the meantime inflation would erode the real value of the base benefits from which to calculate cost-of-living increases. But once Congress enacted into law the principle of indexation, it felt pressured to increase benefits in 1973 and 1974 in order for benefits to keep pace with the steep rises in cost of living during these years. As a result, the base from which indexation began in 1975 was a very high base, in fact the highest base social security had ever attained. If this not very carefully calibrated set of policies resulted in a very substantial reduction of poverty among the elderly, it also meant that social security would constitute an ever-increasing fiscal problem for the federal government.[3]

The indexation of federal taxes occurred in an equally muddled fashion—and with much the same consequences. The problem of bracket creep was on the minds of Republican members of Congress as early as the mid-1970s. But powerful Democratic members of the tax-writing committees of Congress resisted any attempts to index tax brackets on the grounds that indexing would reduce flexibility in the tax system and, by making inflation painless, only reduce pressures on government to keep inflation under control. Moreover, it would eliminate congressional opportunities to pass "tax cuts" that were mere adjustments for bracket creep and did not in fact reduce the revenue flow to the federal government.

Although Reagan, as candidate for president, said he favored tax indexation, he did not include the proposal in his 1981 proposed tax legislation. When he called for a 30-percent cut in taxes over the next three years, he said he did not want to confuse the debate over this tax cut with any other changes in the tax. Also, his advisers were aware that the 30-percent tax cut would be so steep that unless eroded by inflation, it would leave the federal government with inadequate revenues. Like politicians before them, the Reagan administration preferred the appearance of dramatic tax cuts for which it could claim credit to a law that would automatically readjust the tax rate for changes in the cost of living.

When Reagan's proposed legislation came before the Senate, however, senators amended it on the floor by a tax-indexation proposal that had strong support from the many Republicans newly elected to Congress in 1981. Along with many other tax concessions added to Reagan's "pure" bill, the Senate inserted tax indexation into the tax code. Once again, it was to take effect only after the three-year tax cut (now reduced to a 25-percent cut). Once again, it was hoped that inflation would in the meantime erode the size of the tax cut that was being instituted. But as luck would have it, the U.S. economy took a new, recession-minded turn, inflation rates plummeted, and tax indexation began at a rate well below the level estimated by lawmakers at the time Congress passed the legislation (ibid.:ch.9).

By putting the government on automatic pilot—and by setting the pilot levels at points that were either unusually high, as in the case of social security benefits, or unusually low, as in the case of tax rates—Congress and the president created a political context in which balancing the federal budget would be extremely painful. They could not reduce the size of popular programs for the elderly without explicit legislative decision. They could not raise taxes without putting a bill through a complex legislative maze. Pressures to index other governmental programs grew so that by 1980 50 percent of the federal budget was either directly or indirectly indexed (ibid.:1). Congress said good-bye to an era of flexible policymaking when it could silently alter the programs and taxes without explicit acknowledgment of what it was doing. It would now do everything in the open, under the scrutiny of the press, the parties, and the interest groups. It was a rational policymaker's dream. It was a lawmaker's nightmare. The pressures to freeze the status quo were enormous. Congress, prone to stalemate in any case, locked itself in ice.

STATE AND LOCAL POLITICS

If the federal politics of social policy are likely to continue to be a stalemate into the 1990s, the picture is somewhat different at the state and local level. The new configuration in Washington—divided government, automatic policymaking through indexation of entitlements and taxes, trump-card politics, runaway deficits, and unrealistic economic forecasting—are all less evident at the state level. Perhaps the most revealing comparison is state and local behavior during the critical 1981–82 period when the federal government initiated its new regimen of lower taxes, continued high spending levels, and $100 to $200 billion deficits. During this period, states, constrained as they were by constitutional and political requirements that they balance their operating budgets, maintained or even extended their tax bases to cope with the loss of revenue brought about by the economic recession.

When the economy recovered in 1983 and 1984, states realized an unexpectedly large stream of revenue, and they were able to initiate new programs, fund old ones more adequately, and even put some money away for a rainy day. Worried that the economy might turn downward again, leaving them with another revenue shortfall, states generally avoided lowering taxes even when budget surpluses began to accumulate. By 1984, surpluses in state and local general government accounts grew to $20 billion. These surpluses were not the result of reductions in state and local services. The percentage of GNP spent by states and localities was as great in 1986 as it had been in 1980 (Gramlich 1987:303).

The steadiness of state and local policy is all the more remarkable inasmuch as the largest cuts in federal expenditure during the Reagan era were for aid to state and local governments. Federal grants to state and local governments fell by a full 1 percent of GNP between 1980 and 1987 (ibid.:300). For state and local spending to keep pace during the 1980s, expenditures from their own tax revenues had to grow faster than GNP by 1 percent.

Developmental Policy: The Case of Education

The consequences of the more robust policymaking system at state and local levels are nowhere more evident than in the field of education. At a time when Washington's efforts to enhance the quality of

Table 8-4.   Revenue sources of public elementary and secondary schools, 1950–88

Year	Federal	State	Local
		(in percent)	
1950	3	40	57
1960	4	39	56
1970	8	40	52
1980	10	46	45
1983	7	47	43
1988	6	50	44

Sources: U.S. Department of Education 1986:Table 69; National Education Association 1988:43.

American education consisted of commission reports and rhetorical flourishes by the secretary of education, and the federal share of educational expenditures fell from 10 to 6 percent (see Table 8-4), concerted action was evident in many states and localities. The major institutional actor was the state government, which increased from 46 to 50 percent the share of educational costs for which it paid.

The state governments were not only able to pick up the tab no longer covered by the federal government, but they raised per-pupil expenditures by an amount in excess of general increases in the cost of living (Table 8-5). The real dollar increases in per-pupil expenditures were not as steep in the 1980s as in earlier decades, but they seemed to target core educational activities (as distinct from the heating, transportation, and administrative costs that had driven up

Table 8-5.   Total public elementary and secondary school expenditures per pupil, 1950–88

Year	Per-pupil expenditures (1987 $)
1950	872
1960	1,297
1970	2,196
1976	N.A.
1982	2,969
1987	3,697

Source: Peterson 1991:43.

Table 8-6.   Average number of pupils per member of nonsupervisory instructional staff in elementary and secondary schools in United States, 1950–87

Year	Pupils/teacher
1950	24.3
1960	23.4
1970	19.6
1981	16.3
1987	16.2

Sources: Calculated from U.S. Department of Education 1986:Table 26; National Education Association 1988:18, Table C-6.

educational expenditures in the 1970s). Not only did the pupil-teacher ratio continue to decline somewhat (Table 8-6), but teacher salaries climbed to the all-time high they had achieved in 1970 (Table 8-7). In 1970, teacher salaries reached a peak of 20 percent higher than that received by employees in all industries.

During the next decade, teachers lost considerable ground, watching their salaries fail to keep pace either with the cost of living or with general wage increases in other sectors of the economy. But despite the Reagan administration's criticisms of teacher unions and its effort to introduce merit play (tying salary raises to teacher effec-

Table 8-7.   Salaries of instructional staff of public elementary and secondary school systems and of average U.S. employee, 1950–88

Year	Educator salary	Average worker salary	% educator salary greater
1950	12,937	12,937	2.7
1960	17,924	16,046	11.7
1970	23,823	19,764	20.5
1974	24,409	21,053	15.9
1980	21,917	19,791	10.7
1981	21,628	19,399	11.4
1984	22,903	19,900	15.1
1986	24,618	20,696	18.9
1988	26,205	21,524	21.7

Sources: U.S. Department of Education 1986:Table 51; 1986 data estimated from National Education Association 1987:65; 1988 data estimated from National Education Association 1988:20, Table C-11.
Note: Salaries are in constant 1983–84 dollars.

tiveness) into teacher-salary schedules, the average compensation of the instructional staff rose at a rate well beyond both inflation rates and general wage increases. By the late 1980s, salaries for teachers came back to the relative position they had held in 1970 (see Table 8-7).

State and local governments made other efforts to upgrade the quality of educational instruction. In addition to a number of state experiments in merit pay, states and local school districts imposed higher graduation standards, encouraged a more rigorous academic curriculum, and found a variety of ways to allow greater choice to parents and students. Magnet schools and other voluntary programs became the preferred mechanism for carrying out desegregation programs. Minnesota went so far as to allow parents to choose among public schools across local school district lines, an innovation that has so far proven politically popular and could well be a harbinger of similar experiments in other parts of the country.

Redistributive Policy: The Case of Welfare

States have taken up the slack in social policy areas such as education, where the failure to do so could have serious repercussions for the economic well-being of the state. But states have been less willing or able to cut through the stalemate prevailing in Washington on redistributive matters in which states have no particular need to take action. In fact, states have every reason to avoid assuming responsibility for the poor, the disabled, and the homeless. If one state makes a special effort to address these problems on its own, it may only invite a larger indigent population into the state (Peterson 1981).

A review of the trend in financial assistance to families with dependent children can probably best illustrate the difficulty of replacing federal with state action on redistributive policies. This program, called Aid to Families with Dependent Children (AFDC), established in the 1930s, divided the financial responsibility roughly evenly between the federal and the state governments, but the program always left the state governments to decide the level of assistance a family should receive. Between 1940 and 1970, the state governments steadily augmented in real dollar terms the amount of assistance the poor received (Peterson and Rom 1990:8). The size of the benefits that recipients received, however, varied widely from state to state. California, the most generous of the forty-eight contiguous states, provided welfare recipients with as much as five times as large a stipend as did Mississippi, the least generous state.

In the first decades of the program, this interstate variation did not seem to have a large effect on state policymaking or the residential decisions of poor people. But in 1969, the Supreme Court ruled unconstitutional a widespread state practice of denying families migrating into the state any benefits until they had been residents of the state for a year. In subsequent years, poor people seem to have taken into account the level of welfare benefits in a state when making residential choices (Peterson and Rom 1990).

At the same time, states became increasingly concerned about the potential effects welfare-benefit increases could have on the size of their low-income population. The question, for example, became a highly partisan issue in a gubernatorial campaign in Wisconsin, a relatively high-benefit state. Legislators from areas adjacent to the state of Illinois, which had substantially lower welfare benefits, claimed that an influx of poor people from Illinois was having an adverse impact on their community. They called for a reduction in Wisconsin's welfare benefits to keep the problem from becoming more severe. After the defeat of the incumbent Democratic governor, state welfare benefits were in fact modestly reduced in real dollar terms; perhaps more importantly, they fell even further behind the ever-increasing cost of living (Peterson and Rom 1990).

What happened in Wisconsin has become a national phenomenon. Between 1970 and 1985, the real value of welfare benefits declined by 33 percent. Yet the amount of variation in benefit levels remained as great as ever, keeping constant the downward pressure on benefit levels. Perhaps most surprising, these cuts in welfare benefits at the state level were occurring at a time when the average federal food-stamp benefit for the same population was rising in real dollar terms by 31 percent. Even during the Reagan years, food-stamp benefits continued to keep pace with increases in the cost of living, something that was definitely not happening at the state level (Peterson and Rom 1990).

The response of state and local governments to the stalemate in Washington is thus likely to be a nuanced one. In some areas, they are capable of strongly asserting themselves, taking up the slack in ways that will facilitate the economic development of their state or community. This is particularly likely to happen in areas such as education, environmental control, and transportation. But states are less likely to take up the slack in areas such as welfare, health care, and aid for the disabled and homeless. It is not simply or even primarily the financial costs that are involved. States have the flexible tax system that they can draw upon to meet state-defined needs. It is instead the potential cost of creating a greater problem—by attracting to the state those in need of its services—whenever a state attempts to address the problem at hand. Ironically, by doing nothing states can gradually drive their poverty problems away. By doing something about them, they may only make their poverty problems worse. The Washington stalemate gets replicated at the state and local level—not because of divided government but because of the interstate competition for productive labor and industry.

INCREMENTAL CHANGE IN THE 1990s

Social policy changed very little between 1940 and 1965. For more than a quarter of a century, the American political system simply absorbed and digested the great innovations of the New Deal. Then beginning the 1965 it initiated a great expansion of the social security system, established a quasi-national system of health insurance through Medicare and Medicaid, created job-training programs for the poor, provided food-stamp supplements to families on welfare, financed educational programs for the handicapped and disadvantaged, and set up a stable program of assistance for the disabled. Provisions that automatically raised benefits with each rise in the cost of living entrenched many of these programs.

Digesting these innovations has been even more difficult than absorbing New Deal policies, if only because their scope has been so much greater and the increase in their cost has been so much steeper. But the Reagan years, though more tumultuous, partisan, and ridden with ideological appeals, did not differ substantially from those of the Eisenhower administration, which accepted the legitimacy of the New Deal programs while resolutely opposing their expansion. Although Republican efforts to prune social innovations of the past were more persistent in the 1980s than in the 1950s, a Democratic Congress, determined to protect the Great Society it helped to build, checked Republican efforts just about as effectively. If the stalemate of the contemporary period makes significant new policy innovation unlikely, it also makes more certain that the social policy innovations of the 1960s and 1970s will be permanent features of the American political system. The unsuccessful effort of the Reagan revolution to reverse these innovations is probably as powerful a conservative political force as the country is likely to experience.

Small-scale policy innovations are nonetheless still possible. First, one must anticipate greater efforts to control escalations in the cost of health services. The population continues to age, thus maintaining the pressure on health-care facilities. The cost of medical services in rising more rapidly than the cost of living. And the number of costly diagnostic tools and treatments available is constantly expanding. The question is not whether efforts to contain health costs will accelerate, but whether policymakers will extend coverage to groups in the population not currently covered by private insurance, Medicare, or Medicaid.

The controversy surrounding the recent extension of comprehensive health insurance to the elderly provides a clue to the direction future health-care debates will take. Politicians are likely to conclude from this dispute that extending any health care services is so costly that the financing mechanisms necessary to pay for the program will immediately become a matter of political dispute. Since the elderly themselves attacked an extension of health care services as being unnecessarily expensive, politicians will become reluctant to venture further into this fiscally dangerous terrain. The best guess is that a comprehensive solution to health-care costs and coverage will not take place over the next decade, though the issue will gain prominence on the policy agenda. Instead, efforts to contain costs will be carried out mainly by administrative decisions designed to limit the quality of services paid for by Medicare and Medicaid.

Second, political pressure to address the problems of those in extreme poverty will grow. After several decades in which the percentages of the population living in poverty steadily declined from 34 percent in 1949 to 12 percent in 1979 (Danziger 1988:Table 1), the poverty problem, far from disappearing, has become more complicated. Not only is the percentage of those living in poverty as high today as it was a decade ago (10.5 percent of whites and 33.1 percent of blacks in 1987, as compared to 8.7 percent of whites and 30.6 percent of blacks in 1978) (Center on Budget and Policy Priorities 1988:11), but those with income below the poverty line have become younger, more urban, and more likely to members of female-headed households. While poverty among the elderly continued to decline in the 1980s (mainly because social security, Medicare, and other pension programs kept pace with increases in the cost of living), the percentages of children in poverty rose from 14.9 to 19.8 percent between 1970 and 1986 (Reischauer 1988:6). Over 50 percent of black children living in female-headed households were living in poverty (Center on Budget and Policy Priorities 1988: 11). And the percentage of the poor living in the nation's central cities rose from 17 to 23 percent between 1975 and 1985 (Reischauer 1987:Table 2).

Many analysts have thus begun to speak of an underclass—a segment of the population, usually of minority background, living in areas of concentrated poverty within our central cities where male unemployment is high or where men work in the underground economy, where single women are expected to maintain a family largely with public assistance, where housing is substandard and often congested, and where crime is abundant, illness is prevalent, schools are bad, and other social services are virtually absent. This group of the population seems untouched by the great institutions of the welfare state—unemployment insurance, public schools, job-training programs, and disability insurance. Only public assistance, Medicaid, and food-stamp programs seem to provide succor.

Solutions to the poverty problem come in two variants: Universalistic and piecemeal. The Universalistic solution would introduce a set of benefits for all families, regardless of need. This solution has the advantage of integrating all segments of the population into the political order and reducing the separation and stigmatization that is characteristic of the American welfare system. But it has the disadvantage of being very costly. As a result, the preferred political solution to this ever more visible social problem will likely be of the piecemeal variety: raise assistance levels somewhat, perhaps by establishing a national minimum standard, and design educational and training programs that will better prepare the poor to participate in an economy that is nearing full employment.

Other issues will arise, and policymakers will probably attempt partial solutions focused on the specific problem. The American political system is constantly innovative, and the urge to solve problems is never ending. But in the decade of the 1990s, policymakers will address the issues piecemeal and in a fragmented way. Perhaps it is only fitting that they reach a stalemate in the last decade of the century. It is a time when energy flags, old ways seem entrenched, and action is most difficult to initiate. But a new century stands just around the corner. With it will come a sense of rebirth, of renewal, of an unbounded future. Just as Theodore Roosevelt broke the stalemate of late nineteenth-century, business-dominated machine politics at the dawn of the twentieth century, so at beginning of the twenty-first, the creative urge in American politics may reassert itself once again. But it is not yet possible to visualize the political mechanisms that will inaugurate this new age.

NOTES

1. The following four paragraphs are adapted from Peterson 1983:77–78.
2. Calculated from data reported in Ornstein, Mann, and Malbin (1988:72–73, 77).
3. The story of the passage of social security indexation is well told in Weaver (1988:chap. 4).

REFERENCES

"Assessing the Role of Government." 1987. *Public Opinion*, p. 30

Bach, Stanley, and Steven S. Smith. 1988. *Managing Uncertainty in the House of Representatives: Adaptation and Innovation in Special Rules.* Washington, D.C.: Brookings Institution.

Budget of the U.S. Government, Fiscal Year 1988. 1987. Washington, D.C.: U.S. Government Printing Office.

Center on Budget and Policy Priorities. 1988. *Still Far from the Dream: Recent Developments in Black Income, Employment and Poverty.* Washington, D.C.: Center on Budget and Policy Priorities.

"The Coming Tax Revolt." 1978. *Public Opinion*, pp. 30–31.

Congressional Quarterly Almanac. Various issues. Washington, D.C.: Congressional Quarterly, Inc.

Danziger, Sheldon. 1988. "Fighting Poverty and Reducing Welfare Dependency: A Challenge for the 1990s." Paper prepared for the Rockefeller Foundation Conference on Welfare Reform, Williamsburg, Va., February.

Education Week, 16 January 1988.

Fiorina, Morris. 1977. *Congress: Keystone of the Washington Establishment.* New Haven, Conn.: Yale University Press.

Gallup Report. November 1981.

Gallup Report. August 1987 and August 1988.

Gallup Report. July 1988. Report No. 274.

Gramlich, Edward M. 1987. "Federalism and Federal Deficit Reduction." *National Tax Journal* 40:299–313.

Hibbs, Douglas A., Jr. 1987. *The American Political Economy: Macro-economics and Electoral Politics*. Cambridge: Harvard University Press.

Jacobson, Gary C. 1985. "The Republican Advantage in Campaign Finance." In John E. Chubb and Paul E. Peterson, ed., *The New Direction in American Politics*, pp. 143–174. Washington, D.C.: Brookings Institution.

Jones, Charles O. 1988. "Ronald Reagan and the U.S. Congress: Visible Hand Politics." In Charles Jones, ed., *The Reagan Legacy: Promise and Performance*, pp. 30–59. Chatham, N.J.: Chatham House.

Kiewiet, D. Roderick. 1983. *Macroeconomics and Micropolitics: The Electoral Effects of Economic Issues*. Chicago: University of Chicago Press.

Light, Paul. 1985. *Artful Work: The Politics of Social Security Reform*. New York: Random House.

National Education Association. 1987. *Response: Status of the American Public School Teacher, 1985–86*. West Haven, Conn.: NEA.

National Education Association. 1988. *Data Search: Rankings of the States, 1987–1988*. West Haven, Conn.: NEA.

Ornstein, Normal J., Thomas E. Mann, and Michael J. Malbin. 1988. *Vital Statistics on Congress 1987–1988.*, Washington, D.C.: Congressional Quarterly.

———. 1990. *Vital Statistics in Congress, 1989–90*. Washington, D.C.: Congressional Quarterly.

Palmer, John L., and Isabel V. Sawhill, eds. 1984. *The Reagan Record: An Assessment of America's Changing Domestic Priorities*. Cambridge, Mass.: Ballinger.

Peterson, Paul E. 1981. *City Limits*. Chicago: University of Chicago Press.

———. 1983. "Background Paper." In Twentieth Century Fund, *Making the Grade: Report of the Twentieth Century Fund Task Force on Federal Elementary and Secondary Education Policy*, pp. 77–78. New York: Twentieth Century Fund.

———. 1990–91. "The Rise and Fall of Special Interest Politics." *Political Science Quarterly* 105: 539–556.

———. 1991. "Are Big City Schools Holding Their Own?" Occasional Paper 91–4, Center for American Political Studies, Harvard University.

Peterson, Paul E., and Mark C. Rom. 1988. "Lower Taxes, More Spending and Budget Deficits." In Charles Jones, ed., *The Reagan Legacy: Promise and Performance*, pp. 213–40. Chatham, N.J.: Chatham House.

———. 1990. *Welfare Magnets: A New Chase for a National Welfare Standard*. Brookings Institution: Washington, D.C.

Reichley, A. James. 1985. "The Rise of National Parties." In John E. Chubb and Paul E. Peterson, eds., *The New Direction in American Politics*, pp. 175–200. Washington, D.C.: Brookings Institution.

Reischauer, Robert D. 1987. *The Geographic Concentration of Poverty: What Do We Know?* (unpublished paper). Washington, D.C.: Brookings Institution.

———. 1988. "The Welfare Reform Debate as It Will Confront the Next President." Paper prepared for Conference on Welfare Reform, Rockefeller Foundation, Williamsburg, Va., February.

Rosenstone, Steven. 1983. *Forecasting Presidential Elections*. New Haven, Conn.: Yale University Press.

Schick, Allen. 1986. *Crisis in the Budget Process: Exercising Political Choice*. Washington, D.C.: American Enterprise Institute for Public Policy Research.

Shepsle, Kenneth. 1989. "The Textbook Congress." In John E. Chubb and Paul E. Peterson, eds., *Can the Government Govern?*, pp. 238–267. Washington, D.C.: Brookings Institution.

Smith, Steven S. 1990. *Call to Order: Floor Politics in the House and Senate*. Washington, D.C.: Brookings Institution.

Sundquist, James. 1987. "Strengthening the National Parties." In A. James Reichley, ed., *Elections American Style*, pp. 195–221. Washington, D.C.: Brookings Institution.

U.S. Department of Education, Office of Educational Research and Improvement, Center for Statistics. 1986. *Digest of Education Statistics 1985–86*. Washington, D.C.: U.S. Government Printing Office.

U.S. Office of Education. 1979. "Administration of Public Laws 81-874 and 81-815." *Annual Report of the Commissioner of Education, Fiscal Year 1978*. Washington, D.C.: U.S. Government Printing Office.

Weaver, R. Kent. 1988. *Automatic Government: The Politics of Indexation*. Washington, D.C.: Brookings Institution.

Weicher, John C. 1987. "The Federal Budget and State-Local Responses." Paper presented at Ninth Annual Research Conference of the Association for Public Policy Analysis and Management, Bethesda, Md., October 30.

Contributors

Henry J. Aaron is Director of Economic Studies at the Brookings Institution and Professor of Economics at the University of Maryland. He is editor of *Setting National Priorities: Policy for the Nineties* and author, most recently, of *Serious and Unstable Condition: Financing America's Health Care.*

Mary Jo Bane is Director of the Center for Health and Human Resources Policy and Professor of Public Policy at the John F. Kennedy School of Government at Harvard University. She is author, with David Ellwood, of "One Fifth of the Nation's Children: Why Are They Poor?" Her book *Welfare Dependency and Welfare Policy*, with David Ellwood and Thomas Kane, will be published by Harvard University Press in 1992.

Henry J. Bruton is John J. Gibson Professor of Economics at Williams College. His recent writings include *The Political Economy of Poverty, Equity, and Growth: Sri Lanka and Malaysia* and "Import Substitution as a Development Strategy," in *Handbook of Development Economics*, edited by Hollis Chenery and T. N. Srinivasan.

Larry Cuban is Professor of Education at Stanford University. His most recent book is *The Managerial Imperative: The Practice of Leadership in Schools.*

Edward M. Gramlich is Director of the Institute of Public Policy Studies and Professor of Economics and Public Policy at the

University of Michigan in Ann Arbor. He is author of "Social Science Research and Policy: Review Essay" in *The Journal of Economic Literature* and has recently published the second edition of *A Guide to Cost-Benefit Analysis.*

JOHN F. KAIN is Professor of Economics and Chairman of the Economics Department at Harvard University. He is author, with Jeffrey S. Zax, of "Commutes, Quits, and Moves" in the *Journal of Urban Economics* and, with William C. Apgar, Jr., of *Housing and Neighborhood Dynamics: A Simulation Study.*

PAUL E. PETERSON is Henry Shattuck Professor of Government at Harvard University and Director of the Center for American Political Studies. He is editor, with Christopher Jencks, of *The Urban Underclass* and author, with Mark C. Rom, of *Welfare Magnets: A New Case for a National Standard.*

UWE E. REINHARDT is the James Madison Professor of Political Economy at the Woodrow Wilson School, Princeton University. Reinhardt is a member of the editorial board of *The New England Journal of Medicine.* His recent publications include "West Germany's Health-Care and Health-Insurance System: Comanaging Universal Access with Cost Control," in *A Call for Action, Final Report of the U.S. Bipartisan Commission on Comprehensive Health Care,* and "Health Care Spending and American Competitiveness," in *Health Affairs.*